There are many biblical metaphors which may look very similar to those in African target languages yet significantly very different in meaning. A good example is "circumcision of heart" in Romans 2:29. A face-value translation that does not pay attention to conceptual differences between the source language culture and target language culture may yield misleading interpretations. In this book the author demonstrates how the tools of Conceptual Integration Theory and Relevance Theory can be applied to render biblical metaphors in more meaningful ways. This book is very informative and will be of great use to scholars in Biblical Studies, Socio-linguistics and Bible Translation, especially in African cultural contexts where parallels of biblical imagery and rituals are easily encountered and thought to be similar, yet the underlying conceptual meanings are totally different. I highly recommend this book for reference in seminaries, theological colleges and universities.

Diphus Chemorion, DTh
Dean, Faculty of Theology,
St. Paul's University, Limuru, Kenya

Having been a Bible translation consultant for many years, one of the main challenges I have observed translators struggling with is that of effectively rendering both the meaning and impact of metaphors across languages. As has been argued in this book, to adequately address this challenge, it is important to come to terms with the underlying cognitive processes involved. This book not only expounds on a theoretical framework for the interpretation and translation of figures of speech, but also practically demonstrates the effectiveness of such an approach. Indeed, the proposed complementary approach between Conceptual Integration Theory and Relevance Theory is a rewarding way to think about the underlying process that drives and/or hinders projections and inferences to or from the metaphorical blends. I recommend this book to both learning institutions and practitioners as an effective tool for understanding how metaphors work.

Margaret J. Muthwii, PhD
Vice-Chancellor and Professor of Linguistics,
Pan Africa Christian University, Nairobi, Kenya

Interpreting metaphors involves identifying points of comparison between unlike and often superficially incompatible elements. A complex metaphorical expression, like "circumcision of the heart" can be interpreted in various ways by different audiences, depending on the context in which *circumcision* and *heart* are understood. Dr Kamande Thuo convincingly explains how Paul's original audience would have understood this metaphor in Romans 2:29, and he then demonstrates how the same metaphor yields incompatible interpretations for speakers of the Kikuyu language in Kenya, for whom circumcision serves a very different purpose. As a translation consultant with Word for the World Bible Translators, and a speaker of Kikuyu himself, Dr Thuo is uniquely placed to bridge the gap between the Jewish and Kikuyu understandings of the metaphor, which he does by skillfully combining the apparatus of Conceptual Integration (Blending) Theory with the Relevance Theory approach to communication and translation.

Steve Nicolle, DPhil
Director, MA in Linguistics and Translation Programme,
Canada Institute of Linguistics at ACTS Seminaries
and Trinity Western University, Langley, British Columbia, Canada

A Complementary Approach to Interpretation and Translation of Biblical Metaphors

Peter Kamande Thuo

© 2021 Peter Kamande Thuo

Published 2021 by Langham Academic (Previously Langham Monographs)
An imprint of Langham Publishing
www.langhampublishing.org

Langham Publishing and its imprints are a ministry of Langham Partnership

Langham Partnership
PO Box 296, Carlisle, Cumbria, CA3 9WZ, UK
www.langham.org

ISBNs:
978-1-83973-060-3 Print
978-1-83973-199-0 ePub
978-1-83973-456-4 PDF

Peter Kamande Thuo has asserted his right under the Copyright, Designs and Patents Act, 1988 to be identified as the Author of this work.

All rights reserved. No part of this publication may be reproduced, stored in a retrieval system or transmitted, in any form or by any means, electronic, mechanical, photocopying, recording or otherwise, without the prior written permission of the publisher or the Copyright Licensing Agency.

Requests to reuse content from Langham Publishing are processed through PLSclear. Please visit www.plsclear.com to complete your request.

All Scripture translations in this work are the author's own.

British Library Cataloguing-in-Publication Data
A catalogue record for this book is available from the British Library.

ISBN: 978-1-83973-060-3

Cover & Book Design: projectluz.com

Langham Partnership actively supports theological dialogue and an author's right to publish but does not necessarily endorse the views and opinions set forth here or in works referenced within this publication, nor can we guarantee technical and grammatical correctness. Langham Partnership does not accept any responsibility or liability to persons or property as a consequence of the reading, use or interpretation of its published content.

I dedicate this work to colleagues in the ministry of Bible translation, past, present, and future, who have surrendered their lives to translate the word of God into different vernacular languages so that as many people as possible can obey him. May you continue to find joy and fulfillment in this noble ministry.

Contents

List of Figures..ix

Acknowledgments..xi

Abstract..xiii

Abbreviations..xv

Chapter 1 1
   General Introduction
      1.1 Problem Formulation..1
          1.1.1 Cognition and Selective Processing in the Study of
               Biblical Metaphors...2
          1.1.2 Overview of the Interpretation of the Metaphor
               περιτομὴ καρδίας..12
          1.1.3 The Challenge of the Heart Metaphor 14
      1.2 The Research Problem 15
      1.3 The Thesis Statement..18
      1.4 The Research Questions 19
      1.5 Field Data and Research Methodology 20
      1.6 The Scope and Limitations of this Study...........................23
      1.7 Relevance to Field of Bible Translation 25
      1.8 Overview of Dissertation Content 26

Chapter 2 27
   Theoretical Approach
      2.1 Theoretical Framework...28
          2.1.1 The Conceptual Nature of Metaphors 28
          2.1.2 Cognitive Semantics...37
          2.1.3 Conceptual Integration or Blending Theory.........50
          2.1.4 Relevance Theory 63
      2.2 The Theoretical Gap 66
      2.3 Bridging the Gap 69
          2.3.1 The Discourse Space...69
          2.3.2 The Relevance Space 73
      2.4 The Complementary Approach 74
      2.5 Summary 77

Chapter 3 79
   Biblical Conceptualization of περιτομη *and* καρδια
      3.1 The Traditional Frame 80

   3.1.1 Frame Elements 84
   3.1.2 The Heart 98
   3.1.3 Metaphorical Use of the Associated Concepts 100
  3.2 The Modified Frame 105
   3.2.1 Frame Elements 111
   3.2.2 Other Associated Rituals 116
  3.3 The Conceptual Integration Process 119
   3.3.1 Frame Blending 119
   3.3.2 The Outer Spaces 122
   3.3.3 The Source Language Inner Spaces 137
  3.4 Meaning of the Metaphor Περιτομὴ Καρδίας 145
  3.5 Summary 153

Chapter 4 155
 The Conceptualization of IRUA*, HAKIRI *and* NGORO
  4.1 Introduction 155
  4.2 Conceptualization of *IRUA** 157
   4.2.1 The Meaning of *IRUA** 157
   4.2.2 Frame Elements 162
   4.2.3 Frame Shifting 174
  4.3 The Conceptual Integration Process 176
   4.3.1 Association of [*IRUA**] and HAKIRI 177
   4.3.2 Association of [*IRUA**] and NGORO 181
  4.4 Summary 195

Chapter 5 197
 Translating the Metaphorical Blend
  5.1 The Source Language Blended Space 197
  5.2 The Receptor Language Blended Space 198
  5.3 The Translation Space 201
   5.3.1 Target Space Background Framing 202
   5.3.2 Metonymic Links 202
  5.4 Rendering of the Metaphorical Blend 215
  5.5 Procedure for Translating a Metaphorical Blend 218
  5.6 Summary 219

Chapter 6 221
 Conclusions and Recommendations
  6.1 Conclusions 221
  6.2 Further Recommendations 223

Appendixes 225

Bibliography 279

List of Figures

Figure 1: A prototypical diagram of conceptual integration 56

Figure 2: Brady, Oakly, and Coulson's conceptual integration network: Surgeon as butcher 61

Figure 3: A modified integration network 76

Figure 4: The source language discourse and relevance spaces 123

Figure 5: The source language generic and input spaces 138

Figure 6: The source language blended space 140

Figure 7: Integration process of the metaphor *kũgimara hakiri* 179

Figure 8: The receptor language generic and input spaces 191

Figure 9: The receptor language blended space 193

Figure 10: The translation and receptor language target spaces 201

Acknowledgments

Special thanks go to God, who gave humans the gift of languages and made it possible for us to know him through them and also for his provision for indeed "through him all things were made; without him nothing was made that has been made" (John 1:3).

I would like to sincerely thank my supervisor, Dr. Maik Gibson, as well as my second reader, Dr. Andy Alo, for the helpful guidance and valuable comments which helped to improve this work. Of course how the work turned out in the end is entirely my responsibility. I also convey my gratitude to the entire faculty members of the department of Languages, Linguistics and Communication at Africa International University, past and present, who have impacted my life and ministry. They include Prof. Carlson, Prof. Blass, and Dr. Nicolle. I cannot forget the roles of Miss Elizabeth Olsen, Dr. Follingstad, Dr. Ruth Mason, Dan Juma Gambo, Dr. Katy Barnwell, among others, who invested much in my formative years of training. Thank you for your moral support.

To my family, my wife, Sally, and sons, Luke and Nathan, I also dedicate this work. Thank you Sally for having kept me fed and piled with coffee and for allowing me to turn our house into a "writing workshop" as I labored to give birth to this work.

I want to thank Lori Gardener and Sue Pearson for taking time to proofread this work.

I am indebted to the financial support from The Seed Company as well as that of the Summer Institute of Linguistics (SIL) through the SIL Africa Area office in Nairobi, Kenya. Special appreciation goes to Dr. William Gardener for working out all the logistics as far as the running of my scholarship was concerned.

I am grateful for the academic hospitality of the Home of Bible Translators and the Hebrew University in Jerusalem, and in the UK that of Tyndale House and the University Library of Cambridge.

I would like to also acknowledge my colleagues, namely, the second PhD cohort, with whom I shared memorable moments of fellowship, seminars and traveling experiences. I sincerely thank the entire AIU community for their fellowship and the brotherly atmosphere that I and my family enjoyed throughout my studies.

Finally, I thank all the Kikuyu speakers who participated in the field research. My prayer is that the findings of this research will be applicable to many other translations so that the word of God can be understood better. Amen!

Abstract

This work seeks to demonstrate how the associated concepts in the metaphor περιτομὴ καρδίας are construed within the context of Romans 2 and an application made on how best to render this metaphor to a Kikuyu audience, a Bantu language spoken mostly in the central part of Kenya. To this end, a complementary approach between Conceptual Integration or Blending Theory and Relevance Theory has been proposed to detail the integration process and to demonstrate how the interpretation and translation process takes place.[1]

Three main conclusions have been arrived at in this work. The first one is that in the use of the metaphor περιτομὴ καρδίας within the discourse space of Romans 2, Paul is inducing his readers in the process of frame shifting with the meaning of this metaphor intended to be that of fulfilling a cleansing or purification role. This interpretation can be supported further through the process of completion by referring to the Septuagint which renders the Hebrew lexeme מול "circumcision" with the Greek lexeme περιεκάθαρεν "he cleansed/purified." My claim is that Paul is drawing from this background knowledge to narrow the meaning of the metaphor to that of a cleansing or purging ritual which all people need to undergo in order to be cleansed of their sins.

The second conclusion is that the ritual frame associated with the Kikuyu concept [IRUA*] "circumcision," which also activates the organizing frame of [KŨGIMARA] "entering adulthood status," is erroneously recruited in the interpretation of the metaphor translated in the existing Kikuyu Bibles as *kũrua ngoro*, "circumcision of heart," in Romans 2:29. The contextual assumptions

---

1. Fauconnier and Turner, *Way We Think*; Sperber and Wilson, *Relevance, Communication and Cognition.*

that are activated within this organizing frame, which are the same ones that are activated in the interpretation of the SL metaphor *kũgimara hakiri*, "to mature in the mind," lead to the derivation of unintended inferences. To bridge this conceptual gap, I have suggested the need to offer a more definite interpretation as well availing the relevant source language context adjustment material to the targeted readers.

Last, but not least, the complementary approach between Conceptual Integration or Blending Theory and Relevance Theory is a rewarding conceptual undertaking in the interpretation and translation of metaphors. This is mainly because it helps to address the underlying and/or organizing frames, direct projections and inferences activated by the associated concepts in the metaphorical relationship that need to be factored into the translation process.

Abbreviations

BHS	*Biblia Hebraica Stuttgartensia*
BS	Blended space
CEV	Contemporary English Version
CIT	Conceptual Integration (or Blending) Theory
CMT	Conceptual Metaphor Theory
DS	Discourse Space
ESV	English Standard Version
GS	Generic space
IS_1	Input Space 1
IS_2	Input Space 2
KJV	King James Version
LXX	Septuagint (*Rahlfs*)
MT	Masoretic Text
NIV	New International Version
OG	Old Greek Text
RL	Receptor Language
RLBS	Receptor Language Blended Space
RLIS	Receptor Language Input Space(s)
RLTS	Receptor Language Target Space
RS	Relevance Space
RT	Relevance Theory
sg	Singular
SL	Source Language
SLBS	Source Language Blended Space
SLDS	Source Language Discourse Space

SLIS	Source Language Input Space(s)
TEV	Today's English Version
TT	Target Text

CHAPTER 1

General Introduction

In this introductory chapter, I will formulate and state the problem that necessitated this study, provide the thesis statement as well as the research questions which this study is based on, give a brief introduction to the theoretical and methodological framework, state the scope and limitation of this study, propose the relevance of this study in the field of Bible translation, before concluding with an overview of the content of this dissertation.

1.1 Problem Formulation

This section highlights some gaps in the study of biblical metaphors that cause challenges in their interpretation and translation across languages. The first one emanates from the general lack of the use of comprehensive cognitive approaches in analyzing biblical metaphors, and the second, the lack of details as to how given interpretations are arrived at while other equally possible ones are rejected. Some biblical works that address themselves to the interpretation of metaphors are reviewed in this section with the goal of drawing attention to these two related gaps. An overview on how the metaphor περιτομὴ καρδίας "circumcision of heart" in Romans 2:29, which is the focus of this study, has been analyzed by different scholars is also drawn attention to in order to argue for the methodological approach and interpretation proposed in this work. The challenge posed by this metaphor, both in its interpretation and translation to a Kikuyu audience, is also highlighted since this is basically the problem which necessitated this work.

1.1.1 Cognition and Selective Processing in the Study of Biblical Metaphors

In the field of biblical studies, there is a general recognition that the use of a cognitive approach can be beneficial. As Pyysiäinen rightly argues, such an approach has the potential of providing insights as to "how religious concepts are acquired, represented and transmitted."[1] Likewise, Luomanen, Pyysiäinen, and Uro point out that the use of theories from cognitive science could result in the introduction of new perspectives with the authors demonstrating such by applying cognitive science to topics of Christian origins and Early Judaism.[2] A cognitive approach can be instrumental in assisting scholars to figure out how concepts are constructed and construed in the minds of those associated with them since "speakers of different languages have different underlying conceptual systems."[3]

However, general cognitive processes and principles that contribute to meaning construction tend to have been underutilized in the study of biblical concepts, more specifically, when it comes to analyzing biblical metaphors. Only a few attempts have being made using "visualizations, conceptualizations, and orientations" from cognitive science.[4] Even though a number of biblical scholars acknowledge the central role that metaphorical language plays in biblical literature, only a few make an attempt to explore the potential provided by use of cognitive approaches.[5] As a result, most of the biblical works analyzing metaphors treat them as simply stylistic features and in the process fail to give a detailed account as to how the associated concepts

---

1. Pyysiäinen, *How Religion Works*, 8.

2. Luomanen, Pyysiäinen, and Uro, "Introduction: Social and Cognitive Perspectives," 1–2.

3. A "concept" in this work is understood to be "a person's idea of what something in the world is like," Dirven and Verspoor, *Cognitive Exploration*, 14; Evans and Green, *Cognitive Linguistics*, 55.

4. Robbins, "Conceptual Blending and Early Christian Imagination," 161.

5. Most of the works in biblical studies that analyze metaphors focus mostly on analyzing the characteristics of God, since almost all the language that is used to refer to God in the Bible is metaphorical in nature (Caird, *Language and Imagery*, 18). Sally McFague (*Metaphorical Theology*) also captures the central role that metaphors play in religious language and in one of the chapters of her book she analyzes the metaphor of God as a friend. D. Tracy points out of the tendency of major religions to be grounded on certain root metaphors, one such metaphors which he discusses is that of "God is love" which he claims is central to Christianity as a religion (Tracy, "Metaphor and Religion," 89–104). Furthermore, as J. Macquarrie (*God Talk*), points out, metaphorical language abounds in theological discourse, with parables in particular being described as being metaphorical in nature (McFague, *Speaking in Parables*, 30).

in metaphorical relationships are grounded, structured, and also how they relate to one other.[6] Notwithstanding the fact that such works do not claim to follow the traditional pragmatic approach to metaphor interpretation, as will be pointed out in some of the works sampled in this section, there is a tendency to indicate that the meaning of a metaphor derives from the literal meaning of the associated concepts. This tendency, besides failing to detail the cognitive process of metaphor interpretation, fails to account for the metaphor comprehension procedure that results to one interpretation being chosen over other potential ones. Such an approach is grounded on the construal that language simply reflects an objective world "out there," which is not the case, given that the use of language reflects our unique human understanding of the world since reality is not objectively given.[7]

The contemporary scholarship on metaphors is vast and it is beyond the scope of this work to analyze all the existing works. The few works that are sampled here are meant to point out the basic research patterns, if any, with the goal of underlining the need of the use of detailed cognitive approaches as creative components in analyzing biblical metaphors. In analyzing the metaphorical use of "tree" in Isaiah 1–39, Nielsen discusses the association of the domain of the "river [Euphrates]" to that of the "king of Assyria" as found in Isaiah 8:7.[8] In view of the fact that not everything which is associated with the concept RIVER can be mapped to that of the KING OF ASSYRIA, there is need to demonstrate how the some characteristics end up being profiled while other possible ones are suppressed.[9] The tree image is quite flexible and as a result can be used to express different theological ideas, hence there is need to illustrate how or what drives the assumed process of selection. Some of the characteristics of the tree image which are profiled include positive ones such as its use as a building material, its role in bearing fruit, and that of its use in the metaphor "tree of life." The negative ones include related images which speak of YHWH's judgment such as that of the "forest-fire" image,

---

6. Lakoff and Johnson, *Metaphors We Live By*, 106.
7. Evans and Green, *Cognitive Linguistics*, 47–48.
8. Nielsen, *There Is Hope for a Tree*, 54.
9. Concepts are indicated in small caps and point to "the descriptive information that people represent cognitively for a category, including definitional information, prototypical information, functionally important information, and probably other types of information as well" (Barsalou, "Frames, Concepts, and Conceptual Fields," 31).

the use of the concepts THORNS and THISTLES, among others. Nielsen also talks of other characteristics which could be categorized as being negative yet at the same time tend to have the potential of being interpreted positively to represent life, giving the example of a felled tree that has the potential of sprouting again.[10] Furthermore, when the imagery of a tree is evoked, it reflects conceptual structure which includes frames that are associated with given sociocultural experiences. This means that there are a vast number of elements or sub-domains that can be activated as well as varying projections or characteristics that tend to be profiled. Some might be universal while others might vary from one culture to another. Those that might vary include its medicinal nature, the use of its branches as walking sticks, fencing material, shade, and the list goes on. In arriving at given interpretations, especially in instances where negative characteristics acquire positive emergent properties, there is need to demonstrate the underlying process as a means of guiding the readers towards the intended interpretation(s).

Nielsen pegs the change of interpretations on the change of context which she illustrates by the use of the image of the shoot in Isaiah 11:1–9.[11] This imagery may be understood as emphasizing the tender age of King Josiah as he ascended the throne and in another context the same imagery may allow a different interpretation including that of a literal meaning. Again this raises the issue as to how and why certain elements or characteristics end up being profiled in a given context while in others the same characteristics are suppressed. The fact that some of these potential characteristics are blocked from being activated implies that there is an underlying cognitive process involved.

Brettler, in analyzing the biblical metaphor of God as King, rightly points out that it is important to first describe the institution of human kingship as the background framing of exploring the abstract concept of the kingship of God.[12] He further argues that one might not need to know all the details of what transpired in palaces to be able to understand the metaphor of God as king.[13] He talks of the lack of complete correspondence between the concepts GOD and KING and as a result only concentrates on some of the appellations

---

10. Nielsen, *There Is Hope for a Tree*, 225.
11. Nielsen, 233.
12. Brettler, *God Is King*.
13. Brettler, 24–25.

of the human kingship which are applicable to that of God.[14] One of the differences which he argues could assist one to distinguish whether the concept of kingship is used in reference to a human being or to the divine is that of its morphological and syntactical patterning, where the human king is normally addressed as 'ădōnî and God as ădōnāy.[15] The question still remains which mappings are attested and which ones are unattested when comparing the two domains. As will be demonstrated in detail later, the underlying cognitive process is not arbitrary or haphazard but a selective process.

Sohn in examining the marriage metaphor between YHWH and the people of Israel, gives a comprehensive exposition of the ritual or frame of [MARRIAGE] focusing on its synonyms, legal responsibilities, obligations, and ramifications.[16] Some of the sub-domains which he argues are activated by the [MARRIAGE] frame which are used to explain the theological relationship between the people of Israel and their God include the selection of a partner, the engagement ceremony, the marriage feast, the marriage proclamation, the sexual union, the marriage life, divorce, and remarriage. It is important to note that not all of the components that apply to the institution of human marriage are applicable in illustrating God's relationship with the people of Israel, which again underlines the fact that there is an underlying cognitive process involved. Some of the characteristics which are suppressed within this frame when explaining the relationship between Israel and their God include the role of other family members, types of foods served in the marriage ceremony, time that the ceremony is held, the detailed roles and responsibilities of spouses and their children, and so on. This selective process could be better illustrated by pointing to the underlying frame shifting process by use of a cognitive approach.

Baumann also analyzes the same marriage metaphor but focuses on profiling its negative elements.[17] Her claim is that the negative acts associated with the imagery of marriage, such as that of sexual abuse which is profiled in certain texts, are coupled with YHWH's violent acts. She argues that the

---

14. Brettler, 48.
15. Brettler, 49.
16. Sohn, *YHWH, the Husband of Israel*. In this work, rituals and frames will be represented by small capitals in square brackets following the standard way of notation in Linguistics.
17. Baumann, *Love and Violence*.

purpose of the marriage metaphor, especially in the context of the experiences relating to the exile, cannot be explained without invoking YHWH's violent acts. Again, a cognitive approach would go a long way in assisting the reader to see how YHWH's violent acts are associated with the negative elements evoked within the [MARRIAGE] frame.

Lyall, in discussing the legal metaphors in the Epistles, points out that the greatest obstacle in the interpretation of metaphors is that the readers' perceptions are different from those of the original audience.[18] In an attempt to bridge this gap, he explores the background framing of the Roman law as the basis of explaining the words and phrases used by Paul in an attempt to interpret the legal imagery used in the epistle to the Ephesians. Unfortunately, in evaluating the different concepts that are activated in the domain of law, the use of a methodological framework is overlooked.

Strawn, in analyzing the leonine image in the Hebrew Bible, advocates for a methodology that pays attention to both the text and iconography.[19] He observes that this imagery is generally associated with might, hence its metaphorical use by linking it with the monarchy and the deity. According to him, this image is suited in describing YHWH since it activates his attributes as being "good and protecting" and at the same time "judging and threatening."[20] In making general observations on the lion imagery from an ancient Israel/Palestine perspective, he mentions some traits that are suppressed and consequently of secondary interest such as its paws, beard, and mouth.[21] It is also important to note that there are some characteristics or behaviors associated with the leonine image which are not profiled in the Hebrew text, yet form part of the general conceptualization activated in the mind of the readers/listeners.[22] Such include their social relations, one of which has to do with

---

18. Lyall, *Slaves, Citizens, Sons*.
19. Strawn, *What Is Stronger than a Lion?*
20. Strawn.
21. Strawn, 34.

22. The term conceptualization is interpreted broadly as embracing any kind of mental experience which involves the dynamic process of meaning construction. "It is understood as subsuming (1) both novel and established conceptions; (2) not just 'intellectual' notions but sensory, motor, and emotive experience as well, (3) apprehension of the physical, linguistic, social, and cultural context; and (4) conceptions that develop and unfold through processing time (rather than being simultaneously manifested)," (Langacker, *Cognitive Grammar*, 30).

the Lion's mating behaviors.²³ According to his categorization of the leonine image, he concludes that both the positive and negative characteristics are activated in different contexts. The positive ones include that of being mighty or victorious and the negative ones include being wicked and a threat to order among others. Again, this profiling and suppressing of given characteristics can be better illustrated by the use of a cognitive-based theoretical approach.

In analyzing the Hebrew metaphorical instances of the use of the word translated as "circumcision" and how it is rendered in both *Targum Onqelos* (Pentateuch) and *Targum Nebi'im* (Prophets), Derouchie uses a semantic approach to categorize the forms of the use of this word into six different semantic groupings or lexemes.²⁴ They include מול "to circumcise" (31 times), מלל "to circumcise" (1 time), מולה "circumcision" (1 time), ערל "to treat as one having foreskin" (2 times), ערלה "foreskin" (15 times), and עָרֵל "having foreskin" (35 times). In his analysis, he observes that in "instances where the circumcision word-group is clearly metaphorical, the translators of the targums substituted [it with] nonliteral equivalents."²⁵ One such instance is in Leviticus 26:41 where Israel as a nation is called upon to humble its לְבָבָם הֶעָרֵל "uncircumcised heart" which the *Targum Onqelos* renders to mean "obdurate, dull, stupid" hearts. Another example is in Deuteronomy 10:16 where the phrase וּמַלְתֶּם אֵת עָרְלַת לְבַבְכֶם "circumcise the foreskin of your heart" is rendered in *Targum Onqelos* as "removing the obduracy of your heart." Again Derouchie fails to detail the conceptual process that might have influenced the choices made by the Targum translators.

Tsang, in analyzing Paul's use of the slave metaphor in his letter to the Galatians, uses the New Rhetoric method in an attempt to find out how Paul uses this metaphor to persuade the Galatians to heed the gospel.²⁶ He claims that Paul used this metaphor for three purposes, namely, to defend himself and the gospel which he was preaching, to attack the false teachers, and to teach the Galatians. Tsang establishes two bench marks as criteria in deciding the possible meaning of the slave metaphor, namely, that of location and that of context. According to him, context refers to the surrounding material

---

23. Strawn, *What Is Stronger than a Lion?*, 45.
24. Derouchie, "Circumcision in the Hebrew Bible."
25. Derouchie, 182.
26. Tsang, *From Slaves to Sons*.

and how the subject is portrayed in that material, and location to the cultural context of the time. When it comes to analyzing given concepts and how they are conceptualized in different contexts, again a cognitive approach would be a good methodological tool to utilize.

Van der Watt, in analyzing the family metaphor in the Gospel of John, develops a theoretical framework from key passages in this Gospel which he employs to analyze other metaphors used in the same Gospel.[27] His methodological approach is driven by his conviction that modern metaphorical theories should not be used to study ancient texts. He utilizes a deductive approach to come up with what he refers to as "John's theory of metaphor" which he applies to analyze the family metaphor in the Gospel of John. He observes that this metaphor is based on the social reality of a family and notes that "John succeeds in utilizing established and generally accepted knowledge related to family life for understanding and explaining salvific and ethical events on a spiritual level."[28] Watt rightly points out that there is a positive contribution that scholars gain from using approaches from other disciplines. A cognitive-conceptual approach can add more insight in highlighting the ancient imagery of the FAMILY in light of the varying conceptualization associated with this concept by interpreters from different contexts.

There are some works which consider the input of Conceptual Metaphor Theory (CMT) in the interpretation of metaphors.[29] Dille, in analyzing the parental imagery of God in the Deutero-Isaiah writings, argues that this imagery is influenced by both the rhetorical and cultural contexts of other interwoven metaphors used in those writings.[30] The claim that she makes is that the parental imagery of God does not have a consistent meaning within the Deutero-Isaiah writings. In her introductory chapter, she gives a brief survey of the development of what she refers to as a metaphorical theory, which she claims draws from the works of Richards and Black, as well as that

---

27. van der Watt, *Family of the King*.

28. van der Watt, 163.

29. CMT was first proposed by Lakoff and Johnson (*Metaphors We Live By*). They claim that a metaphor is not just a stylistic device of language use, but that it is grounded in thought, which is fundamentally metaphorical in nature. Cognitive linguists define metaphor as a conceptual mapping between two domains, a source domain (or vehicle), and a target domain (or theme), with the target domain being referred with vocabulary from the source domain (Evans and Green, *Cognitive Linguistics*, 296; Coulson, *Semantic Leaps*, 162).

30. Dille, *Mixing Metaphors*.

co-authored by Lakoff and Johnson.[31] She argues that her work derives its systems, categories, and language from Lakoff and Johnson's book and the vocabulary and designation of the two parts of metaphor, namely, topic as "tenor" (what is meant) and image as "vehicle" (how it is said) from Richard's book.[32]

Dille does not detail how the parental imagery is construed and constructed as a way of convincing the readers of her thesis. It is important to note that the concepts translated in English as "father" and "mother" have the potential of evoking endless sub-domains, of course depending on one's sociocultural experience. She only discusses two sub-domains as the ones that are activated within the Deutero-Isaiah writings, namely those of fertility and kinship.[33] There is need to illustrate the process that led to the profiling of these two sub-domains as well as how she arrives at her proposed interpretations. Though she talks of the processes of selection/emphasis, suppression, and organization that take place in the interpretation of a metaphor, she fails to demonstrate how these apply in her analysis.[34] The use of a cognitive approach can go a long way in explaining both how and which sub-domains and elements are highlighted and which ones end up being suppressed.

Howe uses CMT to analyze the moral structure found in 1 Peter by looking at certain image schemas and metonymies as keys.[35] Such keys include slavery, patron-client relationships, restoration of honor, and social balance, among others. She appreciates the role of conceptual metaphors and frames and observes that the NT employs such metaphors such as "Good is Up" and "Evil is Down."[36] Using vocabulary from blending theory, she argues that NT studies and Christian ethics can be bridged by methods and insights from three related fields, which she refers to as input spaces, namely, biblical studies, Christian ethics, and cognitive linguistics.[37] She points out that each of these fields comes with its own methods, theories, and objects of study

---

31. Richards, *Philosophy of Rhetoric*; Black, *Models and Metaphors*; Lakoff and Johnson, *Metaphors We Live By*.
32. Dille, *Mixing Metaphors*, 17, 97; cf. Richards, *Philosophy of Rhetoric*, 100.
33. Dille, 173.
34. Dille, 45.
35. Howe, *Because You Bear This Name*.
36. Howe, 342.
37. Howe, 344–345.

with each borrowing from the other and the input of linguistic theories and methods aiding in the process of running the blend. Dawes also uses CMT to evaluate the concepts ΚΕΦΑΛΗ "head" and ΣΩΜΑ "body" in Ephesians 5:21–33.[38] His argument is that these concepts merge and as a result the commands to be "subordinate" and to "love" apply to both partners (i.e. the husband and the wife).

The use of the CMT approach, as will be discussed in detail later, fails to detail how the underlying process influencing the profiling of a given meaning takes place. It also fails to explain how meaning is constructed in light of the imaginative or creative nature of metaphors, and as Kövecses further points out,

> one of the criticisms of the conceptual metaphor theory (CMT) is that it conceives of metaphors as highly conventional, static conceptual structures (the correspondences, or mappings, between a source and a target domain). It would follow from this that such conceptual structures manifest themselves in the form of highly conventional metaphorical linguistic expressions (like the metaphorical meanings in a dictionary) based on such mappings. If correct, this view does not easily lend itself to an account of metaphorical creativity. Clearly, we often come across novel metaphorical expressions in real discourse. If all there is in metaphor is static conceptual structures matched by highly conventional linguistic expressions, it would seem that CMT runs into difficulty in accounting for the many unconventional and novel expressions we find in discourse.[39]

The metaphorical approach adopted by most of these scholars can be described as being "traditional theological and exegetical" since it tends to assume that the meaning of a metaphor is simply retrieved from the ready-made memory.[40] Such a view is based on the "code model" approach which presupposes that the role of a speaker is to "encode" while that of a hearer is to "decode."[41] It is evident that there is need of the use of a cognitive or

---

38. Dawes, *Body in Question*.
39. Kövecses, *Metaphor in Culture*, 289.
40. Tracy, "Metaphor and Religion," 95; Moreno, *Creativity and Convention*, 1.
41. Wilson and Sperber, "Deflationary Account of Metaphors," 98.

conceptual approach so as to point out the underlying processes that drive the interpretation of metaphors. As Moreno points out, "the human cognitive system seems to be rather selective, at least when it comes to perceiving, processing, memorising and recalling information."[42] This allows an interpreter to focus on the main elements that inform the intended meaning of a given metaphor and at the same time ignore those aspects that happen to be inconsistent with that meaning. One of the examples of this selective process given by Lakoff and Johnson is that of the entailment, LOVE IS A COLLABORATIVE WORK OF ART, which they point out, "requires the masking of certain aspects of love" with aspects such as love emotions "almost never viewed as being under the lover's active control in our conventional conceptual system."[43] Black also discusses this conceptual profiling nature of metaphors by stating that this process "selects, emphasizes, suppresses, and organizes features of the principle subject by implying statements about it that normally apply to the subsidiary subject."[44]

There is the need, therefore, to demonstrate in detail this process as a means of assisting readers to understand why certain metaphors mean what they do in varying contexts. As will be discussed later in the methodological chapter, blending operations which are relevance driven are best suited to explain this creative cognitive process which guides the selection process. The need to reframe biblical studies from a cognitive perspective is captured well by van Wolde who states that such an approach

> . . . focuses on conceptual networks expressed in language and in texts that belong to or function in a specific historical context and are part of culturally bound conceptualizations and categorizations. And it is oriented, as are all disciplines in cognitive studies, on mental activities intimately intertwined with language at all stages of experience, thinking, articulation, and communication in ancient societies. It does not reduce human experiences of the world to the perceiving, experiencing, or knowing of human beings. And it does not explain human experiences as merely responses to external stimuli. Instead,

---

42. Moreno, *Creativity and Convention*, 7.
43. Lakoff and Johnson, *Metaphors We Live By*, 141.
44. Black, *Models and Metaphors*, 44–45.

it focuses on their relation, once (in time and space) a mental connection is made.⁴⁵

1.1.2 Overview of the Interpretation of the Metaphor περιτομὴ καρδίας

This subsection gives a general overview of how different scholars have interpreted the metaphor περιτομὴ καρδίας. The main goal of this endeavor is to find out whether these attempts apply a conceptual/cognitive framework, and if so, whether they address themselves to the underlying selection process that drives the profiling and suppressing of given elements in arriving at the intended meaning of this metaphor in varying contexts.

Berkley, in his book entitled *From a Broken Covenant to Circumcision of Heart*, uses a biblical criticism approach known as intertextual exegesis to analyze Romans 2:17–29.⁴⁶ His goal is to find out some of the gradations which Paul alluded to from the OT which he claims acted as background to the theological themes which inform his arguments and conclusions. Some of the prophetic texts which Berkely alludes to, based on shared common vocabulary, themes and linear developments, include Jeremiah 7:2–11, 9:23–26, and Ezekiel 36:16–27 which he uses to interpret the narrative texts of Deuteronomy 29–30 and Genesis 17.⁴⁷ One of the claims that he makes relates to the role of the Spirit as the agent in the process of the renewal of the heart.⁴⁸ According to him, the concept ΠΝΕΥΜΑ alludes to the promise of spiritual renewal as stated in Ezekiel 36 and consequently this text plays a big role in understanding Paul's interpretation of Romans 2 as far as the relationship between physical and spiritual circumcisions is concerned. He argues that the call for the "circumcision of the heart" through the work of the Spirit should not be interpreted as entirely original to Paul. It is important to note that though this claim might not be original to Paul, he adds new dynamics into the interpretation of this metaphor by going "beyond any first-century Jewish viewpoint in suggesting that physical circumcision is no longer required and in implicitly applying the term Ἰουδαῖος 'Jew' to those who were

---

45. van Wolde, *Reframing Biblical Studies*, 18–19.
46. Berkley, *From a Broken Covenant*.
47. Berkley, 11, 107.
48. Berkley, 145.

not ethnically Jews."⁴⁹ A cognitive-based methodology is well suited, as will be demonstrated in detail in chapter 3, to take on board relevant background texts and assist the reader to arrive at the intended meaning of this metaphor in the context of Romans 2. The suggested conceptual approach will highlight the new elements and links that are activated as well as the background frames and related concepts that are also activated in the process, all of which in one way or another, affect the meaning of this metaphor.

Generally, many of the interpretations suggested about the conventionalized metaphor περιτομὴ καρδίας have to do with drawing further inferences from the general argument that Paul is making in the context of Romans 2.⁵⁰ Such interpretations include a "heart being prepared . . . or marked as belonging to God,"⁵¹ one's "humble response to God's gracious love and election,"⁵² a "distinguishing mark of the true servants of God,"⁵³ a symbol of "a communal recommitment to God and his precepts, resulting in reinstatement of divine favor and return to the land,"⁵⁴ a "circumcision of the spirit and not the flesh, goes to the heart of a man, to his soul, his essence, his attitudes and relationship with God,"⁵⁵ a "figurative expression for inward purity,"⁵⁶ a "circumcision which cleanses the heart,"⁵⁷ "the cutting off the lusts of the heart and life, or parting with the corruption of nature, which rebels against the Spirit,"⁵⁸ a "renewal and purification of the heart,"⁵⁹ a circumcision from its "filthiness and depravity,"⁶⁰ "an inner commitment to God and to his will,"⁶¹ and doing

---

49. Moo, *Epistle to the Romans*, 174–175.

50. Conventionalized metaphors are those metaphors which are associated with the normal use of language and thus become part of the language resources that are shared by speakers' of the language in talking about a specific topic (Cameron, *Metaphor in Educational Discourse*, 101).

51. Newman and Nida, *Translator's Handbook*, 49.

52. Barrett, *Commentary on the Epistle to the Romans*, 60.

53. Beet, *Commentary on St. Paul's Epistle*, 91.

54. Bernat, *Sign of the Covenant*, 127–128.

55. Friedman, "Circumcision of the Heart."

56. Gifford, *Romans*, 80.

57. Godet, *Commentary on Romans*, 131.

58. Keach, *Preaching from the Types and Metaphors*, 993.

59. Murray, *Epistle to the Romans*, 88.

60. Robinson, *Studies in Romans*, 190.

61. Ziesler, *Paul's Letter to the Romans*, 93.

the right things in the heart,[62] to mention just a few. However these interpretations assume that the readers, who happen to come from different cultural backgrounds, will readily derive such inferences and thus the failure to detail the underlying selective process that profiles given inferences and not others. As will be illustrated in the coming chapters, the suggested cognitive-based complementary approach between Conceptual Integration (or Blending) Theory (CIT) and Relevance Theory (RT) goes a long way in explaining how the underlying selective processes take place.

1.1.3 The Challenge of the Heart Metaphor

The metaphorical language of circumcision and uncircumcision in the Bible has been associated to other parts of the body as well, besides the male reproductive organ.[63] These include "lips" (שְׂפָתַיִם עֲרֵל) "uncircumcised of lips" in Exod 6:12, 30), "heart" (לְבָבָם הֶעָרֵל) "their uncircumcised heart" in Lev 26:41), and "ears" (אָזְנָם עֲרֵלָה) "uncircumcised [are] their ears" as in Jer 6:10). The focus of this dissertation is the association of the ritual of circumcision to the heart, which is the most common of these foreskinned metaphors.[64] As will be demonstrated in detail in the later chapters, there are assumed cultural differences that exist between the source and receptor languages when it comes to the implied concepts in this metaphor. It is thus important for a translator to first understand how this metaphor is used within the source culture so as to be able to communicate the religious related assumptions which it is associated with to the receptor audience. I have chosen to focus on the interpretation and translation of the metaphor περιτομὴ καρδίας into

---

62. Gross, "Circumcision in the New Testament," 424.

63. As to whether the phrase περιτομὴ καρδίας is a metaphor or a metonymy, I have taken the view that this is a case of a metaphor with a "built-in" metonymy (i.e. a metonymy within a metaphor) (Goossens, "Metaphtonymy," 350, 363). It is a metaphor with an inbuilt metonymy with the two discrete domains being brought together in a metaphorical relationship ("Metaphtonymy," 352; Ibáñez, "Role of Mappings and Domains," 130). As Radden ("How Metonymic Are Metaphors?" 93) further points out, the distinction between a metaphor and a metonymy is one which is notoriously difficult to differentiate and therefore it is better to think of these two as a continuum with unclear cases in between.

64. Others heart metaphors include וּמַלְתֶּם אֵת עָרְלַת לְבַבְכֶם "and you will circumcise the foreskin of your heart" (Deut 10:16), וּמָל. . . אֶת־לְבָבְךָ "and he will circumcise . . . your heart" (Deut 30:6), הִמֹּלוּ. . . וְהָסִרוּ עָרְלוֹת לְבַבְכֶם "circumcise yourselves . . . and remove the foreskins of your heart" (Jer 4:4), עַרְלֵי־לֵב "uncircumcised of heart" (Jer 9:25; Ezek 44:7, 9), ἀπερίτμητοι καρδίας "uncircumcised hearts" (Acts 7:51), περιτομὴ καρδίας "circumcision of heart" (Rom 2:29).

Kikuyu in the context of Romans 2:17–29 so as to limit this study within a given discourse context.[65] This discourse context will be crucial in analyzing the cognitive process including the relevant frames, elements, projections, and inferences, which influence the meaning of this metaphor.[66]

As Nida rightly points out, "terms associated with social culture pose numerous problems, not only because the basic systems are often so different, but also because the extensions of meaning appropriate to one system rarely work in another."[67] Across these two cultures, as will be demonstrated in details in chapters 3 and 4, circumcision is an important ritual with physical, social and spiritual connotations. There is need, therefore, to have a detailed understanding of the associated concepts of ΠΕΡΙΤΟΜΗ and ΚΑΡΔΙΑ activated in the associated mental spaces in the source language (SL) so as to be able to render appropriately the argument that the apostle Paul is making in the context of Romans 2. On the other hand, it is equally important to understand the relevant concepts activated in the receptor language, which include those of IRUA "circumcision" and NGORO "heart." This is because, as will be demonstrated later, the receptor language (RL) construal which is activated is quite different from the one activated in the SL, leading to the derivation of wrong inferences and subsequently the wrong interpretation of this metaphor.

1.2 The Research Problem

The metaphor περιτομὴ καρδίας in Romans 2:29 is quite a difficult metaphor to translate across languages.[68] In an effort to translate this metaphor, both the old Kikuyu Bible (*Ibuku rĩa Ngai*) and the new one (*Ibuku rĩa Ũhoro ũrĩa Mwega*) have rendered this metaphor literally as *kũrua [kwa] ngoro* "circumcision of the heart." These two translations have the same literal rendering though they fall under two different traditions (i.e. the literal and

---

65. This phrase is a predicate nominative with the subject being joined by an equative verb, meaning "circumcision [which is that] of the heart" (Wallace, *Greek Grammar beyond the Basics*, 40).
66. Dawes, *Body in Question*, 77.
67. Nida, *Towards a Science of Translating*, 216.
68. Newman and Nida, *Translator's Handbook*, 49.

meaning-based translations).⁶⁹ There is a possibility that the translators of the new Kikuyu translation saw the need to maintain the "otherness" for this specific metaphor.⁷⁰ The literal rendering, makes the compared concepts look as if they are simple equivalents that correspond exactly across the two languages, while on the contrary, as will be demonstrated in later chapters, the conventionalized conceptual world that is activated when these associated concepts are evoked across the two languages are not exactly the same. Thus, it is expected that translating this metaphor literally across the two languages without underlining the conceptual differences is bound to lead to the derivation of wrong inferences and implications other than those which were originally intended.

The background framing of the Jewish conceptualization of the concept ΠΕΡΙΤΟΜΗ traditionally activates the frame of covenant fidelity as this ritual was primarily conceptualized as a means of assimilation to the promises of the patriarchs as well as incorporation into Israel's covenant community.⁷¹ The ritual was understood to be a sign of the covenant even before it became part of the law of Moses.⁷² This background framing forms the basis of inferences which the readers were intended to readily draw. As will be argued in chapter 3, these inferences are subsequently adjusted within the context of Romans 2 to narrow the meaning of the metaphor to that of a cleansing or purging ritual which all people need to undergo in order to be cleansed of their sins.

---

69. A literal translation makes a formal correspondence of words from the source to the receptor language and therefore does not make an adjustment of figures of speech while a meaning-based or dynamic-equivalent translation seeks to have the readers respond substantially the same way as the SL receptors and therefore tends to make adjustments in rendering figures of speech (Beekman and Callow, *Translating the Word of God*, 21; Nida and Taber, *Theory and Practice of Translation*, 24; Mojola, "Bible Translation in Africa," 202–213). Though this distinction predominates given translations, translations do not entirely belong entirely to one and not the other when it comes to specific renderings there is a tendency to find traces of both thus translations can only "be placed at some point in a line between extremely literal and extremely free" (Dewey, *User's Guide to Bible Translations*, 33–34).

70. Evans and Krajewska, "Equivalence," 153.

71. Derouchie, "Circumcision in the Hebrew Bible," 186–196; Williamson, "Circumcision," 123.

72. The covenant between God and Abraham is spelled out in Genesis 12:1–3, and revisited in Genesis 15 and Genesis 17. In Genesis 17 alone, the word ברית occurs thirteen times and the background framing of this covenant forms the context of the metaphorical use of this concept in Deuteronomy 10:16 and 30:6. Paul expounds on the same COVENANT frame (which is translated in Greek as διαθηκη in making his argument in the book of Romans (cf. Rom 4; 9:4; 11:27; Gen 17:10–13; Lev 12:3).

On the other hand, the first interpretation which is consistent with the principle of relevance that is evoked in the mind of a Kikuyu reader when the concept IRUA* is evoked is that of a [RITE OF PASSAGE]. This ritual marks a change of status from that of a child to that of an adult member of the society. From this background framing, the readers are bound to draw inferences and also activate other related concepts which are not necessarily those that were originally intended. There is need, therefore, for a translator targeting such an audience with a different construal of the associated concepts in this metaphor, to draw their attention to the similarities as well as differences between these two conceptual frameworks. Where need be, the translator is called upon to take a further step and provide the missing contextual information so that it forms part of the readers' cognitive environment which is relevant to arriving at the intended meaning. These conceptual differences include the physical, social and spiritual connotations evoked in respect to the rituals across the two cultures. The goal of this research is to demonstrate how the associated concepts in the metaphor περιτομὴ καρδίας come together within the context of Romans 2 and how best to render this metaphor to a Kikuyu audience.

There is also a need to come up with a cognitive methodological approach that can assist translators to effectively render metaphors across languages. The CIT conceptual framework proposed by Fauconnier and Turner falls short of giving a satisfactory description on the process in relation to how the proposed blended spaces are composed as well as in detailing how the underlying integration process is run.[73] This framework raises specific questions as to how input spaces are composed or selected, how the selection projection of elements from the input spaces into the blend takes place, how the interrelated cognitive processes of composition, completion and elaboration take place in the blend, as well as how the process comes to a stop when the interpreter successfully arrives at the intended meaning. There is need to provide a full computational analysis of how the integration process takes place as well as how it is driven in an attempt to make this process accessible where need be.

---

73. Fauconnier and Turner, *Way We Think*.

1.3 The Thesis Statement

In this study, I am making three related claims. The first one is that though there are significant differences between CIT and RT as far as the interpretation of metaphors is concerned, these approaches are largely complementary since they tackle different aspects of metaphoric conceptualization. While CIT tends to focus on the structure of a metaphor within the conceptual system, RT sheds light as to how the process of drawing and constraining of inferences and projection of elements takes place within the integration process. As a result, the entire process, from its beginning to its end, is constrained by the principle of relevance (i.e. since people tend to pay attention to information that seems relevant to them), with considerations of cognitive effects and cognitive effort within the relevance theoretic framework being the criterion for evaluating the intended interpretation.[74]

The second claim, which results from the application of the proposed complementary approach, is that the lexical adjusted meaning of the associated concepts in the metaphor περιτομὴ καρδίας within the context of Romans chapter 2 is that of a cleansing or purification ritual. As will be demonstrated in chapter 3, the apostle Paul profiles this meaning by reorganizing the traditional conceptualization of his readers as far as the framing of the associated concepts in this metaphor is concerned, by adding, removing, and altering some elements that they held dearly.

The third claim is that even though the Kikuyu translation tends to imply that the same conceptual framework as that of the SL is activated by translating the metaphor περιτομὴ καρδίας literally as *kũrua [kwa] ngoro*, there are conceptual differences between the associated concepts which the receptor audience needs to be aware of so as to adequately arrive at the intended meaning. There is need, therefore, to bridge the existing conceptual gap by availing relevant SL information to the receptor readers as a means towards assisting them to evoke the relevant frames and inferences so as to arrive at the intended meaning of the use of the SL metaphor περιτομὴ καρδίας in the context of Romans 2.

---

74. Sperber and Wilson, *Relevance, Communication and Cognition*, 158, 260, 263–266.

1.4 The Research Questions

The following are the research questions that this study seeks to address in an attempt to substantiate the above claims:

1. How does the suggested complementary approach between CIT and RT contribute towards a unitary or complementary theory of metaphor? Specific issues to be addressed include how mental spaces are generated and associated within the conceptual system, how inferences, projections and/or suppression of elements are arrived at across the integration network, as well as the process behind running the blend.

2. How does the apostle Paul go about guiding his readers to adjust or shift from their traditional understanding of the associated concepts in the metaphor περιτομὴ καρδίας in Romans 2:29? Issues to be addressed here include pointing out the input spaces and scope network(s) which emerge from the source language conceptual frameworks, showing the schematic scenarios that relate to Paul's argument and how they are cued and blended in the text, as well as highlighting the relevant interpretive frames that Paul is deliberately evoking or profiling in the mind of his readers within the discourse context of Romans 2:29.

3. What are the different cognitive frames, related concepts, and profiled elements that are activated when the concepts *IRUA*, *NGORO* and *HAKIRI* are evoked in the RL? I will seek to point out the inferences which are invited or disallowed by the underlying cognitive frames in light of the social and ethical variations evoked by these concepts as well as discuss the input spaces and scope network(s) which emerge when the above concepts are associated in a metaphorical relationship in the RL. There is need to also point out what is added, removed, and/or altered in the conceptualization of these concepts when compared to those of the SL, in an attempt to suggest how best to translate the metaphor περιτομὴ καρδίας into Kikuyu, so as to evoke the relevant frames and intended inferences in the context of Romans 2.

1.5 Field Data and Research Methodology

Metaphors are culture specific, and so it is important to interpret them within their cultural context as this informs their conceptual content.[75] In an effort to understand better the cultural connotations of the associated concepts in the metaphor *kūrua ngoro*, "circumcision of heart," I conducted a descriptive field research to find out how this metaphor and its associated concepts are construed. I also conducted a field research to find out the meaning of a related metaphor which is commonly used to advise initiates to behave like adults (i.e. *kūgimara hakiri* "to be circumcised in the mind"), since my claim is that the meaning of this metaphor is recruited in the interpretation of the metaphor *kūrua ngoro*. This conceptual-based field research is also intended to find out which frames, sub-concepts, and inferences are activated when these metaphors and their associated concepts, namely, [IRUA] "circumcision," [NGORO] "heart," and [HAKIRI] "mind" are evoked by Kikuyu native speakers. The field data provided primary data on how the ritual of [IRUA*] is construed in its entirety as well as how related concepts in given metaphorical relationship to avoid interpretations that are isolated and out-of-context.[76] I also engaged secondary sources from libraries which also contain data written on the ritual of [IRUA*].

The nature of the field research approach employed is that of a qualitative inquiry.[77] This is informed by the fact that this is a conceptual research intended for an in-depth look at how concepts are construed by the native speakers. This approach also helped in capturing the dynamic nature of this ritual in light of its flexibility and interactive nature. The approach assisted me to arrive at an in-depth wealth of information with the selected groups that formed my sampling frame.[78]

In conducting the field research, I used a non-random purposeful or judgmental sampling approach.[79] One group that formed my sampling frame was that of men who were in their late 60s and early 70s. They were purposefully

---

75. Charteris-Black, "Contrastive Cognitive Perspective," 156.
76. Patton, *How to Use Qualitative Methods*, 18.
77. Williams and Chesterman, *The Map*, 59; Mertens, *Research and Evaluation*, 399.
78. Mertens, *Research and Evaluation*, 311, 323.
79. Hennink, Hutter and Bailey, *Qualitative Research Methods*, 85; Patton, *How to Use Qualitative Methods*, 52; Creswell, *Qualitative Inquiry and Research*, 118; Gay, Mills and Airasian, *Educational Research*, 600.

selected to provide information mostly concerning the ritual of [IRUA*] in light of their knowledge and experience having undergone the traditional ritual themselves. The age groups following this, including those who were in their forties, had undergone the hospital surgery and the information which they have is in the form of *kĩrĩra* "passed-down teachings" from the previous age groups. I interviewed eleven men in total and stopped gathering more information when I noticed I had reached a point of information saturation as the same information started to repeat itself and provided no new insights.[80] Though there are no specific guidelines as far as "determining the size of purposeful samples" is concerned, there is growing evidence that to understand and uncover core categories in a cultural domain, ten to twenty knowledgeable people are enough.[81] I also took the opportunity to inquire from the same group the meaning of the metaphor *kũgimara hakiri* since the context of discussing the ritual of [IRUA*] provided the right setting for the participants' frame of reference.[82]

I also conducted a specific research among eighty Christians to find out their understanding of the metaphor *kũrua ngoro* "circumcision of heart" in the context of Romans 2. The reason for focusing on Christians as one of the groups in my sampling frame is in light of the fact that they are the only ones who might have encountered this metaphor in one way or another and also because they are likely to feel obligated to understand and interpret it. I used the approach of recruiting respondents through what is referred to as the gatekeepers or snowball-sampling approach by recruiting pastors to identify them.[83] This is because I needed a bridge to gain their confidence and also since I was new in these areas, I needed help in locating them. I also conducted interviews with two church leaders as well as read relevant literature written on [IRUA] to find out how this ritual is construed and conducted among Christians today.[84] I did not consider the level of education or age as

---

80. Hennink, Hutter and Bailey, *Qualitative Research Methods*, 88; Charmaz, *Constructing Grounding Theory*, 113.

81. Patton, *How to Use Qualitative Methods*, 58; Gay, Mills and Airasian, *Educational Research*, 154.

82. Marshall and Rossman, *Designing Qualitative Research*, 92.

83. Hennink, Hutter and Bailey, *Qualitative Research Methods*, 92; Mertens, *Research and Evaluation in Education*, 322.

84. Cf. Gachiri, *Rite of Passage for Christian Boys*; Githura, "Factors That Influence"; Njiraini, "Mentoring."

varied factors affecting the respondents' conceptualization of these concepts so as to reduce the possibility of any sampling bias. As I conducted this research, I found out that as the number of the respondents increased, I was not gathering any new information and therefore had to stop. I first exposed the respondents to the context of the metaphor by reading Romans 2:17–29, before asking them to give their understanding of the metaphor *kūrua ngoro* with the goal of making sure that their responses were context-bound.

I chose all the respondents from three counties, namely, Murang'a, Kiambu, and Nyeri. The reason is that these counties are the traditional strongholds where the people of Kikuyu live, and it is from here that the Kikuyu people dispersed to other locations.[85] I also wanted to find out whether there are important differences in how the ritual of [IRUA*] is construed across these counties.

In conducting the interviews, I used open-ended questions in an effort to direct and avoid manipulating the responses as well as to extract detailed information including that of the associated perceptions and attitudes activated in the mind of the interviewees.[86] I also used further probing and follow-up questions to seek for elaborations and more details. A sample of some probing questions can be found in appendix B. I did not work on the probing questions in advance which enabled me to creatively come up with the wording as well as the sequence of asking them in the course of the interviews.[87] The in-depth, open-ended direct questions went a long way in avoiding the bias of having predetermined categories.[88] These questions were semi-structures and were guided by the objectives of the study as well as the topics that needed to be covered.[89] The main five open-ended questions that I posed (see appendix A) were intended to find out the respondents' understanding of the concepts IRUA*, HAKIRI, and NGORO, as well as their association in the metaphors *kūrua hakiri* and *kūrua ngoro*.

The data relating mostly to the ritual of [IRUA*] was collected in the form of tape recordings and important parts were transcribed for analysis. One

---

85. Fedders and Salvadori, *Peoples and Cultures of Kenya*, 117.
86. Weiss, *Learning from Strangers*, 3; Mugenda and Mugenda, *Research Methods*, 197–200.
87. Patton, *How to Use Qualitative Methods*, 111.
88. Patton, 7, 9.
89. Gay, Mills and Airasian, *Educational Research*, 158.

such extract can be found in appendix B. The responses relating to the understanding of the associated concepts in the metaphorical relationship (i.e. HAKIRI and NGORO) were mostly taken through written notes with the same process being used to take note of key concepts and follow-up questions in the course of the interviews. The church interviews were mostly in the form of written responses.

The data analysis was inductive and involved generating and organizing data into categories according to the responses on the questions posed.[90] The goal of this approach was to develop a conceptual understanding of the entire ritual by linking the core concept and other related sub-concepts or dominant categories to a broad conceptual framework.[91] I looked for concepts that fell under different thematic conceptual sub-categories that go together as they emerged out of the data which mostly involved putting together responses to a particular evaluation question.[92] I then categorized the collected data into cognitive frames. Evaluations, claims and interpretations have been derived from the field data as I sought to bring out meaning and insights from the same.

1.6 The Scope and Limitations of this Study

There is need to clarify and delimit the scope of this study. This research is not intended to be a detailed exploration nor an extensive survey of the respective source and receptor cultural rituals of circumcision or other related rituals. As a result, not every aspect of these rituals is discussed here, but only those aspects of the associated concepts which contribute towards the interpretation and translation of the metaphor περιτομὴ καρδίας in the context of Romans 2. I have also avoided discussing all the underlying semantic motivations behind the grammatical constructions of each and every word found in the text of Romans 2 but only a few which in one way or another contribute to the arguments which I am making.

I have also not endeavored to discuss the historicity of the theories of metaphor from Plato to Aristotle to Aquinas, nor have I indulged much in

---

90. Patton, *How to Use Qualitative Methods*, 149.

91. Boeije, *Analysis in Qualitative Research*, 84, 109.

92. Patton, *How to Use Qualitative Methods*, 15; Strauss and Corbin, *Basics of Qualitative Research*, 16, 64, 112.

surveying the extensive literature on metaphor or in discussing the whole spectrum of contemporary theories of metaphor, a task which Howe addresses himself to.[93] Additionally, I have not discussed how metaphors relate to other figures of speech such as metonymy, irony, etc., a task which Goossens adequately addresses.[94] I have also not discussed every detail of RT but have only referred to relevant portions of the theory which are central in bridging the gaps left by the blending process in light of the complementary approach that I have proposed. Finally, I have only highlighted relevant aspects in the vast field of cognitive linguistics to try and offer a reasonable complementary metaphor theory on the basis of data collected. Tendahl and Gibbs in their article entitled "Complementary Perspectives on Metaphor" give a detailed analysis of cognitive theories of metaphors.[95]

This study is far from being a theological reflection detailing the purpose of this ritual in both the source and receptor languages, especially as it relates to its origin and practice. Similarly, this study is not intended to be a historical narration regarding the ritual of circumcision as recorded in both the Hebrew and Greek Bibles. For an overview of the origin, practice, and significance of circumcision from both source and receptor languages, I recommend the works of Williamson,[96] Kline,[97] Hegg,[98] Derouchie,[99] and Wambũgũ, Ngarariga, and Kariũki,[100] among others. For those who might be specifically interested in knowing how to incorporate the Kikuyu traditional rite of passage from a Christian perspective, Gachiri's book entitled *Rite of Passage for Christian Boys*, details how to go about it.[101] This study is also focused on the Kikuyu people and not on the other neighboring communities since they have, or are about to have, their own Bible translations. I also do not discuss the corresponding ritual of girls in Kikuyu since it has

---

93. Howe, *Because You Bear This Name*, 11–106.
94. Goossens, "Metaphtonymy," 349–377.
95. Tendahl and Gibbs, "Complementary Perspectives on Metaphor."
96. Williamson, "Circumcision."
97. Kline, *By Oath Consigned*.
98. Hegg, "Circumcision as a Sign."
99. Derouchie, "Circumcision in the Hebrew Bible."
100. Wambũgũ, Ngarariga, and Kariũki, *The Agĩkũyũ*.
101. Gachiri, *Rite of Passage for Christian Boys*.

disappeared over time and therefore when the concept [IRUA] is recalled, only that relating to boys is strongly activated.

1.7 Relevance to Field of Bible Translation

Biblical metaphors, especially those whose associated concepts involve rituals and customs, are a big challenge when it comes to translating them across languages. This challenge results from differences in cultural and semantic associations of the related concepts which are quite difficult to reproduce across languages. Since rituals are quite common among African cultures, this study should provide a helpful approach which will go a long way in assisting translators on how to go about rendering them across languages. The application of the notion of Frame Semantics, specifically that of frame shifting, in the blending process is also a major contribution to the work of Bible translation. I hope that translators will appreciate the fact that translation is a process which mostly involves adjusting the target peoples' conceptual frames. This is in light of the fact that frames do not match neatly across languages, in view of the fact that they are experiential, dynamic, and culture specific.

The proposed complementary approach between CIT and RT is intended to offer a more comprehensive cognitive approach when it comes to the interpretation and translation of metaphors. This study is unique in that it suggests a complementary approach specifically to the translation of biblical metaphors, by providing details as to how the selection processes is driven as well as how emergent properties are generated. As Moreno points out

> . . . very little work has been done to explain how emergent properties are derived. In fact, experimental work which deals explicitly with the issue . . . has mostly been concerned with presenting evidence for the existence of emergent features rather than explanation of the cognitive processes involved in their derivation.[102]

While CIT generates the input spaces and the information contained in these input spaces, RT establishes the links within the spaces and illustrates how relevant elements, projections and emergent properties are generated in

---

102. Moreno, *Creativity and Convention*, 77.

the blended space. My hope is that the suggested complementary approach will provide some insights as to how creativity takes place in the interpretation and translation of metaphors.

1.8 Overview of Dissertation Content

In the second chapter of this book, which is the theoretical chapter, the central role that conceptual frames have in the interpretation and translation of metaphors is highlighted. I also argue for the merits of the suggested complementary approach between CIT and RT by pointing out gaps and how they can be bridged.

In chapter 3, I discuss the schematization of the concepts ΠΕΡΙΤΟΜΗ and ΚΑΡΔΙΑ as input spaces in the blending process, and then argue for the meaning of these associated concepts in the context of Romans 2. These include profiling elements that are activated or semi-activated, both from the traditional as well as modified frames which Paul is comparing, as well as the inferences that are allowed in the process.

In chapter 4, the Kikuyu conceptualization of the associated concepts IRUA, NGORO and HAKIRI is discussed in light of findings from the field research. In the integration process relating to these RL concepts, the elements, links, and inferences that are allowed in the integration process are discussed and those that are projected to the blend highlighted.

In chapter 5, I compare the two resulting blended spaces from the source and receptor languages within the translation space with the goal of underscoring elements and relations that are made salient. I then suggest the best way to translate the SL metaphor περιτομὴ καρδίας into Kikuyu.

Chapter 6 summarizes the findings as well as answers the questions raised at the beginning of the study. This chapter also derives some general conclusions and gives further recommendations.

CHAPTER 2

Theoretical Approach

Since cognitive linguistics is more of an approach that has shared guiding principles, perspectives and assumptions, and not a specific theory, there is a diverse range of overlapping, complementing, and sometimes competing theories, which have been proposed as ways of arriving at how meaning is constructed in the mind.[1] Such approaches include cognitive grammar,[2] cognitive semantics,[3] mental space theory,[4] conceptual blending theory,[5] and relevance theory,[6] to mention just a few. This chapter expounds the theoretical basis for the complementary approach adapted in this study, more specifically as it relates to the construction of the meaning of metaphors.

As previously mentioned, it is beyond the scope of this work to discuss each and every conceptual theory of metaphor, but the focus in this theoretical framework is that which is fundamental to the suggested complementary approach. These include cognitive semantics, more specifically, the related topics of frame semantics and frame shifting and aspects of the two theories which are the focus of this study, namely CIT and RT. I will point out the methodological gaps in the integration process and the crucial role that the suggested outer spaces, namely the discourse and relevance spaces, play in

---

1. Evans and Green, *Cognitive Linguistics*, 3.
2. Langacker, *Foundations of Cognitive Grammar*, vol. 1; Langacker, *Concept, Image and Symbol*; Langacker, *Cognitive Grammar*.
3. Lakoff, "Cognitive Semantics"; Saeed, *Semantics*.
4. Fauconnier, *Mental Spaces*; Fauconnier, *Mappings in Thought and Language*; Fauconnier and Sweetser, *Spaces, Worlds and Grammars*.
5. Fauconnier and Turner, "Conceptual Integration Networks"; *Way We Think*.
6. Sperber and Wilson, *Relevance, Communication and Cognition*.

the construction of the meaning of a given metaphor. I will then point out how the complementary approach will be used in this work before making some concluding observations.

2.1 Theoretical Framework

The cognitive nature of metaphors poses a challenge in adequately rendering them across languages. This conceptual nature of metaphors discussed below informs the complementary approach between cognitive linguistics and RT proposed in this work.

2.1.1 The Conceptual Nature of Metaphors

One of the definitions that points to the conceptual nature of metaphors is given by Barcelona who defines metaphor as a "cognitive mechanism whereby one experiential domain is partially 'mapped,' i.e. projected, onto a different experiential domain, so that the second domain is partially understood in terms of the first one."[7] Two other cognitive linguists, Lakoff and Johnson point out that the process of interpreting a metaphor is driven by conceptualizing experiences which enable an interpreter to pick out the important aspects that are relevant and at the same time disregard those that are not.[8] The Conceptual Integration or Blending Theory (CIT), which informs the approach adapted in this work, also refer to metaphors as "arising from complex blending processes that reflect ad hoc, creative thought processes."[9] Since metaphors are a result of a cognitive creative process, they tend to be based on one's experiences, meaning that the background framing of the associated concepts cannot exist outside a cultural framework.[10]

Dille acknowledges the effect of culture in the interpretation of metaphors by pointing out that even though a concept such as that of CHILDBIRTH is a widely experienced ritual across all cultures, in its conceptualization, it is first

---

7. Barcelona, "Introduction," 3.

8. Lakoff and Johnson, *Metaphors We Live By*, 83.

9. In this work, the term "Conceptual Integration" is used rather than "Blending" thus the acronyms CIT (Fauconnier and Turner, *Way We Think*). This approach is referred elsewhere as "conceptual integration," "mental binding," "space structuring model," or simply as the "blending theory" (Coulson and Oakley, "Blending and Coded Meaning"; Coulson, *Semantic Leaps*; Tendahl, *Hybrid Theory of Metaphor*, 143.

10. Lakoff and Johnson, *Metaphors We Live By*, 19.

and foremost culturally shaped.[11] Some of the universal elements associated with this ritual shared across cultures include the pregnancy period, birth pains, and role of midwives. On the other hand, every culture has a distinctive conceptualization of this ritual, an example being the Kikuyu who announce the birth of the babies differently according to their gender, with a boy attracting five ululations and a girl three. The context of a metaphor does not only refer to its co-text, be it spoken or written, but also to that of a speaker and her audience as well as to the purpose for which the metaphor is used.[12] There is no doubt that a given context has an important role in determining the meaning of a given metaphor, and as Cormac further points out, "one cannot explain the operation of communicative meaning in metaphors without paying attention to the . . . context in which the metaphor occurs, and its wider cultural context."[13]

In her book written to train translators, Barnwell points out that for a translator to uncover the meaning of a metaphor, he needs to identify its three componential parts, namely, the topic, the illustration, and the point(s) of similarity.[14] She gives an example from Hebrews 11:12 which talks of Abraham as the one from whom came descendants who are as many as the stars of heaven and as the sand of the seashore. The "descendants" is the topic, the "stars of heaven" is the illustration, and the fact that both are "many" is the point of similarity. This view is based on the "code model" approach in the translation process in which the role of a translator is that of encoding the message and that of the hearer/reader that of decoding that message. The weakness of this model is that it does not give ample emphasis to the context factor for, as Wilson and Sperber point out, for any "communication to be achieved purely by coding and decoding, each signal in the code must unambiguously convey exactly the same context on all occasions."[15] One cannot interpret a given linguistic utterance without referring to its context of communication, meaning that a context might not be automatically communicated through the coding process alone.

---

11. Dille, *Mixing Metaphors*, 17.
12. Booth, "Ten Literal Theses," 174.
13. Cormac, *Cognitive Theory of Metaphor*, 192.
14. Barnwell, *Bible Translation*, 141–142.
15. Wilson and Sperber, "Deflationary Account of Metaphors," 98.

In the conceptual nature of metaphors adopted in this study, there is no clear division that can be drawn between the literal and figurative meaning of words. The issue of whether it is possible to draw a line between the literal and figurative meaning of words in a metaphorical relationship has drawn a heated controversy between scholars. Davidson argues that in order to determine the meaning of a given metaphor, one needs to only appeal to the literal meaning of words that constitute the metaphor and nothing more.[16] He argues that it is from the literal meaning that words obtain their metaphorical meaning through acquiring new extensions, implying that a word does not acquire a new meaning through its metaphorical use. He gives the example of the statement "the Spirit of God moving upon the face of the waters" in which he argues that the word "face" acquires a new extension by being applied to "waters."[17] I find this view to be oversimplified as well as erroneous since the literal meaning of the associated concepts in a metaphorical relationship tend to normally conflict with the meaning of the metaphor given that "waters" do not have a "face." There are examples where the use of a lexical unit is clearly metaphorical as in the case in Luke 13:32 where Jesus referred to Herod as a fox. In this instance, it is clear that Jesus did not refer to Herod as being literally a fox and a reader is invited to discover what Jesus meant by the use of this comparison. Some of the interpretations expressed include Herod being cunning and treacherous,[18] destructive,[19] worthless,[20] contemptuous,[21] or a political nuisance.[22]

The challenge with Davidson's approach is that one may be tempted to think that it is possible to draw a clear line between the literal and figurative meaning of a word in a metaphorical relationship. This might not be the case, and as Soskice points out, "[w]hile it is possible to specify literal senses for terms, the metaphorical meaning pertains not to the individual terms but

---

16. Davidson, "What Metaphors Mean," 30; the word "literal" here means the ordinary use of language in expressing concrete objects and events (Cormac, *Cognitive Theory of Metaphor*, 73).

17. Gen 1:2; Davidson, "What Metaphors Mean," 32.

18. Evans, *Luke*, 216.

19. Bock, *Luke*, 247.

20. Louw and Nida, *Greek-English Lexicon*, 755.

21. Morris, *Luke*, 249.

22. Ryken, Wilhoit, and Longman III, *Dictionary of Biblical Imagery*, 30.

to the complete utterance."²³ Establishing a neat dividing line between these two is a difficult task, since as Cormac points out, "such a criterion must be linguistic as well as cognitive; we have to show how the literal can be experienced or perceived as literal and the metaphorical as metaphorical."²⁴ Leezenberg further states:

> The notion of literal meaning, then, expresses an ideal academic discourse rather than the reality of everyday communication. Word meaning may be relatively stabilized by oft-repeated usages, but this semblance of a literal meaning should not be confused with literal meaning as a precise and decontextualized notion. Word meanings are context-dependent, imprecise, and variable . . . the different applications of a word in different contexts need not have any one aspect of meaning in common, nor does any one application in a specific dimension have to be logically prior to, or more important than, others. The concept of literal meaning may serve as a regulatory ideal for education and lexicography, but it has no use in either everyday linguistic behavior or in semantic or conceptual theorizing. Literal meaning, in other words, is a myth: as convenient as it may be, it is, in the final analysis, a fiction.²⁵

The attempt to make a distinction between the literal and metaphorical senses of words fails to take on board the possibility that a given lexical unit can have both of these senses depending on the situational context of the utterance. Take the example of the use of the word שתה in Obadiah 1:16. This concept can be understood as having a literal sense referring to someone who has swallowed some amount of alcoholic substance.²⁶ It can also be interpreted

---

23. Soskice, *Metaphor and Religious Language*, 84.
24. Cormac, *Cognitive Theory of Metaphor*, 15.
25. Leezenberg, *Contexts of Metaphor*, 304.
26. Other objects that indicate the verb שתה has been used in a literal sense include its association with water (Gen 24:14; Num 20:11), (fermented) wine (Gen 19:33; Jude 13:4, 7, 14), milk (Ezek 25:4), and urine (2 Kgs 18:27; Isa 36:12). The context of the book of Obadiah rules out water, milk, and urine as being the likely objects of the verb שתה since the context is not about the people of Edom quenching their thirst, being refreshed, or being under siege. The context is about their wrong doing against the people of Israel and therefore the most probable object is that of wine.

as having a metaphorical sense to refer to a number of figurative uses.[27] Since there is no cut-off point that would involve different interpretive mechanisms for the literal and metaphorical senses, my claim is that both senses have been blended together within the same context. On the one hand, the people of Edom did indeed hold a "merry party" on the mountain of God, with this act of drunkenness being associated with victory. There is the possibility that after the victory, the Edomite army went ahead to celebrate using the spoils such as food and drinks from their defeated enemy. On the other hand, a metaphorical interpretation would bring out the irony that what they were really drinking was the wrath of God.[28] This paves way for the possibility of their celebration quickly turning into a drunkenness of another kind, that which was associated with the "cup of wrath" symbolizing the Lord fighting the Edomites for treating their brothers, the people of Israel, with cruelty.[29] We find the same figurative sense occurring elsewhere, both in the OT as well as in the NT, symbolizing both God's anger and Christ's suffering.[30]

The conceptual approach of metaphors diminishes the distinction made between the literal and the metaphorical senses of a word, and at the same time allows one to make the decision, if need be, whether the use of a word is clearly metaphorical within a given context. From this perspective, metaphors are treated "as simply a range of cases at one end of a continuum that includes literal, loose and hyperbolic interpretations" having "no sharp cut-off point

---

27. The verb שתה is used figuratively a number of times in the Scriptures. It is associated with "blood" to refer to the water which David's men risked their lives to bring to their king symbolizing the sacrifice they undertook on behalf of their king (1 Chr 11:19), with blood associated elsewhere with the verb שתה to represent an act of slaughter (cf. Num 23:24; Isa 49:26; Deut 32:42). The verb שתה also takes "poison" as its object, an example being that of Job confessing to drinking "poison" from God's arrows as a figurative way of communicating the sufferings that he was going through (Job 6:4). The verb שתה is also used figuratively in the phrase "drinking water from one's own cistern" symbolizing enjoyment of sexual relations with ones wife only (Prov 5:15). Another object of שתה which points to its figurative use is its association with the abstract object "shame" to symbolically point to the fate that awaited the Babylonians for the violent acts they did against many nations (Hab 2:16). Other abstract objects used with the verb שתה include wickedness (Job 15:16), slander (Job 34:7), violence (Prov 26:6), and "the cup of God's wrath" (Isa 51:17, 22; Jer 25:16, 26–27; 49:12; 51:7; Ezek 23:32–34; Obad 1:16; Job 21:20; Ps 11:6; 75:8; Lam 4:21; Hab 2:16) among others.

28. McComiskey, *Minor Prophets*, 536.

29. Coggins and Re'emi, *Israel among the Nations*, 91.

30. Cf. Jer 25:15–29; 49:12; Ps 75:8; Hab 2:16; Rev 14:10; 16:19; Mark 14:36; John 18:11.

between them."[31] To illustrate this lack of a sharp cut-off point, Wilson uses the following sentence as an example:[32]

(1) The audience slept through the lecture.

This sentence can be interpreted literally to mean that the audience was asleep throughout the lecture, as an approximation by arguing for a slightly weaker claim that the audience was on the point of falling asleep, metaphorically as making still a weaker claim of a physical state of drowsiness, and also by making an even more weaker metaphorical claim that the audience was extremely bored with the lecture. The choice between which of these possible interpretations is intended is context dependent. Furthermore, the construction of meaning as either literal or metaphorical does not involve two different kinds of mental processes, as Fauconnier and Turner point out:

> The language forms that lead to intuitively literal meanings can also give us intuitively metaphorical meanings that seem to belong to radically different constructions of meaning. And those mapping schemes compose in identical ways, regardless of whether the ultimate meanings are flatly literal, poetically metaphorical, scientific analogical, surrealistically suggestive or opaque . . . grammar is a set of prompts for guiding us quite precisely in our use of imaginative mental operations. The grammar indicates a kind of path. But what ultimately happens on that path depends on what specifically is encountered and on the imaginative operations conducted along the way. The results may subjectively seem to occupy different realms of thought, even though we are unconsciously carrying out the same mapping schemes.[33]

Metaphors as figures of language involve relating what would otherwise be interpreted as independent semantic domains, allowing for creativity of one's long-term semantic memory so as to bring out the meaning of the associated concepts in a vibrant fashion resulting in new insights that light

---

31. Wilson and Sperber, "Deflationary Account of metaphors," 97; Wilson, "Parallels and Differences," 44.
32. Wilson, "Parallels and Differences," 46.
33. Fauconnier and Turner, *Way We Think*, 154.

up the discourse.³⁴ Despite Davidson's claim that the "attempt to give literal expression to the content of the metaphor is simply misguided," it is important to first come to terms with the semantic and cognitive content of the concepts associated in a metaphorical relationship.³⁵ This is because from such background knowledge, certain elements are composed, selected and projected into the blend and at the same time others end up being suppressed. In relation to the analysis of the metaphor περιτομὴ καρδίας in Romans 2:29, the background understanding of the associated concepts in the SL is equally important, for as Derouchie observes in his analysis of the use of the circumcision terminology in the Hebrew Bible, the meaning of the physical ritual "directly influenced the application and the resulting meaning in contexts where the associated words are used metaphorically."³⁶

Since translation is a mental activity, it also requires the use of cognitive-based approaches.³⁷ The traditional approaches mainly require the translator to concentrate on the semantic components of the associated concepts in a metaphorical relationship which erroneously lead them to look for the closest natural equivalent expressions into the RL.³⁸ These approaches tend to be informed from a position that treats figures of speech as linguistic phenomena or stylistic feature rather than a conceptual undertaking.

Newmark proposes some prescriptive translation procedures which are listed here as they appear in his list of the order of preference.³⁹ The first one is to reproduce the same image in the RL as it appears in the SL, normally referred to as a word-for-word or literal translation. The second option is to replace the image in the SL with a standard RL image. This option is mostly recommended when the use of the SL image clashes with the use of the same image in the RL culture. The third option is to translate a metaphor using a simile, which according to him leads to the modification of the shock of the metaphor and at the same time retention of the image of the metaphor. An example is translating the associated concepts of HEROD and FOX in Luke

---

34. Aaron, *Biblical Ambiguities*, 6; Cormac, *Dognitive Theory of Metaphor*, 136; Macquarrie, *God Talk*, 97.
35. Davidson, "What Metaphors Mean," 45.
36. Derouchie, "Circumcision in the Hebrew Bible," 176.
37. Wilss, *Knowledge and Skills*, 137.
38. Nida, *Towards a Science of Translating*, 185; Newmark, *Textbook of Translation*, 114.
39. Newmark, *Textbook of Translation*, 87–91.

13:32 by stating that "Herod is *like* a fox (αλώπηξ)." The fourth option is to translate the metaphor with a simile plus a sense statement (or occasionally a metaphor plus sense). This would result in the translation "Herod *behaves like a fox.*" Newmark claims that the use of such a compromise avoids comprehension problems, though it should be noted that such renderings result in the loss of the intended effect. The fifth option is to convert the metaphor to its sense, which would result in such a statement as "Herod is a crafty person." This procedure is recommended when the RL image is too broad in sense or not appropriate to the register, but again the emotive aspects of the use of a metaphor may get compromised in the process. The sixth option is that of modifying the metaphor, and the seventh that of deleting the metaphor together with its sense components, especially in a case where the metaphor is redundant. The eighth option is that of retaining the same SL metaphor but adding a gloss in order to enforce the image.

Nida recaps some of Newman's proposals in the translation of metaphors but adds a couple of other options.[40] His options include that of using an equivalent metaphor in the RL, rendering of a metaphor with a simile, and using a non-metaphorical statement. He adds the option of translating a non-metaphor with a metaphor, an option which he demonstrates by translating the hymn "Stand up, stand up, for Jesus" to a people group called Lahu. He points out that the action of standing before Jesus among the Lahu is somewhat silly since junior people do not stand up before their leaders, leading to the rendering which when back translated means to "stand firm." An example where a simile is used to translate a metaphor is in Mark 4:20 where most of the English translations render the metaphor as "some are *like* seeds that increase to thirty" with the focus being on resemblance between the compared elements.[41] The option of translating a metaphor with a non-metaphor especially in instances where a metaphor has no parallels in the receptor language is controversial since such an adaptation involves some kind of loss of information. Nida demonstrates this by giving two examples.[42] One is the expression "his countenance fell" which in Subanean language of the Philippines is translated as "he became sad." The other is the metaphor

---

40. Nida, *Towards a Science of Translating*, 219.
41. Beekman and Callow, *Translating the Word of God*, 12.
42. Nida, *Towards a Science of Translating*, 220.

"uncircumcised heart" in Acts 7:51, which in the Cakchiquel language is translated as "with your hearts unprepared," which to me is still metaphorical since the heart does not literally undergo preparation. An example of an instance where a non-metaphor phrase is translated by the use of a metaphor is the example where the Maya people translate instances where references are made to an insane person by use of the metaphor "hot head."[43]

The challenge posed by the traditional approach to translating metaphors across languages is the assumption that metaphorical expressions can be isolated and therefore all that a translator needs to do is to find semantic equivalents or components that match those of the SL in the RL. Such an approach is erroneous since "variation across languages suggests that languages encode very different kinds of conceptual systems."[44] In view of the fact that words do not match across languages, it is important to understand them within the confines of the language which they are used. Thus a claim as that made by Harries that "the semantic resources on which the metaphor rests are not tied to a particular language" is far from reality and taking such a view can have dire consequences in the resulting translation.[45] The translation practice requires that concepts be understood in a cultural frame of reference and therefore it is misleading to think of metaphors as transcending cultural boundaries.[46] In translating biblical metaphors, a translator should not overlook the fact that the Bible is a culture-specific document and as a result demands a culture-oriented approach. As McElhanon further points out:

> What is important is that the natural integration of knowledge and flow of information in the target language requires that primacy be given to the construal of an event according to the exigencies of that language, not according to some attempt to match low-level units of translation. The salient features of coherent conceptualization within the target language are more determinative than are any attempts to preserve *incidental*

---

43. Nida, 221.
44. Evans and Green, *Cognitive Linguistics*, 56.
45. Harries, "Many Uses of Metaphor," 166–167.
46. Wilss, *Knowledge and Skills*, 84.

components from the SL scenarios, whether explicitly stated or implicitly conveyed.[47]

2.1.2 Cognitive Semantics

The main aspects of the conceptualist view of meaning of words was developed by Lakoff and Johnson followed by their respective individual works.[48] Generally, cognitive semantics can be said to be motivated by an attempt to bridge the distinction made between linguistic expressions and encyclopaedic knowledge, or what Saeed refers to as "real-world" knowledge, in the construction of meaning.[49] What is meaningful to a person is related to his or her daily experience(s), which points to the fact that meaning is connected to the mental entities of an individual and therefore meaning cannot be said to be objective.[50] As Lakoff further argues, the meaning of a word is associated with an environment of some sort and for that reason a concept cannot be meaningful in itself without considering its context.[51] Take the example of the action by the tax collector of "beating his breast" as he sought God's forgiveness as recorded in Luke 18:13. Within the biblical context, the action symbolized the fact that the tax collector was sorrowful about his sins, while the same action from a Kikuyu speaker's perspective would associate the tax collector with being "proud" or "stubborn." This highlights the importance of considering all the information that is associated with a concept by a given community as forming its meaning potential.[52]

The assumption associated with generative grammar that the knowledge of linguistic structures and rules can be formed and applied independently from other mental processes is far from the reality.[53] This is because morpho-syntactic structures cannot be analyzed without reference to their underlying semantic content and thus the meaning of a lexical unit cannot be separated

---

47. McElhanon, "From Word to Scenario," 52.
48. Lakoff and Johnson, *Metaphors We Live By*; Lakoff, *Women, Fire, and Dangerous Things*; Johnson, *Body in the Mind*.
49. Saeed, *Semantics*, 343; Kertész, *Cognitive Semantics and Scientific Knowledge*, 22.
50. Gärdnefors, "Some Tenets of Cognitive Semantics," 19; Boeve, "*Linguistica Ancilla Theologiae*," 19.
51. Lakoff, *Women, Fire, and Dangerous Things*, 292.
52. Allwood, "Meaning Potentials and Context," 43.
53. Chomsky, *Language and the Problems of Knowledge*, 90.

from its encyclopaedic knowledge.[54] A cognitive semantic approach seeks to investigate the underlying conceptual structures and processes involved in the interpretation of a given lexical unit by profiling selected contextual factors that dictate which encyclopaedic meaning is to be made salient. This is in line with the principle that not all of the encyclopaedic knowledge is made accessible in the interpretation of a given lexical unit or concept.[55]

As far as the interpretation and translation of metaphors is concerned, cognitive semantics underscores the important role played by contextual factors, which allow for the possibility of the addressee to draw relevant inferences in light of his or her context. Cognitive semantics as an approach helps one to be more conscious of the translation process as a planned semantic change and to become "more creative, trying to recreate or replicate the metaphorisation process found in the original language in an analogous way, rather than finding the equivalent."[56] One of the cognitive approaches that has been used in the construction of the meaning of metaphors is that of conceptual structures which are referred to as "image-schemas." An image schema is defined as "a recurring pattern of experience which is abstract and topological in nature."[57] Following the cognitive model of image-schemas, Lakoff and Johnston give an example by grouping together spatial metaphors that use the UP-DOWN image-schema as pointed out in summary table 1 below.[58] This image schema makes use of the human-based experience of "lying down" and "getting up" which give rise to a number of meaningful concepts.

---

54. Saeed, *Semantics*, 216.
55. Evans and Green, *Cognitive Linguistics*, 220.
56. Yri, "Recreating Religion," 191.
57. Cervel, *Topology and Cognition*, 42.
58. Lakoff and Johnson, *Metaphors We Live By*, 15–21.

Table 1: A spatial orientation of the up-down image schema

UP	DOWN
HAPPY - I'm feeling *up*. - That *boosted* my spirits. - You're in *high* spirits. - My spirits *rose*.	SAD - I'm feeling *down*. - I am *depressed*. - He's really *low* these days. - My spirits *sank*.
CONSCIOUS - Get *up*. - Wake *up*. - He *rises* early in the morning. - I'm *up* already.	UNCONSCIOUS - He *fell* asleep. - He *dropped* off to sleep. - He's *under* hypnosis. - He *sank* into a comma.
HEALTH AND LIFE - He's at the *peak* of health. - He's in *top* shape. - Lazarus *rose* from the dead.	SICKNESS AND DEATH - He *fell* ill. - He's *sinking* fast. - He came *down* with flu.
HAVING CONTROL - I have control *over* her. - He's at the *height* of his powers. - He's in a *superior* position.	BEING SUBJECT TO CONTROL - He is *under* my control. - He *fell* from power. - He is my social *inferior*.
HIGH STATUS - He has a *lofty* position. - She'll *rise* to the *top*. - He's at the *peak* of his career.	LOW STATUS - He has little *upward* mobility. - She *fell* in status. - He's at the *bottom* of the social hierarchy.
GOOD - Things are looking *up*. - We hit a *peak* last year. - He does *high* quality work.	BAD - It's been *downhill* ever since. - Things are at an all-time *low*.
VIRTUE - He is *high* minded. - She has *high* standards. - She is an *upstanding* citizen.	DEPRAVITY - That's a *low* trick. - Don't be *underhanded*. - I wouldn't *stoop* to that.

This example points to the fact that humans tend to understand the abstract concept of better quality and greater quantity in terms of vertical elevation or increased height, and on the other hand, that of bad quality and lesser quantity in terms of decreased height. The UP-DOWN image-schema can be said to be based on the general observation that when people add matter into a container, say a liquid, there is the simultaneous tendency for the matter to increase in height and quantity. This means that image schemas as relatively abstract conceptual patterns are grounded in everyday experiences or embodied experiences as people interact and observe the world around them, hence they are far from being innate knowledge structures that a child is born with.[59] Other image schemas associated with SPACE include FRONT-BACK, LEFT-RIGHT, NEAR-FAR, CENTRE-PERIPHERY, among others.[60] McElhanon applies the same UP-DOWN image-schema in the Bible where concepts such as HEAVEN,[61] HOLY,[62] STRENGTH,[63] HONOR,[64] PROSPERITY,[65] and PRIDE[66] are conceptualized as being UP, while SHEOL,[67] EVIL,[68] WEAKNESS,[69] DEFERENCE,[70] POVERTY,[71] and HUMILITY[72] are conceptualized as being DOWN.[73]

2.1.2.1 Frame Semantics

One of the factors that influence the meaning of a given lexical unit is that of the underlying cognitive framing associated with it since "frames provide the fundamental representation of knowledge in human cognition."[74] A cognitive frame is a detailed knowledge structure or schema that "represent a schematisation of experience (a knowledge structure), which is represented at the conceptual level and held in long-term memory, and which relates elements and

---

59. Evans and Green, *Cognitive Linguistics*, 178.
60. Evans and Green, 190.
61. Ps 14:2.
62. Isa 57:15.
63. Ps 21:13.
64. Deut 26:19a.
65. Ps 49:1–2.
66. Job 40:11–12.
67. Ps 55:15.
68. Prov 14:19.
69. Ps 88:4.
70. Gen 43:28.
71. 1 Sam 2:7.
72. Prov 29:23.
73. McElhanon, "From Simple Metaphors," 40.
74. Barsalou, "Frames, Concepts, and Conceptual Fields," 21.

entities associated with a particular culturally embedded scene, situation or event from human experience."[75] Frames as knowledge structures are shaped by how particular societies view the world and hence include beliefs, values, and emotions.[76] The linguist Fillmore advocates the idea that the meaning of a word has much to do with one's schematization of the world, thus establishing the view that every word is connected to its respective background frame.[77] This frame is evoked as reference whenever a given lexical unit is activated in the mind.[78] Consider the example of the concept IRON LADY which is evoked in example sentence 2 given by Fauconnier and Turner.[79]

(2) "But Margaret Thatcher would never get elected here because the labor unions can't stand her."

The concept Margret Thatcher, a former Prime Minister of Britain who was in office from 1979 to 1990, also evokes that of IRON LADY, which automatically evokes a [POLITICAL] frame. Another example where a frame is recruited to help interpret a given scenario can be derived from what Fauconnier and Turner refer to as the Regatta example.[80] In this example two boats are compared as competing against each other following the same course and having departed from San Francisco on the same day, even though they happened to have sailed many years apart. One is a modern catamaran which sailed in 1993 and the other is a clipper which sailed back in 1853. The familiar frame of a [RACE] emerges in the blend which allows for the conceptualization of the two ships as competing against each other. This same frame of a [RACE] is also recruited when the reader comes across words in the discourse such as "winning," "leading," "losing," and "gaining," which are used in the context of a racing contest.

Another example of the recruitment of a frame in the interpretation of a given lexical unit has to do with the mention of the word "safe" in example 3

---

75. Evans and Green, *Cognitive Linguistics*, 211.
76. López, "Applying Frame Semantics to Translation," 312.
77. Fillmore, "Frame Semantics"; Fillmore, "Frames and the Semantics of Understanding."
78. Fillmore, "Frame Semantics," 124.
79. Fauconnier and Turner, *Way We Think*, 18.
80. Fauconnier and Turner, 63.

below which is uttered in the context of a child playing on a beach with a shovel.[81]

(3) "The child is safe."

As the concept SAFE is evoked in the sentence above, the abstract frame of [DANGER] is automatically activated with its related roles and elements such as victim, instrument, as well as the resulting action of harm. This is as a result of the creation of an imaginary scenario from the encyclopaedic knowledge with the property of "harm" being associated with children allowing for the interpretation that the child will not be harmed. This same frame of [DANGER] is not activated when concepts such as "SHOVEL" and "BEACH" are associated with the concept SAFE since the cognitive knowledge relating to what it means to be safe does not allow the interpretation of beaches or shovels coming to harm.

When a given element in a frame is evoked in the course of a discourse, all the other related elements in that frame are also made available in the minds of both the speaker and the addressee. This can be illustrated by Fillmore and Atkins's use of the concept SELL, a concept which automatically evokes the recurring experience of the familiar [COMMERCIAL EVENT] frame. In this transaction, the organizing scenario of acquisition of possession(s) from one party to another through the exchange of money is made salient.[82] This frame also makes available a number of other elements associated with it which include props and players such as "goods," "seller," "buyer," "money," etc. Some properties can be highlighted so as to focus on certain aspects of the [COMMERCIAL EVENT] frame. If the verb "buy" is evoked, the actions of "paying," "buying," and "spending" are made salient. Furthermore, when sets of related words are evoked, such as "pay," "spend," "sell," "buy," "charge," "tender," etc., they end up automatically evoking the [COMMERCIAL EVENT] frame which provides "the background and motivation for the categories which these words represent."[83] Another example of related words evoking

---

81. Fauconnier and Turner, 26.
82. Fillmore and Atkins, "Towards a Frame-Based Lexicon," 79.
83. Fillmore, "Frame Semantics," 116–117.

their respective frame(s) can be derived from the illustration of the "Debate-with-Kant" blend quoted below.[84]

(4) I claim that reason is a self-developing capacity. Kant disagrees with me on this point. He says it's innate, but I answer that that's begging the question, to which he counters, in *Critique of Pure Reason*, that only innate ideas have power. But I say to that, What about neuronal group selection? And he gives no answer.

In this scenario, the use of words such as "claim," "disagrees," "answer," and "counters," evoke the [DEBATE] frame. Even though in both input spaces there is no mention of the word "debate," in the resulting blend into which the two philosophers are projected, the [DEBATE] frame allows for the two to engage in an argument and to exchange opinions. This frame gives further structure to the interaction between the two philosophers by making them aware of the existence of each other in the blend allowing for the possibility of coming up with a potential winner of the debate.

It is important to point out that even though related elements in a given frame tend to be activated when one of the elements in the same frame is evoked, only those elements that are relevant in a given context end up being made salient in the mind of the speaker and addressee. Staying with the illustration of the [COMMERCIAL EVENT] frame, consider the example of a person trying to explain the events that led to a pedestrian being knocked over by a vehicle. Although the speaker may point out that the pedestrian was on the way to buy some commodity from a shop, the exact type of commodity might not be made salient in such a context. In a later section, I will seek to demonstrate in detail how RT makes it possible for some salient elements in a given frame to be projected while others end up being ignored or suppressed.

Since words have the potential of evoking a number of different cognitive frames to which they are connected, the principle of relevance plays a crucial role in determining the right frame to be evoked in a given context. As an example, consider example 5 below, uttered in response to an inquiry as to whether my wife is a Kikuyu.

---

84. Fauconnier and Turner, *Way We Think*, 59–60.

(5) *Ngũranĩte na mwena wa Nandĩ* – "I have married [literally bought a wife] from [the people of] Nandi."

Though the word *kũgũrana*, has the root meaning "to buy" and involves some sort of exchange, in the context of my response in example 5 above, this word does not evoke the [COMMERCIAL] frame in reference to the amount of dowry that I had to pay, but profiles the place where my wife comes from. This means that even though the concept GŨRA "buy" has the potential of being evoked in both the [MARRIAGE] and [COMMERCIAL] frames, a given communication context plays a crucial role in determining which of these frames is activated. It is therefore important to establish the connection between words and their respective cognitive frames in view of the fact that frames offer the conceptual underpinnings of any element within it including those of related senses and words.[85] This process of associating words to their corresponding frames is normally unconscious and entirely automatic. It is only when one has a problem in figuring out their meaning that the underlying conceptual process is made accessible through retrospection.

Though there is the possibility of a number of frames being universally shared, it is important to note that even in such circumstances, most, if not all, of these universally shared frames have elements that are unique due to the fact that they are experienced within specific cultural groups.[86] This results from the fact that there is a link between frames and cultures, with people who share the same cultural and historical background likely to also share the same conceptual frames or schemas. Coulson illustrates this using the concept BACHELOR which, as she points out, is a universally shared frame.[87] In the cultural model of a spiritual setting, say, that of a Catholic priest who has given up his right to marriage for the sake of serving the church of Jesus Christ, the stereotypical assumptions that are evoked by this concept tend to naturally exclude such a person from being described using the tag "bachelor." Therefore frames are very important in the interpretation and translation of a given lexical unit since they direct one to consider the

---

85. Petruck, "Frame Semantics and the Lexicon," 279.
86. Yao, "Application of Frame Theory," 1142–1143.
87. Coulson, *Semantic Leaps*, 243.

component of background knowledge and experience(s) from the perspective of a given speech community which end up informing or influencing their understanding.

The interpretation and/or translation of a given lexical unit may vary across different contexts as a result of a number of factors. One of them is the speaker's modulation and ability to maneuver the cultural background knowledge, beliefs, and experience(s) evoked by that lexical unit, the intended audience(s), as well as the surrounding discourse context where it is found.[88] These factors, among others, determine which frame(s) and framing elements are activated or semi-activated in a given context. Coulson and Kutas provide the following example as a demonstration by pointing out that the meaning of the lexical unit "bouncing" in the (a) sentences is determined by Paul's responses in the (b) sentences.[89]

(6) (a) Jaimie came bouncing down the stairs.
    (b) Paul ran over to kiss her.

(7) (a) Jaimie came bouncing down the stairs.
    (b) Paul rushed off to get the doctor.

The meaning of "bouncing" in 6a in light of Paul's response in 6b is different from the meaning of "bouncing" in 7a in light of Paul's response in 7b. The sentences in example 6 evoke the frame of [JOYFUL REUNION] and those in example 7 the [DANGER] frame. Each of these frames would require a different response from an onlooker who might be around at the time of these events with the context directing their reactions. Let us assume that the context of utterance in example 6 above is that of Paul, Jaimie's husband, having returned from a work-related assignment which might have taken him away from his family for a number of days. In this context, an onlooker would recruit the [JOYFUL REUNION] frame and one of the resulting inferences that might be communicated strongly is that Paul and Jaimie might need some privacy. On the other hand, the context of example 7 above which evokes the [DANGER] frame would require an onlooker to come to the aid of Jaimie, and if need be,

---

88. Coulson and Kutas, "Frame-Shifting and Sentential Integration," 2; Kövecses, *Metaphor in Culture*, 69.

89. Coulson and Kutas, "Frame-Shifting and Sentential Integration" 2.

assist Paul to rush Jaimie to a hospital. Consider this other pair of examples from Kikuyu on the next page, which share the organizing frame [GŪTUA MATA] "to spit saliva."

(8) *Thoguo athiĩ gũtua mata* – "Your father has gone to urinate."
(Literally: "Your father has gone to spit saliva.")

(9) *Thoguo aratuĩra mata gĩthuri* – "Your father is blessing you."
(Literally: "Your father is spitting saliva on his own chest.")

In the context of this being uttered in response to a son inquiring of his father's whereabouts, two different frames are evoked. In light of example 8 above, the frame of [MŨGIRO] "taboo" is evoked since it is forbidden for a son to see his father's nakedness. On the other hand, utterance in example 9 automatically recruits the frame of [KĨRATHIMO] "blessing" and the son would feel more than welcome to witness the ritual, especially if he happens to be a beneficiary. Therefore since some lexical units might be ambiguous, it is important to make sure that the right frames are evoked so as to avoid the derivation of wrong inferences.

2.1.2.2 Frame Shifting

Frame shifting results from the difficulty that a reader/hearer of a text/speech faces after failing to make sense of a certain lexical unit using the contextually evoked frame paving a way to the setting up of a new frame in an attempt to try and resolve the conflict.[90] This mostly happens when an addressee comes across new information that they fail to make sense of using a previously acquired frame. Example 10 below given by Coulson illustrates such a dilemma that leads to a change of frames.[91]

(10) "Everyone had so much fun diving from the tree into the swimming pool, we decided to put in a little water."

An interpreter will have no problem in interpreting the first part of the sentence. It is in the second part of the sentence that they would find difficulty after realizing that the swimming pool mentioned in the first part of the

---

90. Coulson, *Semantic Leaps*, 56–57.
91. Coulson, 55.

sentence does not have water. Since the previously held frame of a [SWIMMING POOL] has "water" as an essential element, the interpreter is forced to change or reorganize the previously held frame of a [SWIMMING POOL] with water to one that has no water in an attempt to interpret utterance in example 10 above. This process of reorganizing a previously held frame in order to accommodate a new meaning is what Coulson refers to as "frame shifting."[92]

Another common cause of frame shifting is when a word loses its former meaning and acquires a new one hence calling for the revision of any previously held frame associated with such a word. This change/adjustment of such a frame is made possible by the fact that cognitive frames are open to change and thus given aspects of a previously held frame can keep on changing in light of the new meaning that a word acquires. Take, for example, the English word "cool," which is traditionally associated with "calmness," "steadiness," and "temperate moderation." This word has acquired a new meaning among young people and is now associated with being fashionable and trendy. Sometimes the use of this word has an underlying tone of rebellion to mean "doing something radical" and is normally associated with an action that makes a person "stand out" from the crowd. Since this new meaning does not fit in the old framing associated with concept COOL, it calls for the reorganization of the entire frame into a new one, requiring people to make a conceptual shift to be able to accommodate this new acquired meaning.

The creation of a new frame, or that of the reconstruction of an old one in light of encountering a new meaning, also necessitates the reorganization of all of the elements within the frame. Coulson gives an example using the ethical conceptualization of the concept ABORTION.[93] In instances where the pregnancy is construed as the responsibility of the mother, it entails that she is expected to carry the pregnancy to term even if the pregnancy might have resulted from a rape incident. In order to convince a woman holding such a view that it is okay to abort, one has to first persuade her to reorganize the elements that inform her existing frame. In instances where a new frame is constructed to accommodate a newly acquired meaning, related words are also accommodated within this new frame. Using the example of the concept COOL discussed above, words that would have been previously considered as

---

92. Coulson, 34.
93. Coulson, 244.

antonyms to the concept COOL, such as "disturbance," "messing up," "upsetting the status quo," and "unsettling," are accommodated in this new frame and given a positive nuance. Consequently, events that would have been traditionally categorized using the old frame as being "disorganized" or "rough" are now depicted in this new frame as being "cool." Therefore, the process of frame shifting, which results in the creation of a new frame, is triggered by the failure to accommodate a new lexical unit under an existing conceptual frame with the newly acquired frame also resulting in other new words being associated and accommodated within the frame and given new semantic nuances.

2.1.2.3 Application to Translation

A given text or discourse unit is constrained by a given frame network(s), which act as the organizing frame(s) when it comes to addressing issues of relevancy, interpretation of related words and events, as well as analyzing the role of the elements that are involved. A translator needs to thoroughly understand the underlying frames associated with the concepts in both the source and receptor languages since such frames filter wrong meanings, inferences or assumptions that may find their way into the translation process. It is also important to note that the same word in different contexts might evoke different interpretive frames in the mind of addressees and therefore one should be careful how they render such words since they end up dictating how the entire discourse is construed.[94] Therefore, a translator who ignores background frames as an important component in the translation process is bound to make mistakes since frames shape the meaning of the words.

Wendland suggests four options that are available to choose from as a translator seeks to evoke the right framing in the mind of their readers.[95] The first option is that of "re-framing," where a translator tends to pay more attention to the semantic and pragmatic significance of the original and thus ends up looking for similar conceptual frames in the RL to match those of the SL. Care should be taken to make sure that one does not render a frame without considering the differences that might exist between the source and receptor languages. An example is that mentioned previously of the tax collector in Luke 18:13 where *Ibuku rīa Ngai* adopts a literal approach by rendering the

---

94. Coulson and Kutas, "Frame-Shifting and Sentential Integration," 2.
95. Wendland, "Framing the Frames," 34.

Greek phrase ἔτυπτεν εἰς τὸ στῆθος αὐτοῦ as *kwĩgũtha gĩthũri* "to beat his chest." This choice is unnatural and misleading since this gesture is culturally associated with someone who is arrogant and proud. The second option is that of "de-framing" where the translator favors the cognitive frames of the RL over those of the SL. An example is the idiom of "loving with all intestines" among the Sabaot in Kenya, which replaces that of "loving with all the heart."[96] The third option is that of "hyper-framing" where the translator seeks to enrich or correct the RL frames by the use of para-textual means such as footnotes, illustrations, cross-references, glossary entries, etc. to try and match the cognitive frames that are assumed to have been evoked in the SL text. The last option is that of "co-framing" where the translator seeks to complement the prevalent frames by use of other socio-culturally oriented applications. An example is that of the word translated as "sex" which is rendered in the Kikuyu translation by the use of the euphemism *gũkoma na atumia* "sleeping with women."[97] The translation process that has to do with analyzing background frames in both the source and receptor languages require the translator

> . . . to adjust his/her analysis to the comprehension process, taking into account that his/her task is to project the SL frames onto the TL linguistic elements that activate a knowledge which should be, as much as possible, semantically, pragmatically and stylistically equivalent to that activated by the ST elements. Only if the [target text] TT linguistic elements activate the relevant frames for the interpretation of the text, will the readers be able to draw the correct contextual inferences on the basis of their frame-based knowledge. From this point of view, the translator becomes a kind of bilingual and bicultural "mediator" between two different conceptual systems.[98]

---

96. Matt 22:7
97. cf. Gen 19:5; Lev 18:6–30.
98. López, "Applying Frame Semantics," 315.

2.1.3 Conceptual Integration or Blending Theory

CIT mainly draws from Fauconnier's previous research on mental spaces theory with the crucial insight "that meaning construction typically involves integration of structure that gives rise to more than the sum of its parts."[99] In an attempt to demonstrate how meaning is constructed, this theory keeps track of links or relations between spaces, elements in the spaces and their counterparts, and also specifies the nature of the underlying operations that take place in the formation of a conceptual network.[100] This theory, as a basic mental demonstration, seeks to demystify, so to speak, how meaning is constructed "online" allowing the setting up of mental spaces, the setting up of an integration process across these mental spaces, the projection and/or blockage of elements from the input spaces to the blend and vice versa, as well as the recreation of new structures in the blend through the processes of composition, completion and elaboration.[101] In the following sub-sections, I will discuss different types of networks that are involved in the integration process, how mental spaces that form the basis of the integration network are formed, give a general description of CIT, discuss the "emergent issue" detailing how meaning is generated in the blend, and lastly point out the role of CIT in the interpretation of metaphors.

2.1.3.1 Types of Networks

Fauconnier and Turner discuss four types of integration networks, namely, the simplex, mirror, single-scope, and double-scope.[102] These networks are not separated or unrelated to one another, but in a continuous landscape, one can point to prominent points that distinguish one from another.[103] A simplex network, so called because it is the simplest kind of integration network, is where one input provides the frame with roles while the other input provides the specific elements or values in that frame. An example is where the concept FAMILY forms one of the input spaces and the participants Paul and Sally appear in the other input. After realizing that Paul is Sally's father,

---

99. Fauconnier, *Mental Spaces*; Fauconnier and Sweetser, *Spaces, Worlds and Grammars*; Evans and Green, *Cognitive Linguistics*, 400.
100. Coulson, *Semantic Leaps*, 24.
101. Fauconnier and Turner, *Way We Think*, 37, 44.
102. Fauconnier and Turner, 119–135.
103. Fauconnier and Turner, 139.

we find that in the blend, the structuring frame of the [FAMILY] is projected and integrated with the elements Paul and Sally as specific elements within the frame. For mapped elements between two input spaces, we find that the [FAMILY] frame projects the roles and the elements as values matching the roles within the blend. As a result, the roles of father and Paul are matched in the blended space as well as those of Sally and daughter. As Fauconnier and Turner further point out, "in simplex networks there are no clashes between the organizing frames of the inputs, because the input with the values (*Paul* and *Sally*) has no organizing frame that competes with the organizing frame provided by the other input (*father-ego*)" and thus "these networks perform indispensable role compressions."[104]

Mirror networks occur in instances where all the spaces in the network (i.e. the generic space [GS], the inputs, and the blend) share a common organizing frame, which makes it easier to establish the corresponding cross-space mapping between the two input spaces. In the boat race integration network also discussed above, we find two corresponding elements in the input spaces under the organizing frame [BOAT SAILING ALONG AN OCEAN COURSE] that share the role of "boat," namely, the nineteenth-century Clipper and the late-twentieth-century, exotic Catamaran.[105] Since the inputs share the same [RACING] frame, there are no clashes expected at the general level with such clashes only coming after filling in more details, an example being the oddity of racing the two types of the boats, one old and one more newer, which do not usually race against each other.

Single-scope networks have input spaces that do not share a common frame, with one of the frames being selected to structure the blend. The input that provides the organizing frame is referred to as the "source" and the other one, which is usually the focus of understanding, being referred to as the "target" input. An example is given by Fauconnier and Turner of the scenario of a boxing competition that gives a vibrant and compact frame in compressing the understanding of two CEOs in business competition.[106] One CEO is portrayed as having landed a blow while the other one as having recovered, one as having tripped while the other takes advantage, and one of

---

104. Fauconnier and Turner, 122.
105. Fauconnier and Turner, 63.
106. Fauconnier and Turner, 126–127.

them having knocked the other out cold. The construal of this situation builds up a conceptual integration network with a cross-space mapping between the boxing input and the business input. This integration network maps, for example, each boxer to a CEO, a punch to an effort by one of the CEOs, a blow to an effective action, and staying in the fight to that of continuing in business. In short, the projection to the blend in a simple single-scope network is highly asymmetric with one of the inputs, here the boxing frame, organizing the blend. The respective frames from the two inputs (i.e. that of [BOXING] and that of [BUSINESS]) are different and are not connected historically since "there are no vital relations of Time, Space, Change, Cause-Effect, and Intentionality that connect the input spaces directly, and no outer-space Identity connections between organizing frames, roles or elements below that level of typology in the two different inputs."[107] Since the two frames together with their elements are not directly identical, this offers conceptual clashes that are highly visible. Such clashes are solved by use of one of the frames as the organizing frame giving insight into the focus input, in this case, the boxing input giving insight into the business or CEOs input.

Double-scope networks have "inputs with different (and often clashing) organizing frames as well as an organizing frame for the blend that includes parts of each of those frames and has emergent structure of its own."[108] One such example is that of same-sex marriages in which the

> ... inputs are the traditional scenario of marriage, on the one hand, and the alternative domestic scenario involving two people of the same sex, on the other. The cross-space mapping may link prototypical elements such as partners, common dwellings, commitment, and love. Selective projection takes frame structure from each input. It takes social recognition, wedding ceremonies, and mode taxation from the first input of "traditional marriage," and same sex, absence of biologically common children, and the culturally defined roles of the partners from the second input. Emergent properties will characterize this new social structure reflected in the blend.[109]

---

107. Fauconnier and Turner, 127.
108. Fauconnier and Turner, 131.
109. Fauconnier and Turner, 134.

Another example is that of the "computer desktop" interface where the two frames, namely that of [OFFICE WORK] and that of [COMPUTER COMMANDS] are both projected as organizing frames in the blend.[110] As a result, the frame in the blend ends up drawing from actions in the office frame such as those of opening files and throwing away trash, as well as from the computer command frame, which include commands such as "find," "replace," "print," and "save." This kind of network may also result in blend elements that might be different in some aspects from those found in either of the two input spaces resulting in an "emergent structure" of its own (i.e. a meaning that is more than the sum of its component parts).

2.1.3.2 Mental Spaces

Mental spaces, which were first introduced by Fauconnier, form the basis from which CIT was primarily developed.[111] In the conceptual integration framework, mental spaces are activated in the working memory and are the ones which allow for meaning construction to take place. Fauconnier and Turner describe mental spaces as "small conceptual packets" that are constructed in the working memory as one thinks, talks, and acts in different settings.[112] Coulson further defines them as "temporal containers for relevant information about a particular domain . . . as perceived, imagined, remembered, or otherwise understood by a speaker."[113] They are structured as frames and are derived from background knowledge as well as from related contextual information.[114]

An example is given by Fauconnier and Turner of the frame [WALKING ALONG A PATH] which can be drawn from the long-term memory of someone climbing Mount Rainier in the year 2001.[115] The resulting mental space includes elements such as the climber, Mount Rainier, and the time of the event (i.e. the year 2001), information which can be activated in a variety of ways for different purposes. A mental space "You climbed Mount Rainier in 2001" could be set up to report a past event. Another mental space "If you

---

110. Fauconnier and Turner, 22–23.
111. Fauconnier, *Mental Spaces*.
112. Fauconnier and Turner, *Way We Think*, 40.
113. Coulson, *Semantic Leaps*, 21.
114. Fauconnier and Turner, *Way We Think*, 102.
115. Fauconnier and Turner, 40.

climbed Mount Rainier in 2001," could be set up on the basis of a counterfactual situation, and another mental space "Max believes that you climbed Mount Rainier in 2001" could be set up to state what a person named Max believes. The same information could be recalled by creating the mental space "Here is a picture of you climbing Mount Rainier in 2001" in the context of talking about a picture that might have been taken during that same event. All these are examples of how the same information could be activated through creating different mental spaces for different purposes. This demonstrates the fact that mental spaces are contextual since they are molded by a given communicative context. Furthermore, since they are dynamic in nature, they could be revised in the course of the discourse in an attempt by the hearer to find optimal matches within the activated integration network.[116]

In the process of building an integration network, mental spaces, which are referred to as input spaces, are projected to another mental space referred to as the blended space, hence the process of blending generally "operates on two Input mental spaces to yield a third space, the blend."[117] Though found in the working memory, familiar mental spaces usually end up being entrenched in the long-term memory in the form of structured frames, elements, and relations. Such mental spaces are usually attached to other related mental spaces that are likely to be activated at the same time. Consider example 11 below given by Fauconnier and Turner.[118]

(11) "Jesus on the cross."

This utterance could evoke such frames such as [ROMAN CRUCIFIXION], [JESUS THE SON OF GOD], and also that of [JESUS THE BABY]. In the integration process, elements are activated within their respective frames since they are intertwined to their respective frames.[119] Take the example of the frame [JESUS THE BABY], which naturally activates familiar elements including participants and props together with their respective roles. The participants include "Mary" and "Joseph" in their role as the parents, the "shepherds" in their role as the ones who spread the news of the birth of the Savior, the "angels" in their role as the ones who broke the news to the shepherds, "Herod" in his role as the

---

116. Fauconnier and Sweetser, *Spaces, Worlds and Grammars*, 12.
117. Fauconnier, *Mappings in Thought and Language*, 149.
118. Fauconnier and Turner, *Way We Think*, 103.
119. Fauconnier and Turner, 252.

one who wanted to kill the baby Jesus, and the list goes on. An example of a prop is that of the "manger," which is symbolic of Jesus's humble upbringing. Therefore, activating a frame also includes knowing how related elements and relations operate within it.

Although mental spaces are usually motivated by linguistic data, language forms are themselves products of general cognitive processes.[120] To this end, language users do not just focus on retrieving frames from the long-term memory that are ready-made but are also constantly involved in the process of constructing meaning through building and blending existing frames.[121] Consequently, they are continuously involved in the process of selecting which background frames are relevant in the understanding of linguistic utterance(s) that they encounter, how to blend these frames if need be, as well as selecting relevant elements and ascribing to them roles, some of which are projected into the blended space (BS). The construction of utterances involves the integration of existing frame-based grammatical structures in the mind of the speaker, which substantiates the claim that derivation of mental spaces happens within the framework of a particular culture, and as Fauconnier further points out

> In order for thinking and communication to take place, elaborate constructions must occur that draw on conceptual capacities, highly structured background and conceptual knowledge, schema-induction, and mapping capabilities . . . languages are designed, very elegantly it would seem, to prompt us into making the constructions appropriate for a given context with a minimum of grammatical structure. Language does not itself do the cognitive building – it "just" gives us minimal, but sufficient, clues for finding the domains [read: mental spaces] and principles appropriate for building in a given situation. Once these clues are combined with already existing configurations, available cognitive principles, and background framing, the appropriate construction can take place, and the result far exceeds any overt explicit information.[122]

---

120. Coulson, *Semantic Leaps*, 24.
121. Coulson, 32.
122. Fauconnier, *Mental Spaces*, xviii.

2.1.3.3 A General Description of CIT

A crucial insight from CIT is that meaning construction involves the integration of mental spaces and that the meaning that emerges in the blend might not be connected directly back to input spaces. CIT has at least four basic mental spaces in its network, namely, a GS, at least two input spaces, and a BS as demonstrated in figure 1 below.[123] The circles represent mental spaces, the black dots represent elements in the spaces, the solid lines represent mappings between the inputs, the dashed lines link the correspondences between the elements, and the hollow dots represent emergent structures in the BS.

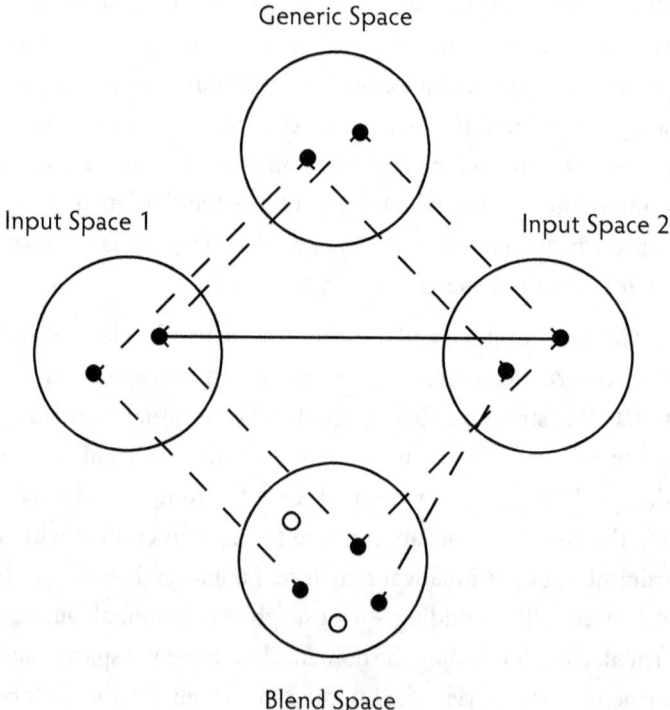

Figure 1: A prototypical diagram of conceptual integration

The GS contains the general conceptual structure and represents properties and elements that are common to all the other mental spaces in the network since it is the core cross-space that dictates the mapping between

---

123. cf. Fauconnier and Turner, *Way We Think*, 46.

these spaces.[124] By uniting the spaces, the GS gives coherence to the whole integration network by connecting elements that are activated in the input spaces. Let us consider the "Debate with Kant" example, which talks about a debate between a German philosopher named Kant who wrote back in 1784 and a modern philosopher who engages with Kant back in 1995.[125] In the GS, we find that the general element "thinker" equated to Kant in input space 1 (IS_1) and to a modern philosopher in input space 2 (IS_2), the general element "mode of expression" being filled by "writing" in IS_1 and by "speaking" in IS_2, the general element "language" being filled in by "German," which is the language that Kant used in his writings in IS_1, and "English" in IS_2, etc.

As mentioned above, the prototypical integration network has two input spaces. In the "Debate with Kant" example, the two input spaces are that of a modern philosopher and that of a German philosopher. The fourth space in the integration network is the BS, or simply referred to as the blend, which "*inherits partial structure* from the input spaces and *has emergent structure* of its own."[126] In the illustration of the "Debate with Kant" we find that both philosophers are projected into the BS allowing for the possibility of the two philosophers holding a debate with one another even though they happened to have lived many years apart. It is important to note that the information that is projected or generated in the blend might seem unrealistic. Consider the metaphorical utterance in example 12 used by Grady, Oakley, and Coulson.[127]

(12) "My surgeon is a butcher."

In the BS, we find the butcher being projected as operating on a patient, information that seems impractical. A detailed discussion as to how the meaning of this metaphor is constructed within the blend is discussed in the next section.

2.1.3.4 *The Emergent Structure*

Within the blend, there is the possibility of the development of new emergent structures that are more than the sum of the information contained in

---

124. Fauconnier, *Mappings in Thought and Language*, 149; Fauconnier and Turner, *Way We Think*, 47.
125. Fauconnier and Turner, *Way We Think*, 59–62.
126. Fauconnier, *Mappings in Thought and Language*, 149 (italics his).
127. Grady, Oakley, and Coulson, "Conceptual Blending and Metaphor."

either of the input spaces. This process takes place through three interrelated processes, namely, that of composition, completion, and elaboration.[128] The process of composition involves projections being made from each of the input spaces, which results in the creation of new relations that did not exist before within the respective input spaces. This might take place either through the fusion of elements or through single elements being projected from the input spaces into the BS. Take the example of the Buddhist monk given by Fauconnier and Turner that envisions a Buddhist monk walking up a mountain and strolling back again a few days later.[129] In this example, we see the projection of single elements in the BS from the input spaces with the two "monks" being projected separately as single elements into the blend. The two journeys that the monk took (i.e. to and fro), are fused and projected into the blend as one journey which the "two monks" took. Furthermore, the two different days that the journeys took are fused and projected into the blend as the same day.

A classic example in the Bible that demonstrates the process of composition is that of the living creatures recorded in Ezekiel 1:5–11 where we find elements from all the input spaces being projected to the BS. The input spaces are that of "man," "lion," "ox," and "eagle," with some selected elements from each of the input spaces being merged resulting in the creatures that are described in this text. In the integration process, some elements in the blend are allowed to flow back into their respective input spaces. In this case, the four faces of the creatures are linked back to the four respective input spaces representing the four different animals (i.e. that of a man, that of a lion, that of an ox, and that of an eagle). The feet are said to be those of a calf and therefore this element is prohibited from flowing back into any of the other input spaces. Through the emergent process, we find the virtue or the imaginative world being accommodated in the blend. The creatures resulting in the blend might not make sense, especially in light of fact that each of the creatures had four faces and four wings, but this does not mean that the blend is not a success.

---

128. Fauconnier, *Mappings in Thought and Language*, 150–151; Fauconnier and Turner, *Way We Think*, 48; Coulson, *Semantic Leaps*, 122–123; Evans and Green, *Cognitive Linguistics*, 404.

129. Fauconnier and Turner, *Way We Think*, 39–40.

The process of completion is where background framing as well as cognitive and cultural models from the long-term memory are projected from the input spaces into the blend with the goal of "completing" the structure in the blend, a process which is mostly unconscious.[130] This process allows for a composite structure to be projected into the blend, which is completed into a larger emergent structure than that of the input spaces often resulting in the creation of an emergent content in the blend. Take the example from the "desktop interface" discussed above. We find the process of completion in the blend in that from the background knowledge of the [OFFICE WORK] frame, actions such as moving and dropping documents and files into new folders are projected into the blend. The completion process can also be found in the construction of the meaning of the metaphor "my surgeon is a butcher" where the stationing of the butcher in an operation room allows the inference of incompetence to be projected into the blend, an inference which is derived from the background understanding that a butcher is not trained to operate on human beings.

The process of elaboration is said to have taken place when the structure in the blend results in its own emergent logic, through a process referred to as "running the blend." Again, borrowing from the illustration of the "desktop interface," we see some new structure emerging in the blend such as the activity of double-clicking to open a folder, the dragging of files, copying and pasting of folders, etc. These actions cannot be traced back from any of the input spaces pointing to the fact that the desktop blend has come up with its own emergent logic. From the metaphor "my surgeon is a butcher," the blend can develop a possible trajectory of a butcher packing human flesh in the same way that a butcher packs beef. Another example of the process of elaboration can be illustrated from the "Buddhist monk" blend where the possibility is given of the same monk meeting with himself on the path and engaging in a chat, actions which are arrived at without caring whether they are possible or not.[131] The process of elaboration might go on indefinitely, therefore there is need to constrain it, which is an issue that is addressed by the principle of relevance. In summary, it is clear that the creative process

---

130. Fauconnier and Turner, 48.
131. Fauconnier and Turner, 48.

recruited by CIT is suited to the construction of the meaning of metaphors, for as Fauconnier points out,

> Metaphor is a salient and pervasive cognitive process that links conceptualization and language. It depends crucially on a cross-space mapping between two inputs (the Source and the Target). This makes it a prime candidate for the construction of blends, and indeed we find that blended spaces play a key role in metaphorical mappings. That is, in addition to the familiar Source and Target of metaphorical projection, blends are constructed in which important cognitive work gets accomplished.[132]

2.1.3.5 CIT and Metaphors

The interpretation of metaphors calls for innovation on the part of both the speaker and the hearer. Since CIT involves the projection of the content of input spaces into a separate BS, it is well suited to account for this creative online process. This innovative process is captured in figure 2 below, taken from Grady, Oakley, and Coulson illustrating the interpretation of the metaphor "my surgeon is a butcher."[133] The two input spaces in this integration process are that of the "surgeon" and that of a "butcher," with the surgeon in the blend being associated with the brutality of a butcher. CMT talks of the mapping of elements from the two domains as the solution towards arriving at the intended meaning as elements from the source input are mapped to their counterparts in the target input space. This would mean that the cleaver of the butcher is mapped to the scalpel of the surgeon, the cutting of meat to the cutting of flesh, the dead animal to the patient, the abattoir to the operation room, and so forth. However, the processes of mapping elements across the input spaces cannot entirely explain how inferential meaning such as the incompetence of the surgeon is arrived at, pointing to the fact that the meaning of metaphors is more than the mapping of the source domain to the target domain. Also take the example of the conceptual metaphor ARGUMENT IS WAR where the concept ARGUMENT is understood in terms of that of WAR with the structure of "war" being mapped to that of an "argument"

---

132. Fauconnier, *Mappings in Thought and Language*, 168.
133. Grady, Oakley, and Coulson, "Blending and Metaphor," 4.

in an effort to draw similarities between the two.[134] We find that the process of mapping between the two domains does not give specific guidance as to how and why different properties or elements are chosen or highlighted while others are not. There is no specific guidance as to which properties of "war" should apply to the "argument" domain and which ones do not.

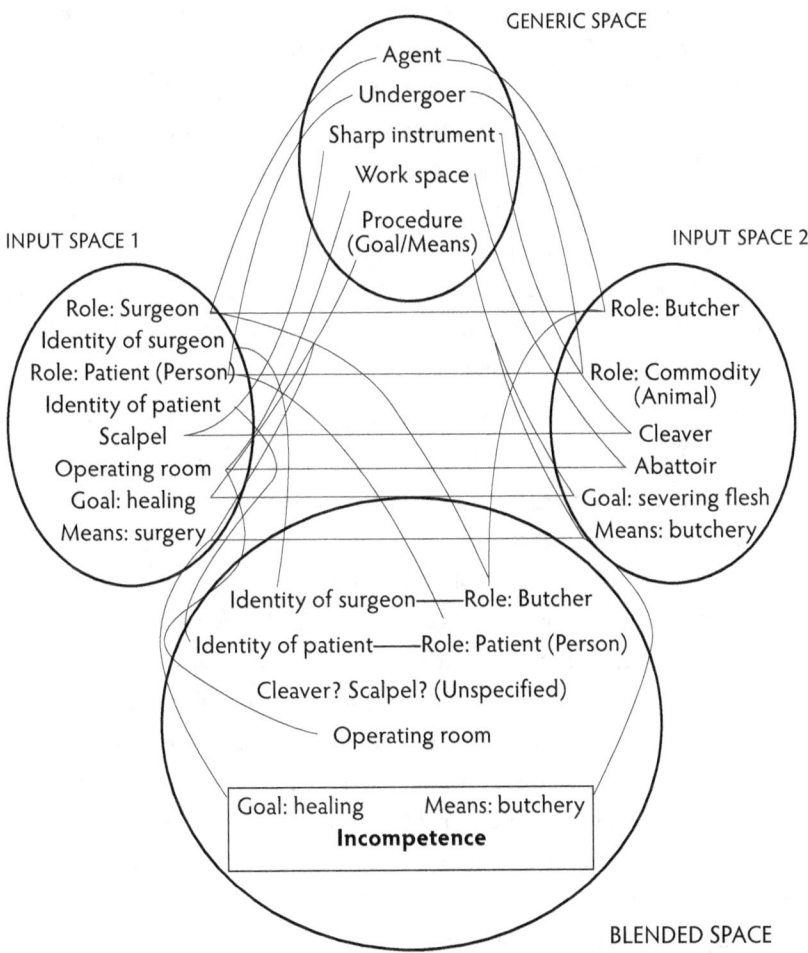

Figure 2: Brady, Oakly, and Coulson's conceptual integration network: Surgeon as butcher[135]

---

134. Lakoff and Johnson, *Metaphors We Live By*, 5.

135. Text in this figure taken from Joseph Grady, Todd Oakley, and Seana Coulson, "Blending and Metaphor," in *Metaphor in Cognitive Linguistics: Selected Papers from the 5th*

On the other hand, CIT provides an account as to how the emergent meaning in the blend is arrived at by proposing that emergent meaning is arrived at in the BS by projections from the input spaces as well as a result of the blend developing an "emergent" content of its own. The fact that the behavior of the surgeon is compared with that of a butcher requires the reader to draw from their background knowledge, through the process of completion in the blend, that since a butcher is associated with severing flesh from bones they cannot be trusted with performing surgery on patients.

Unlike the conventional metaphor account that emphasizes a uni-directional mapping from a source to a target domain, CIT treats these domains as inputs to the BS providing a more comprehensive account of links that exist between the long-term memory and other spaces in the integration network.[136] CIT also allows for the derivation of inferences that do not originate from either the source or the target domains, especially in situations where the construction of new meaning requires the adjustment of some culturally held thoughts and expectations, for as Wilson and Sperber point out

> If we treat the relationship between an utterance and its interpretation as inferential, then the issue is whether the properties that seem to "emerge" in the metaphorical interpretation can in fact be inferred. It should be obvious that the answer is "yes." Surgeons and butchers both characteristically cut flesh, but in quite different ways. Surgeons cut live flesh; they cut as little as possible, and with the utmost care to avoid unnecessarily severing blood vessels, nerves or tendons, thus causing irreparable damage. Butchers cut dead flesh to produce pieces of meat for cooking; this places no principled restriction on how much should be cut (or minced, broken, pounded, etc.), and puts a premium on severing nerves, tendons, and other hard tissues. So a surgeon who treats flesh as a butcher does would indeed be grossly incompetent and dangerous.[137]

International Cognitive Linguistics Conference, Amsterdam, 1997, edited by Raymond W. Gibbs Jr. and Gerard J. Steen, p. 105. Published by John Benjamins Publishing Company, Amsterdam/Philadelphia, 1999, https://benjamins.com/catalog/cilt.175. Used with permission.

136. Coulson, *Semantic Leaps*, 196–197.
137. Wilson and Sperber, "Deflationary Account of Metaphors," 114–115.

Another example that demonstrates the working of CIT is the case of the tax collector discussed above where in the Jewish culture the "beating of chest" signals "humility" while such an action among the Kikuyu would be associated with "arrogance" or "pride." There is no way the two domains, namely, that of "tax collector" and that of "chest" would result in these interpretations if the approach of mapping the source domain to the target domain is the only one applied. As will be discussed in more details later, there are elements from the background knowledge that might not be relevant in a given context, which are prohibited from entering the blend as well as from floating back to the input spaces. In the example of the "tax collector beating his chest" elements such as pain, length of time that the action takes place, whether the tax collector used their right or left hand, to mention a few, are some of the elements that are hindered from being projected to the blend. As Dancygier further points out

> ... blending as a theory makes us better at describing just how new meanings can be creatively constructed out of the existing knowledge structures. The framework aligns itself with cognitive approaches to the construction of meaning in that it treats language expressions (but also visual images, sounds, gestures, and all other meaningful forms of human expression) as prompts which the human mind uses in an act of meaning construction and comprehension. The central assumption, rather than a corollary, is, then, that meaning is best described as dynamically constructed in a mental process which is by definition creative and imaginative. This is the reason why blending is particularly appealing to the research aimed at the explanation of the mechanisms of creativity, which includes literary analysis, and, more specifically, stylistics and poetics.[138]

2.1.4 Relevance Theory

Relevance Theory (RT) was originally developed by Sperber and Wilson and mainly applied to translation by Gutt and Blakemore.[139] Some key works that

---

138. Dancygier, "What Can Blending Do For You?," 6.
139. Sperber and Wilson, *Relevance, Communication and Cognition*; Gutt, *Translation and Relevance*; Gutt, *Relevance Theory*; Blakemore, *Understanding Utterances*.

have analyzed metaphors from an RT perspective include those by Moreno, Wilson and Carston, and Alo, among others.[140] RT makes two general claims in respect to how humans cognitively process information as well as how they tend to naturally communicate that information. The first claim, referred to as the "cognition principle of relevance," is that human cognition is geared towards maximization of relevance, and the second claim, which is referred to as the "communicative principle of relevance," is that utterances raise expectations of relevance.[141] According to this theory, the linguistic meaning of an utterance only acts as a clue to the speaker's communicative intentions. As Wilson and Carston claim, the lexical meaning of an utterance involves the construction of an occasion-specific ad hoc concept which involves an interaction between the encoded concepts, the contextual information, and the expectation of relevance.[142]

The main claim that RT makes is that human cognition is oriented towards achievement of relevance. The achievement of cognitive effects within the relevance theoretic framework takes place in three different ways. First is that of strengthening existing assumptions through providing further evidence, second is the elimination of existing false assumptions in light of new evidence, and third is the derivation of new contextual implications through interaction with existing information. To illustrate these three ways, suppose someone told me on the eve of the Election Day in Kenya that,

(13) Tomorrow is the Election Day.

Suppose I happen to have known that tomorrow is an Election Day and as a result had already planned to go and vote, then utterance 13 above would achieve relevance by strengthening what I already knew. Suppose that I was thinking that the Election Day would take place a week later and had planned to spend the whole day writing my dissertation. In such an instance, utterance 13 would contradict what I knew concerning the date of the elections, thus eliminating my existing assumption. Lastly, if I had already planned to go and vote and had decided to pass by my friend's house to pick him up on

---

140. Moreno, *Creativity and Convention*; Wilson and Carston, "Metaphor, Relevance, and the 'Emergent Property,'"; Alo, "Translating the Metaphor."
141. Sperber and Wilson, *Relevance, Communication and Cognition*, 158, 260, 263–266.
142. Wilson and Carston, "Metaphor, Relevance, and the 'Emergent Property,'" 230.

the way to the polling station, then example 13 above would combine with this existing assumption to yield to the contextual implication that I can go ahead and pass by my friend's house on my way to vote. RT seeks to achieve these goals by guiding the interpreter to the achievement of cognitive effects using the least processing effort. If less processing effort is used to achieve more cognitive effects, then the utterance is said to be more relevant, and if one spends more processing effort and ends up achieving minimal cognitive effects, the utterance is said to be less relevant.[143] The utterance in example 13 above would be more relevant if I had a voter's card and was planning to vote on Election Day and thus would yield a range of contextual effects. On the other hand, suppose the person who uttered example 13 above continued and said,

(14) The polling clerks will be conducting the elections.

I do not need to be reminded that polling clerks conduct elections, since that is their mandate. This means that the extra processing effort that I might spend processing this information will not be rewarded with any extra contextual effects, and therefore utterance 14 will not be relevant to me. For any information to be relevant, a speaker takes into account the hearer's accessible background assumptions as well as inferences the addressee can readily draw so as to arrive at a hypothesis concerning the intended informative intention.

According to the relevance theoretic comprehension procedure, one is apt to follow the path of interpretation that uses the least effort in deriving cognitive effects and naturally tends to stop when the expectation of relevance is satisfied.[144] In obedience to the communicative principle of relevance, a communicator attempts to formulate their utterance in such a way as to guide listeners to access the intended assumptions in order to draw the intended conclusion(s) and in the process save the addressee from spending any extra processing effort.[145] According to RT, the interpretation that comes first is usually the one that is most relevant in a given context since it naturally requires the least processing effort.[146] It is only when the first interpretation

---

143. Sperber and Wilson, *Relevance, Communication and Cognition*, 261–266.
144. Wilson and Sperber, "Relevance Theory," 613.
145. Tendahl, *Hybrid Theory of Metaphor*, 239.
146. Gutt, *Relevance Theory*, 21, 24; Moreno, *Creativity and Convention*, 40.

is not satisfactory that the interpreter moves to the next one in line, and so forth. Take the example of the following utterance uttered by a lady to a bride in a Kikuyu Christian wedding ceremony:

(15) "*Ta   mũiru waku   nĩndakwamũkĩrĩte   na   moko merĩ.*"
     As   co-wife yours   I.you.have.received   with   hands two.
     "As my co-wife, I receive you with both hands."

One of the interpretations that could be accessed as far as the ambiguous reference *mũiru* "co-wife" is concerned, is that of a second wife. In the context of a Christian wedding where such a relationship is not entertained, this interpretation is rejected giving way to the second possible interpretation, namely that of a wife to one of the brothers to the groom. This interpretation is chosen because as a result of the background assumptions derived from both the immediate environment as well from the cultural knowledge shared at the time.[147] Hence the interpretation that satisfies the expectations of relevance is the one that the hearer chooses. The basic interpretation process requires the addressee to "(a) Follow a path of least effort in computing cognitive effects: Test interpretive hypotheses . . . in order of accessibility. (b) Stop when your expectations of relevance are satisfied (or abandoned)."[148]

2.2 The Theoretical Gap

Though Schmid claims that CIT in its present state "is sufficiently detailed to allow for fairly reliable predictions on how humans deal with situations forcing them to combine familiar but previously unrelated concepts in one novel concept,"[149] my claim is that CIT is somehow weak in detailing how the resulting processes take place. Scholars working on CIT have not explicitly provided details as to what informs the composition of blends in the interpretation of metaphors.[150] This vagueness also includes, among other concerns, that of detailing the constraining process which determines how input spaces are composed, how the selection and projection of elements takes place, as well

---

147. Wilson, "Relevance and Understanding," 41.
148. Wilson and Sperber, "Relevance Theory," 613.
149. Schmid, "Conceptual Blending," 219.
150. Tendahl, *Hybrid Theory of Metaphor*, 152.

as how emergent properties are derived in the blend.[151] The fact that human cognition is a selective process means that the projections from the input spaces to the BS are not arbitrary or random but are somehow constrained by given factors to allow for local understanding.[152]

In the "Debate with Kant" example discussed above, we find that there is selective projection to the blend which results in Kant himself, his debate counterpart, and some of their ideas being projected to the blend. On the other hand, we find elements that are not being projected into the blend, such as the time that Kant lived, the language he used in his writings, the fact that he could not have been aware of such a debate taking place many years after his death. In the Regatta illustration, which has also been discussed above, the selective process allows for the two boats, their positions in the course, the time they spent on the way, among other relevant elements to be projected into the blend, while on the other hand, factors such as the 1853 date, the existing weather conditions of the time, to name just a few, are not projected into the blend. CIT scholars also fail to detail the factors that influence the choice of interpretive frames and also how an addressee is meant to identify which interpretation is the right one since varying interpretations can be arrived at using the same mental spaces. Take also the example from the utterance "the child is safe" mentioned in the context of a child playing on a beach with a shovel which is discussed in example 3 above. We find that the ocean, which is a potential source of danger, is not projected into the blend, even though it might be activated in the background knowledge as one of the potential dangers. In the metaphorical utterance "my surgeon is a butcher," also discussed above, we find that mappings from the source domain of "butcher" to the target domain of "surgeon" does not explain how a hearer is able to derive the interpretation of the surgeon as being incompetent and consequently accused of malpractice. By using the process of mapping alone, there is no doubt that butchers are also skilled in their work just as surgeons are in theirs. It is therefore important to come up with a workable solution as to how to constrain this selective process so that only relevant projections and interpretations are allowed to take place in the integration process.

---

151. Moreno, *Creativity and Convention*, 77; Tendahl, *Hybrid Theory of Metaphor*, 160.
152. Evans and Green, *Cognitive Linguistics*, 409.

The simple acknowledgment that emergent features result from adding information from the long-term memory does not provide a good solution to the problem of what motivates the selection process since the process of retrieving background knowledge could as well lead to interpretations that may not be intended by the speaker. Consequently, the conceptual integration process raises a further question as to what factors drives the BS to inherit selected elements from the input spaces as well as to generate new properties, a question which CIT does not answer satisfactorily. As Moreno further points out

> One important problem with Blending Theory, and with many psycholinguistic approaches to metaphor is that it does not take seriously into account the speaker's communicative intentions . . . a single metaphor . . . can be used to convey a number of different meanings on different occasions. In order to explain this in terms of Blending Theory, one would have to say the hearer forms a different blend in every occasion. It is not clear how this can be done. Since the projection from input spaces to the blended space is taken as based on structural similarities between spaces and not in the search for the recognition of speaker's intentions, there is no apparent reason why different elements from an input space would be projected into the blended space on different occasions. In fact, even if the explanation of different interpretations were to be given in terms of different types of completions of the blend, the theory cannot explain what determines these different completions.[153]

In response to this criticism, Fauconnier and Turner have proposed a set of optimality or governing principles, which they claim restricts the blending processes.[154] These include the "topology" principle that claims that relations in the blend should match the relations of their counterparts in the other spaces, the "pattern completion" principle, the "integration" principle (which claims that representations in the BS can be manipulated as a single unit), the "maximization and intensification of vital relations" principles, the "web"

---

153. Moreno, *Creativity and Convention*, 81.
154. Fauconnier and Turner, *Way We Think*, 309–346.

principle (which claims that representations in the BS should maintain mappings from the input spaces), the "unpacking" principle (which allows for the reconstruction of the network connections between the spaces in the blend), and the "relevance" principle (which creates pressure to attribute significance to elements in the blend). Satisfying these principles is said to be selective, thus, satisfying one might be inconsistent with satisfying another, with the most likely one being adopted.

Unfortunately, these optimality principles do not offer specific guidance as to which mechanisms govern the selection process, how the determination of input spaces is done, how frames are recruited, or how emergent properties arise, among other concerns. They seem more of playing the role of a check-list, which is only applicable at the end of the interpretation process given that they address the resulting blended spaces as end products. These principles are not intended to constrain the process of the formation of blends as it happens. Therefore, there is need to detail the factors that lead to the formation of these blends in our minds and specifically how the selection process, which determines what our minds focus on in the construction of meaning, takes place, an issue I address next.

2.3 Bridging the Gap

As a result, in addition to the traditional spaces addressing relations within the integration network as far as the interpretation of metaphors in concerned, I have included two outer spaces, namely the discourse space (DS) and the relevance space (RS), as relations that constrain the integration process. Within the DS, the role of context is highlighted providing the structure and function that contribute towards the entire argument in which the metaphor is found. The RS is central in providing the framing that guides mappings and selections in the network. These two are interconnected, with the argument in the DS forming the basis that determines the background knowledge or framing which is activated within the RS. Let us look in details the role of these two outer spaces.

2.3.1 The Discourse Space

The discourse approach adopted in this study is the mental models approach, which as Smith points out, "posits a mental representation which models the state of affairs expressed in the text."[155] Using this approach, words will be treated as "sound sequences that conventionally express concepts that are within conceptual schemas."[156] The reason behind using this approach is to try as much as possible to take on board the "context-based processing constraints," which are part of the author's and the reader's mental worlds serving as clues necessary to the interpretation of metaphors.[157] Identifying the discourse context of a metaphor is important for as Kittay points out

> The question of how we identify a metaphor has never been adequately treated, in part, I believe, because writers have not correctly identified the unit of discourse that constitutes a metaphor. Language can only be identified as metaphorical by virtue of linguistic and contextual conditions that require that we interpret it differently from its surrounding discourse; therefore, we cannot give the conditions by which we recognize metaphors without identifying that unit of discourse which constitutes a metaphor.[158]

Langacker refers to this mental world as the "current discourse space" in which both a speaker and a hearer have a shared construal of elements and relations that form the basis of their communication at a given moment.[159] It is also referred to as the "base space" or as the "speaker reality space."[160] Incorporating a DS within the integration network is recognizing the role of discourse participants who in one way or another influence the construal of the mental spaces that are activated as well as how these mental spaces are developed and revised in the course of the development of the discourse.[161] In a given DS, utterances come to mean what they mean because of the DS structures and arguments which influence the semantic content of words.

---

155. Smith, *Models of Discourse*, 55.
156. Lakoff and Turner, *More than Cool Reason*, 109.
157. Cameron, *Metaphor in Educational Discourse*, 42.
158. Kittay, *Metaphor*, 40–41.
159. Langacker, *Cognitive Grammar*, 59.
160. Brandt, *Explosive Blends*, 7; Fauconnier, *Mental Spaces*, xxvii.
161. Brandt, *Explosive Blends*, 11; Fauconnier and Sweetser, *Spaces, Worlds and Grammars*, 12.

Mental spaces are dynamically constructed with relevant concepts being profiled in the course of a discourse. Prompts that serve as clues in the construction of mental spaces, which in one way or another contribute to the emerging meaning of a discourse, include "names of authors, forms of address, pronouns, tenses, the choice of vocabulary, interactional properties, or visual images."[162] These clues might be recalled in the course of the discourse to refer back to previous mental spaces in other discourse spaces that are recalled or made salient to advance the argument that the speaker is making within the current DS. This mostly happens in the integration process through the process of completion in the running of the blend, as background knowledge is also recalled to draw further inferences. If an interpretation requires a different background from that of the current discourse space, the existing space is extended to accommodate this information, and if this extension results in contradictory information, a new mental space is set up, which might maintain some of the aspects of the previous mental space.[163] The integration process also takes into consideration the schematic scenarios including values, beliefs, and attitudes which are blended within a given DS or unit. Since metaphors bring to the DS traces of their previous uses in other discourse spaces, which may need to be taken on board in the current DS, I will be alluding to how the metaphor translated as "circumcision of the heart" has been used, analyzed, and interpreted in previous discourses.[164]

The textual unit of this study, as has been mentioned previously, is Romans 2 mainly focusing on verses 17–29. This unit will serve as the immediate context that informs the interpretation of the metaphor περιτομὴ καρδίας. This DS will help in accounting for the blending strategies applied in the text, which include making observation of how the reorganization of elements is done through the introduction of new elements that are instrumental in adjusting the scenarios that are crucial in the interpretation of this metaphor. The meaning of a metaphor is context-bound since a metaphor only appears in a given DS, and as Tendahl points out

> The blended space is especially dependent on the context due to the main operations involved in constructing the blend. In

---

162. Dancygier, "What Can Blending Do For You?," 11.
163. Coulson, *Semantic Leaps*, 23.
164. Cameron, *Metaphor in Educational Discourse*, 27.

completion background knowledge is recruited to structure the blend in addition to the composed structure that derives from mappings from the input spaces. *Elaboration* further determines a blended space. This means that the blend might be further developed by simulation and imagination and thus it is again modified by an extra-linguistic source. Moreover, the operations of composition, completion and elaboration may lead to emergent structure which is not derived by any of the input spaces alone, but rather by interactions of the input spaces and operations such as completion and elaboration. Last but not least, emergent structure certainly includes implicatures, and implicatures are without doubt context-dependent.[165]

Since as Sperber and Wilson point out the notion of context is more than just the immediate context in which a linguistic unit is embedded, the adopted discourse approach will also focus on the state of affairs from both the external and internal worlds of the text (i.e. the history behind the text as well as that of the community that is in front of the text including their historical and cultural contexts).[166] Context includes the sum knowledge and conceptual framework that are accessed in the process of interpreting an experience, and as a result include "expectations about the future, scientific hypothesis or religious beliefs, anecdotal memories, general cultural assumptions, [and] beliefs about the mental state of the speaker."[167] When it comes to the translation process, context is important for as Wendland points out

> Recent explorations in translation theory and practice, especially cognitive-based studies, have underscored the importance of context in communication. Without an adequate understanding of the surrounding circumstances that motivate a text, it is difficult, if not impossible, to understand it as intended by the original author. This is true to a greater or lesser extent even when communicating in the same language, and the difficulties

---

165. Tendahl, *Hybrid Theory of Metaphor*, 168.
166. Sperber and Wilson, *Relevance, Communication and Cognition*, 15–16; Reed, "Discourse Analysis," 192; Green, *Hearing the New Testament*, 218; Georgakopoulou and Goutsos, *Discourse Analysis*, 8.
167. Gutt, *Relevance Theory*, 22.

only increase where translation from one language and sociocultural setting to a different one is involved. In short, then, the meaning of a translated text is always contextually conditioned with respect to both its composition and interpretation.[168]

By analyzing the surface structure of Romans 2:17–29 as the primary textual unit, I will be seeking to take note of the clues that the author profiles that constrain the inferences he intends his readers to draw, which accordingly contribute towards the rhetorical function of the text. It is also by analyzing a given discourse unit that one is able to recognize how the author brings together the different parts of the integration network in the text which are basic in recreating the mental spaces that are foundational in the arrangement of the DS. I will also analyze the RL use of metaphors in their contexts. It is important to note that the selectivity of profiled elements in a given text naturally follows the path of relevance.[169] Therefore, as one seeks to construct the mental spaces in the integration network following the author's specifications provided in the text, one is able to arrive at relevant inferences which lead to a greatly enriched mental model(s) leading to a better understanding to what the speaker/author is trying to model in the mind of their addressee(s).

2.3.2 The Relevance Space

The concept of background framing in the integration process automatically activates that of relevance. This is because it is on the basis of its relevance that some of the information in the background knowledge ends up being projected in a given situational context.[170] Without the input of relevance, it would be hard to determine which background frame(s) to activate and by extension which among the possible meanings is the speaker's intended one. In the blending process, a listener tends to naturally seek to follow the path of maximizing relevance and in the process ignores those connections as well as elements in the integration framework that go against this principle. Therefore, it is in consideration of the relevance framing space that some elements are made salient and hence selected to form the basis on which

---

168. Wendland, *Life-Style Translating*, 263.
169. Moreno, *Creativity and Convention*, 7.
170. Brandt, *Explosive Blends*, 12.

inferences are constructed and also the basis on which projections are made into the BS.[171]

The RS is a major input into the integration process in view of the fact that it brings on board the background framing of concepts in a given communication context. The entire integration process is constrained by relevance (i.e. one tends to pay attention to information that seems relevant to them), with considerations of cognitive effects and cognitive effort as a criterion for evaluating the intended interpretations. As Evans and Green point out, RT "relates to the processes that mental spaces and blending theorists refer to as projection, mapping, schema induction and integration."[172] This means that the formation of the input spaces involved in the integration process is relevance driven with the consideration of the roles of the speaker and the hearer in negotiating the message and determining its meaning taken on board.[173] Within the RS, the contribution of context in the interpretation of metaphorical utterances is also highlighted since "words, phrases, entrenched background assumptions taken from long-term memory and situation-specific assumptions are all clues needed to come up with an interpretation of an utterance."[174] In the selection of projections into the blended space, relevance comes in handy in the selection of projections into the blended space by directing which properties are chosen or highlighted since the inferential comprehension process is geared towards relevance. Take the example of a preacher speaking in a church service for the first time. There are different observations that one might arrive at concerning them, some of which are not intended as part of what they intend to communicate. Say for instance that they appear to be nervous. There is no doubt that the preacher would prefer their audience not to take notice that they're nervous but that they should pay attention to their message. In the same way, the interpretation of metaphor requires the hearer to adhere to the strongly manifest assumption(s) which are intended by the speaker.

---

171. Sperber and Wilson, *Relevance, Communication and Cognition*, 158; Brandt, *Explosive Blends*, 13.
172. Evans and Green, *Cognitive Linguistics*, 463.
173. Sperber and Wilson, *Relevance, Communication and Cognition*, 142–144.
174. Tendahl, *Hybrid Theory of Metaphor*, 167.

2.4 The Complementary Approach

The theoretical basis proposed in this work is a complementary approach between CIT and RT. Even though there are some significant differences between these two approaches as far as the interpretation of metaphors is concerned, my argument is that these theories can complement each other since they tackle different aspects of metaphoric conceptualization process. On the one hand, while CIT focuses on the structure of a metaphor within the conceptual system, on the other hand, RT sheds light on how the integration process is run in light of the communication aspect of a given metaphor. The two theories agree in a number of aspects and therefore are well suited to complement each other. These include the fact that they are cognitively based, hence both acknowledge the fact that linguistic representations of metaphors are only clues to the interpretation process. They are also in agreement that the construction of meaning is online allowing for local contextual cognitive processes. CIT refers to the resulting online spaces as "mental spaces" while RT refers to them as "ad hoc concepts." According to CIT, mental spaces are a "structured set of knowledge that includes such forms as mental frames possibly containing several individual concepts, whereas ad hoc concepts are a particular kind of concept."[175] This means that mental spaces are generally bigger than ad hoc concepts. Both theories agree that these online spaces (i.e. mental spaces and ad hoc concepts), are constructed for local understanding. In addition, both theories allow for drawing of emergent properties and inferences as well as concur that the process of the construction of meaning is somehow constrained.

The proposed complementary approach between these two theories allows for mental spaces to be governed by pragmatic rules with the integration process adhering to the achievement of relevance. As will be demonstrated in the following chapters, the integration process can benefit by embracing the input from RT, a factor that most CIT scholars fail to take into account when coming up with their integration networks. Figure 3 below, shows the proposed modified conceptual integration network.

The proposed complementary framework will be used in this study to detail the composition of input spaces in the integration process in both the source and receptor languages as well as in detailing the constraining

---

175. Tendahl, 168–169.

process which determines how the selection and projection of elements takes place, as well as how emergent properties are derived in the blend for local understanding. Using this approach, the elements within the SL input spaces of ΠΕΡΙΤΟΜΗ and ΚΑΡΔΙΑ will be highlighted with the underlying process behind the selected projections to the BS discussed. The background frames that give rise to these input spaces will be discussed together with the modified ones which the apostle Paul is arguing for in the construct in the context of Romans 2. The approach will help to detail the conceptual integration process behind the interpretation of the metaphor περιτομὴ καρδίας which include profiling links between the associated concepts as well as the intended inferences.

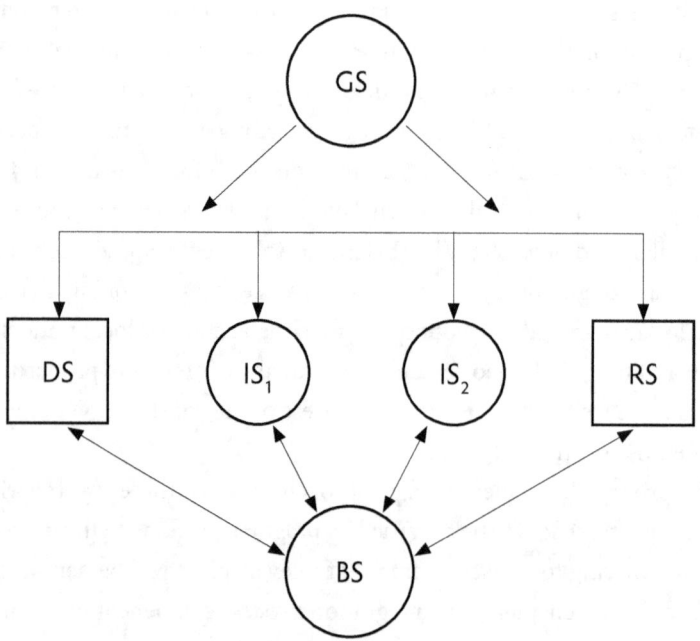

Figure 3: A modified integration network

Also, as far as the RL language is concerned, the proposed complementary approach will help in pointing out the integration process behind the associated concepts of IRUA* "[male] circumcision," HAKIRI "mind" and NGORO "heart" including highlighting the underlying conceptual structures and background frames that are evoked in the process. In the translation chapter, using the suggested complementary approach, the two blended spaces from the SL and RL will be associated as input spaces within what is referred to conceptually as the translation space.[176] In the process, the relevance projections and intended inferences that need to be projected to the RL target space will be highlighted. The application of this complementary approach will therefore inform the proposed rendering of the SL metaphor into the RL in the context of Romans 2.

In the two outer spaces introduced within the conceptual framework, namely the discourse and relevance spaces, the constraining context of the metaphors both in the source and receptor languages will be discussed. Within the DS of Romans 2 where the SL metaphor περιτομὴ καρδίας occurs, the rhetorical function of the metaphor will be discussed by also looking at related concepts and lexical units made salient in the course of the discourse, which shape the meaning of this metaphor. The cognitive frames and related concepts that are also activated in the RL when the concepts IRUA, NGORO and HAKIRI are associated in a metaphorical relationship in given discourse contexts' will be discussed. The other outer input space is that of RS, which highlights the pragmatic factor involved in the integration process that directs the interpreter on which connections to go for and which ones to ignore in the integration process. The two outer spaces from the source and receptor languages contain information from their respective background framing, which informs the conceptual framework of the associated concepts and they are therefore crucial in determining the meaning of metaphors.

2.5 Summary

There is need to detail the mechanisms governing the selection process or the direction which the integration process takes. These include how input spaces are determined, how the processes of composition, completion, and elaboration are constrained in the integration process, and also how the above processes come to a halt since they can go on forever. The proposed complementary approach between CIT and RT is able to assist one to figure out how the properties in the input spaces emerge in the course of the interpretation process as well as how the hearer is able to derive inferences which lead to the

---

176. McElhanon, "From Simple Metaphors," 69–70.

interpretation intended by the speaker. As will be pointed out in the application of the complementary approach in the following chapters, in order to arrive at the intended meaning of a given metaphor, listeners are guided by the path of relevance within a given discourse space. This path offers guidelines as to which background knowledge/framing to access, which elements to profile, as well as which among many are the speaker's intended inferences.

CHAPTER 3

Biblical Conceptualization of ΠΕΡΙΤΟΜΗ and ΚΑΡΔΙΑ

This chapter demonstrates how the meaning of the metaphor περιτομὴ καρδίας is constructed in the blend by use of the complementary approach between CIT and RT. In this theoretical framework, the two background frames of ΠΕΡΙΤΟΜΗ and ΚΑΡΔΙΑ are treated as inputs to the integration process with the discrepancies between the two domains mediated by a BS. Since frames as interpretive resources are culture based, there is need to first come to terms with the underlying frames in the SL, which are activated by the associated concepts in a metaphorical relationship.[1] This step is crucial in understanding the new meaning that Paul was leading his audience to construct in the context of Romans 2 as he creatively sought to reshape the conventional cultural frame that his readers held.

The first section of this chapter analyzes the traditional Jewish world view as far as the related concepts of ΠΕΡΙΤΟΜΗ and ΚΑΡΔΙΑ are concerned. This includes profiling the related frame elements that are activated, highlighting the sequence of events that are activated when the ritual of [ΠΕΡΙΤΟΜΗ] is evoked, and pointing out related beliefs as well as accompanying values and emotions that are activated in the process. The second section of this chapter will seek to analyze the modified frame that Paul was arguing for and leading his audience to construct in their minds in the context of Romans 2. This section will demonstrate how he went along in modifying both the generic role associated with the traditional frame, referred to here as the [OLD COVENANT]

---

1. Coulson, *Semantic Leaps*, 35; López, "Applying Frame Semantics," 312.

frame, as well as the specific traditional role associated with the ritual frame of [ΠΕΡΙΤΟΜΗ]. The third section of this chapter will seek to lay out in detail the conceptual integration process that is at work in the construction of the meaning of the metaphor περιτομὴ καρδίας in light of the suggested complementary approach. I will demonstrate how the new meaning of this metaphor is constructed by modifying the elements associated with the existing traditional frame in light of the background knowledge associated with the ritual of [ΠΕΡΙΤΟΜΗ]. In the process, the new inputs or prompts that Paul profiles will be highlighted. Given that what is represented by this metaphor is a prepackaged blend, so to speak, the various mental spaces will be identified, links between them traced, and the intended inferences highlighted. I will then conclude by pointing out the meaning of this metaphor in light of the argument Paul is making in Romans chapter 2.

3.1 The Traditional Frame

The old semantic frame associated with the concept ΠΕΡΙΤΟΜΗ "to cut around" is that of [RITUAL], with its generic frame being that of the [OLD COVENANT].[2] In translating the metaphor περιτομὴ καρδίας, one needs to thoroughly understand the relevant aspects associated with the ritual of [ΠΕΡΙΤΟΜΗ] in order to understand what is implied by that of the heart. The more generic frame that is activated when the ritual of [ΠΕΡΙΤΟΜΗ] is evoked is that of [ΔΙΑΘΗΚΗ] "covenant," a rendering which is also chosen in the Septuagint (LXX) for the Hebrew concept בְּרִית. This meaning keeps the old connotation of a "compact, treaty, mutual agreement" between God and his people.[3] As Behm points out, the LXX translators

---

2. One of the synonyms of περιτομὴ is the verb ὀρθοτομέω which means "to cut straight." It is used in 2 Timothy 2:15 to figuratively describe the action of expounding the word of God in a correct manner. The substantive κατατομή "mutilation" in Philippians 3:2 is used sarcastically to attack false teachers who were insisting in combining the gospel with the law and were specifically insisting that the Gentile converts had to be circumcised so as to be accepted as believers. The practice of mutilation was practiced in pagan cults and is explicitly forbidden in the Torah (Lev 21:5). The idea of a general and specific frame is discussed by Norrick (Norrick, "Discourse and Semantics") who refers to the [BOXING] frame as being a more specific frame than that of [FIGHTING], with the frame of [COMPETITION] being even more generic than that of [FIGHTING].

3. Muraoka, *Greek-English Lexicon*, 150.

Must have felt that the originally legal term בְּרִית had come to convey stronger and specifically religious thoughts which went far beyond the idea of a contract between God and man and suggested the idea of a free declaration of the divine will to man's salvation. διαθηκη, too, was a legal term which might compromise different forms of a binding expression of will, e.g., testamentary disposition (which is alien to the OT), a contract between two parties and divine dispositions and sacred ordinances of the most forceful kind. If they thus used διαθηκη for בְּרִית, the one term certainly seemed to be no less rich than the other, but there was a shift of accent through the predominant use of διαθηκη in the religious sense. In other words, the exclusively determinative will of the divine author emerged in clearer focus . . . in Jer. 31:31 ff., to mention the instance which is most important from the NT standpoint, and which represents both the climax and end of the OT idea of the covenant, the concept καινήδιαθηκη allows us to conceive of the religion of the age of salvation, to which the gaze of the prophet is directed, only as the free gift of God, as the declaration of His saving will, as the revelation of grace, in relation to which Israel can be only a recipient. "Disposition," "declaration of the divine will," "the divine will self-revealed in history and establishing religion" – this is the religious concept of the διαθηκη in the LXX, and it represents a significant development of the Hebrew term even while preserving its essential content.[4]

The predominant meaning that is strongly activated when the concept ΔΙΑΘΗΚΗ is evoked is that of a relationship based on obligations established under divine sanctions.[5] The divine-human relationship which is activated could either be a bilateral relationship between God and a human being, or, a relationship that goes in one direction (i.e. from God to a human being).[6] The covenant ritual in Genesis 17 is an example of a bilateral relationship

---

4. Behm, "The Greek Term διαθήκη," 127.
5. Hugenberger, *Marriage as a Covenant*, 171.
6. Soggin, *Israel in the Biblical Period*, 55.

that is unequal.[7] God, who is the stronger party, promises Abraham and his descendants, the weaker parties, that they would be fruitful and inherit the promised land, and goes ahead to place an obligation on the weaker party, namely, that of circumcising all male descendants as a reminder of the covenant that he entered with them.[8]

In Genesis 17 alone, the word בְּרִית occurs thirteen times, and for that reason unless one understands a covenant as a means of passing-on covenantal privileges and obligations from one generation to another, it is hard to relate why circumcision is described as its sign and why it has been observed devotedly by the descendants of Abraham over the years. Another example of a bilateral relationship made within the framework of a covenant is that of the covenant made between God and the Israelites.[9] In this covenant, which is also referred to as the Sinai or Mosaic covenant, the action of God was met with a human commitment to obey its obligations. This is different from the covenant made with Noah, referred to as the Noahic covenant, which is a one directional relationship since it is God who commits himself not to destroy the inhabitants of the earth with flood waters.[10]

Another meaning that is activated when the concept ΔΙΑΘΗΚΗ is evoked is that of a "half-legal and half-sacral form of a fellowship between man and man" which involves "sacral assurances in the form of oaths or sacrifices" with a name of a divine being evoked in the process.[11] An example is that of the covenant entered between David and Jonathan.[12] Even though they entered into this covenant in their capacity as private individuals with equal bargaining power, the resulting mutual obligations were binding legal agreements

---

7. The Genesis 17 event is a climax of what was initiated in Genesis 12:1–3 and revisited in Genesis 15 (Cotter, *Genesis*, 109). Even though Genesis 15 and 17 are recorded as two separate accounts belonging to different traditions, (i.e. chapter 15 being attributed as having resulted from the Yahwist ["J"] and/or Elohist ["E"] sources and chapter 17 from the Priestly ["P"] materials) these two accounts are better interpreted as complementing each another (Moberly, *Genesis 12–50*, 25, 57–58). In chapter 15 God, being the stronger party, is committing himself to the covenant obligations, while in chapter 17 Abraham, as the weaker party, is committing both himself and his male descendants to observe the ritual of circumcision as an outward sign of accepting the obligations of the covenant (Cotter, *Genesis*, 97).

8. Huey, Jr., *Jeremiah, Lamentations*, 281; Delaney, *Abraham on Trial*, 96.

9. Exod 19–24; 32–34.

10. Gen 9:1–17.

11. Quell, "διαθήκη," 109.

12. cf. 1 Sam 18:3; 20:8; 23:18.

under sacral guarantees.¹³ Another example of a covenant made between individuals which was half-legal and half-sacral is the peace covenant made between Jacob and Laban, with the name of Yahweh being invoked as a witness and a memorial stone pillar erected as a sign.¹⁴

The [OLD COVENANT] generic frame also evokes other types of covenants which include the one made in the plains of Moab, the one made at Mounts Ebal and Gerizim, the one made at Shechem, the one made with Phinehas, the Davidic covenant, the marriage covenant, and the covenant between God and the eschatological Israel.¹⁵ The covenant institution among the people of Israel points to the fact that legal obligations played an important role in fashioning the entire social life of the people of Israel as a community of Yahweh.¹⁶

The ritual of circumcision is described as a בְּרִית אוֹת "sign of the covenant" made between God and Abraham, and by extension Abraham's descendants, which fulfills both the functions of a mnemonic cognition sign as well as an identity sign.¹⁷ According to Wenham, the Hebrew word אוֹת is used in three different ways.¹⁸ First, it is used as reference to a proof aimed to convince someone about something. An example is that of the plagues that occurred in the land of Egypt, which were intended as signs to persuade Pharaoh that YHWH is sovereign.¹⁹ Second, the word אוֹת is used to refer to acted prophecies which resemble the situations they describe. An example is when the prophet Ezekiel placed an iron griddle between him and the city of Jerusalem as a sign of the coming siege.²⁰ The third use of the word אוֹת is that of reminding someone of something. Examples include that of eating unleavened bread, which is a reminder of the exodus and the need to observe the law or that of the Sabbath, which was a reminder to the Israelites of the holiness of God and that they were called to be holy.²¹ The rainbow is also referred to as בְּרִית

---

13. Huey, Jr., *Jeremiah, Lamentations*, 280; Quell, "διαθήκη," 112.
14. Gen 31:44–55.
15. Deut 29–31; Josh 8:30–35; Josh 24; Num 25:12–18; 2 Sam 7:11b–16; 23:5; Mal 2:14; Jer 31:31; Isa 42:6; 49:6–8; 55:3.
16. Quell, "διαθήκη," 114.
17. Derouchie, "Circumcision in the Hebrew Bible," 184; cf. Gen 17:11.
18. Wenham, *Genesis 16–50*, 23.
19. cf. Exod 7:3–5.
20. cf. Ezek 4:3.
21. Exod 13:9; 31:13–17; Deut 6:8; 11:18.

אוֹת "a sign of the covenant" since it was embedded in the clouds to remind God not to destroy all the living creatures with another flood.[22] The ritual of circumcision falls under this third category, namely, that of reminding someone about something. Therefore, circumcision is not the covenant itself, despite the fact that it is referred in some instances as if it is *the* covenant itself.[23] Such references should be understood as metonymic since the ritual of circumcision is used to refer to the covenant with which it is associated.

The relevant question might be raised as to whom the sign of circumcision is intended for; is it for the Israelites, for the foreigners, or for God himself? The answer to this question is pegged on first establishing what this sign is supposed to accomplish. The interpretation that it is intended to be a reminder to God of his promises, in the same way that a rainbow does, is problematic because a sign is expected to function primarily as a reminder to the one(s) who affixes it. This means that the sign of circumcision was meant to act as a reminder to a covenant member, so that whenever he sees this sign on his body, he is reminded to obey the very covenant for which it is a sign.[24] It is in observing the ritual of circumcision that a male child is symbolically inducted to be a partaker of the promises made to the patriarchs and also assimilated as a child of Abraham with the ritual acting as a sign of commitment to follow God's commands.[25]

3.1.1 Frame Elements

This section highlights the main elements and relations that are evoked from the traditional understanding of the source domain activated by the ritual frame of [ΠΕΡΙΤΟΜΗ]. These include participants and props, attendant circumstances, deontic status and ethical values which are associated with this ritual. Also highlighted are other related concepts and sub-frames that are made available when this concept is evoked.

---

22. Gen 9:11–16.
23. cf. Gen 17:10; Acts 7:8.
24. Wenham, *Genesis 16–50*, 24; cf. Gen 17:11, 13–14.
25. Bernat, *Sign of the Covenant*, 38; Williamson, "Circumcision," 123.

3.1.1.1 Participants and Props

As far as the [OLD COVENANT] frame of [ΠΕΡΙΤΟΜΗ] is concerned, God is evoked as its main agent since he is the initiator of this ritual. As the stronger partner in the covenant made between him and Abraham, his position is that of a guarantor "of the covenant and its institution, as in a legal covenant . . . He is also the subject to it, to the degree that the question of protective lordship is not left open."[26] Abraham and the male descendants after him are also activated within this ritual frame and are expected to observe it as a reminder of God's promises, failure of which there are consequences, including that of being cut off from the community of God's people.[27]

The other participants made available in this ritual frame include the parents of the male child undergoing the ritual. The father figure is given the primary responsibility to see to it that the male child undergoes the ritual, with most circumcisions in the biblical era been performed by a member of the family.[28] Abraham is said to have circumcised his son Isaac when Isaac was eight days old, Isaac did the same to his son Jacob, and Jacob to his twelve sons.[29] Though the third singular form of the verb וַיָּ֫מָל "and he circumcised" is used in Genesis 17:23, considering the large number of men to be circumcised, it is likely that Abraham might have been assisted in performing the physical circumcision to all the male members born in his household.[30]

There are also indications that mothers too performed this ritual. Zipporah is said to have circumcised one of her sons as a desperate act of evading death.[31] The context that led to this incident was an attempted attack on the life of

---

26. Quell, "διαθήκη," 118.
27. cf. Gen 17:14.
28. Bloch, *Biblical and Historical Background*, 9.
29. Gen 21:4; Acts 7:8: Note that the Greek text in Acts 7:8b is ambiguous and could either be interpreted to mean "Isaac was the father of Jacob, and Jacob was the father of the twelve patriarchs" or that "Isaac circumcised Jacob, and Jacob circumcised the twelve patriarchs." Some translations including the KJV, the NIV, the ESV, etc., follow the former alternative, while the TEV, the CEV, among others, follow the latter option by filling in the explicature from the first part of the verse where Abraham is said to have circumcised his son Isaac on the eighth day after birth. This is also the understanding of the Jerusalem Bible which states "So when his son Isaac was born he circumcised him on the eighth day. Isaac did the same for Jacob and Jacob for the twelve patriarchs."
30. Note the same use of the verb in the third person singular is used in Genesis 18:8 whereby the word עשה most probably means that Abraham had ordered for the food to be prepared and not that he himself prepared it.
31. Exod 4:24–26.

Moses by the Lord for what seems to have been a failure on the part of Moses to circumcise his son within the prescribed time limit.[32] A number of issues are not made clear in the reporting of this incident, which include the exact reason behind the intended killing, whether it was Moses or one of his sons who was threatened with death, and the reason why it was Zipporah who had to perform the act and not Moses. As far as the last issue is concerned, one of the allegorical interpretations given is that she had to do it herself so as to symbolize the termination of any link with the Midianite religion and in so doing connect herself together with her sons with the God of Israel.[33] The Hebrew pronouns used in this text are ambiguous making it hard to figure out who does what and to whom. Part of resolving this ambiguity as to whom Zipporah circumcised would involve first establishing whether or not Moses was circumcised. There is a possibility that Moses was already circumcised prior to this event, either as an infant, since he was brought up by his mother, or at a later date following the Egyptian manner, since there is evidence that Egyptians practiced circumcision.[34] This then could only mean that it is Moses's son who Zipporah circumcised. We also find mothers circumcising their male children in the Hasmonean period as part of their normal routine as they brought them up.[35]

In instances where the parents failed to execute this responsibility, the role was taken over by the rabbinic court.[36] There are also occasions where community leaders are said to have performed this ritual. One such example is that of Joshua, and just as in the case of Abraham discussed above, it is inconceivable to think of him performing all the operations alone without some people assisting him.[37] The apostle Paul is said to have circumcised Timothy so as to reach out to the Jewish people with the gospel of Jesus Christ since Timothy had a Jewish mother and therefore was considered as being Jewish.[38]

The intended beneficiaries are male children who are descendants of Abraham, either born free or born to their servants, whether they may be

---

32. Kugel, *Traditions of the Bible*, 518.
33. Blumenthal, "Circumcision Performed by Zipporah," 259.
34. cf. Jer 9:25–26.
35. 1 Macc 1:10–60.
36. Cohen, *Guide to Ritual Circumcision*, 6.
37. Josh 5:2–8.
38. Acts 16:3; Cohen, *Beginnings of Jewishness*, 373–375.

sons of hired workers or those of aliens.³⁹ The distinction between the sons of the ones born free and those born by slaves is said to have come from a later period than that of Abraham when such a difference had became an important issue, as Westermann points out

> The extension to the prescription to circumcise to the household can only mean that for P the whole household is a cultic unity, and that the circle of worshippers of Yahweh is expanded by the slaves beyond the members of the Israelite people. This shows a certain openness, conditioned by the strong bond of family unity, which includes the slaves. At the same time the significance of circumcision undergoes adaptation and it becomes explicitly religious. This is to meet a concern that the slaves can take part in family worship.⁴⁰

Even though the sons of slaves and foreigners could undergo the ritual of circumcision and practice their master's religion, they did not merit the same benefits and privileges as the sons born to Israelites, which include the promise of land and of many descendants.⁴¹ Other participants who were activated by the ritual frame of [ΠΕΡΙΤΟΜΗ] include neighbors and relatives, who would also join in the celebration of the ritual.⁴² The instruments used to perform the ritual were צֻרִים חַרְבוֹת "flint knives," with the old Greek (OG) translator in Joshua 5:2, pointing out that these knives were μαχαίρας πετρίνας ἐκ πέτρας ἀκροτόμου "stone knives made from sharp rock."⁴³

3.1.1.2 Attendant Circumstances

The ritual of [ΠΕΡΙΤΟΜΗ], as expected of any other ritual, has to be performed at the right time so as to attain its status as well as meet its goal.⁴⁴ The normative Jewish practice is to perform this ritual on the eighth day after birth.⁴⁵ The fact that it is performed on an eight-day-old child means

---

39. Gen 17:12–13; cf. Exod 12:44, 48.
40. Westermann, *Genesis 12–36*, 266.
41. Bernat, *Sign of the Covenant*, 45; Gunkel, *Genesis*, 265; cf. Gen 12:1–3.
42. Luke 1:58.
43. Josh 5:2.
44. Gruenwald, *Rituals and Ritual Theory*, 10.
45. Gen 17:12; 21:4; Lev 12:3; Luke 1:59; 2:21; Acts 7:8; Phil 3:5.

that it is imposed since the child is not old enough to consent to or dissent from undergoing the ritual. It was performed during day time hours with its observation superseding that of the Sabbath or any other holy days if they happen to fall on the same day.[46]

Outside the prescribed norm, there were instances where the ritual had to be performed on adult males, instances which can be explained in one way or another. In the Genesis 17:23–25 account, where we find that Abraham being circumcised at the age of ninety-nine years old and Ishmael at thirteen, it is as a result of the fact that when the order was given, they were already passed the prescribed age. In the Joshua 5:2–7 account, where all the men who were born during the wilderness journey from Egypt had not been circumcised, the reason for not performing the ritual when they were supposed to have done so was because "Israel was in a state of *apostasy*, and during that time the children bore the reproach of the same by being *denied* the 'token' or 'sign or the covenant' . . . Israel was a rejected people and therefore their children were not entitled to bear the mark of covenant-relationship to God."[47]

The spatial delimitation of this ritual during the biblical period seems to have been primarily at home, with the ritual in a later period transferred to the synagogue where it was performed in the presence of the whole congregation.[48] There was an instance where it was performed on the way to a lodging place, which again could be explained as an exception to the rule.[49] In the Joshua 5 event, we find the possibility of the existence of special places where circumcision was performed since it is mentioned that the Israelites were circumcised at a place called *Gibeath Haaraloth*, which when translated means "the hill of foreskins."[50] This could have been a referent to an ancient place where other nations performed circumcision as a rite of puberty in preparation for marriage.[51]

The meaning of the Greek verb περιτομὴ which means "to cut round" points to the manner in which the ritual is performed, namely, that of cutting off the foreskin of the penis in a circular manner. The fact that it is performed

---

46. Cohen, *Guide to Ritual Circumcision*, 9; John 7:23.
47. Pink, *Gleanings in Joshua*, 123–124.
48. Cohen, *Guide to Ritual Circumcision*, 6; cf. Gen 17:23; Luke 1:59; 2:21.
49. Exod 4:24.
50. Josh 5:3.
51. Fox, "Sign of the Covenant," 591.

on the sexual organ is said to be an indication that the "significance of the rite – both as a sign of malediction and of consecration – had reference to the descendants of the vassal who swore the circumcision oath-curse."⁵² The view that the ritual was performed for a שֵׁנִית "a second time" in the Masoretic Text (MT) of Joshua 5:2 raises the question as to whether the men underwent circumcision for a second time, and if they did, how that could have been possible. In addressing this concern, Sasson argues that the interpretation that the men underwent circumcision for a second time is a varied interpretation since their foreskins had to be removed completely.⁵³ According to him, this was an improved circumcision to that done in Egypt, which he claims is substantiated by the mention of the removal of the reproach of Egypt from the Israelites in Joshua 5:9.

The old Greek (OG) translator(s) seems to have had difficulty in translating the word שֵׁנִית for fear of communicating the idea that the adult males were subjected to circumcision for a second time. Instead they read the verb שֵׁנִית as וְשׁוּב "and return/again" and went ahead to render this verb with the Greek word καθίσας "sat down," which points to the posture that the patients took when undergoing the ritual.⁵⁴ One of the possible reasons behind this decision by the OG translators was that they could have mistakenly read the word וְשֵׁב "sit down" from the source text instead of וְשׁוּב "again."⁵⁵ Another possibility could have been that the Hebrew *vorlage* behind the OG text of Joshua had more details from the one behind the MT source text to the extent of mentioning the posture of the one performing the ritual.⁵⁶ This is informed by the observation that the Greek text of Joshua is 5 percent shorter than the parent text behind the MT, which could be a pointer that OG translators depended on an older textual variant from a different recession since "the shorter or more difficult the reading is judged to be the earliest recoverable one."⁵⁷

A related sub-ritual that is activated when the ritual of [ΠΕΡΙΤΟΜΗ] is evoked is that of the naming of the patient undergoing this ritual. This

---

52. Kline, *By Oath Consigned*, 87.
53. Sasson, "Circumcision in the Ancient Near East," 474.
54. van der Meer, *Formation and Reformulation*, 341.
55. Butler, *Joshua*, 55.
56. Soggin, *Joshua*, 18.
57. Tov, *Greek and Hebrew Bible*, 387; Nelson, *Joshua*, 23.

tradition seems to have originated back from the time of Abraham since it is in the context of the giving of the command of circumcision that his name was changed from Abram to Abraham.[58] We also find this same tradition of naming continued in the NT where in the observation of the ritual of circumcision both John and Jesus were named.[59]

The ritual of [ΠΕΡΙΤΟΜΗ] is associated with other roles, other than that of being incorporated into the covenant community. One such primitive role is that of marking one's readiness for marriage as well as that of inclusion into the communal life of ancient Israel.[60] This is demonstrated by the circumcision ritual in Genesis 34 where it seems that the ritual was commonly observed among ancient tribes given that the Shechemites did not have a problem in giving in to this requirement. According to the Israelites, the giving of Dinah to be married to Shechem, a man who was uncircumcised, would have been a disgraceful act which could have brought shame and dishonor to them.[61] Of course it turned out that Jacob's sons had an ulterior motive since it turned out to be a pretext to render the Shechemites incapable of defending themselves and consequently kill them for what one of their own had done against their sister.[62] Another instance where there is a connection between the ritual of circumcision and that of marriage is in Exodus 4:18–26 where we find the use of the phrase "bridegroom of blood," which could be understood to mean that circumcision signaled Moses's fitness for marriage.[63] The relationship between the rituals of marriage and that of circumcision is also alluded to in the story of David's marriage to Saul's daughter Michal.[64] We find here Saul demanding from David a bride price of a hundred foreskins from the Philistines, which

---

58. Gen 17:5; The choice of names is not arbitrary since as Cotter (Cotter, *Genesis*, 108–109) points out

> In reality "Abram" and "Abraham" are simply variants of the same name, the second a slightly longer form than the first, but this story invests the change with great significance. Throughout the books, names have carried a person's meaning... The change of name here is intended to convey a real change in Abram's identity. So, just as his people is to be made great, his name is "made great," i.e., lengthened.

59. Luke 1:59; 2:21.
60. Hamilton, *Book of Genesis*, 363.
61. cf. Gen 34:14.
62. Westermann, *Genesis 12–36*, 536.
63. Gray, *Joshua, Judges and Ruth*, 69.
64. 1 Sam 18:20–27.

could be interpreted as a sign that David was ready to start a family.[65] We also find the association between בְּרִית "covenant" and the ritual of marriage in the use of the allegory of marriage to point to the covenantal relationship between YHWH and his chosen people.[66]

3.1.1.3 Deontic Status and Ethical Value

As mentioned above, the traditional understanding associated with the ritual of circumcision is that of incorporation by establishing a covenantal relationship by linking future generations to the promise that God had made to the patriarchs.[67] It was intended to be the "medium through which covenant privileges and responsibilities were passed on from one generation to the next," and just as the mark remains in the body, so is the covenant that God made with his people.[68] This means that the ritual of circumcision has the power to change one's identity, social status and the reality of things, given that as a result of undergoing this ritual, the descendants of Abraham could inherit the blessings of prosperity and progeny.[69] A good example of this change is in the life of Abraham and his wife Sarah whose situation was changed from that of barrenness to that of having many descendants.[70]

It is mandatory for a Jewish male child to undergo this ritual in order to be included into this covenant relationship. Those who do not bear this mark are conceptualized as having no part in the covenant community since circumcision is conceptualizes as a sign of being adopted and loved by the God of Israel. It was therefore important for those who were uncircumcised from other nations to undergo the ritual and become proselytes as a demonstration that they had the zeal for the law as well as that they were willing to embrace the Jewish faith without reservation.[71] The author of Jubilees underlines the importance of circumcision as a sign of the covenant by pointing out that

---

65. Bernat, *Sign of the Covenant*, 51.
66. Beeby, *Hosea*, 21; cf. Hos 1–3; Mal 2:13–16.
67. Butler, *Joshua*, 58.
68. Williamson, "Circumcision," 123.
69. Gruenwald, *Rituals and Ritual Theory*, 14; cf. Gen. 17:9–14; 23–27.
70. Gen 17:2–6, 8, 16.
71. McKnight, *Light among the Gentiles*, 82.

> Anyone who is born whose own flesh is not circumcised on the eighth day is not from the sons of the covenant which the Lord made for Abraham since (he is) from the children of destruction. And there is therefore no sign upon him so that he might belong to the Lord because (he is destined) to be destroyed and annihilated from the earth and to be uprooted from the earth because he has broken the covenant of the Lord our God.[72]

Even though Jewish women are not expected to undergo the physical ritual of circumcision, they are enjoined as recipients of the covenant blessings and therefore bound by its obligations through their fathers, and later on through their husbands when they get married. They are considered to be an extension of a male's authority given that they are part and parcel of the household which has embraced the covenant stipulations.[73] The male figure is regarded as the representative head of the household unit, and for that reason when a man partakes of the covenant mark, he does so on behalf of the female members in his family. Furthermore, a man is perceived as the one who produces seed and subsequently as having the power to transmit life with a woman being the object where the seed is implanted.[74]

Within the [OLD COVENANT] frame, the ritual of circumcision was understood to be more than just a sign of racial purity. The prophets prophesied that other nations would be beneficiaries of this covenant as long as they submitted themselves to the obligations of its stipulations.[75] This means that the implied covenantal blessings and responsibilities, especially that of the ministry of the coming Messiah, could now be claimed by those who are *not* biologically related to the patriarchs but who have submitted themselves to the terms of that covenant. This is in light of the fact that "a person's foreignness was determined by social allegiance as much as [it was] by purely racial considerations."[76] Given the fact that this ritual is understood to be a prerequisite in accessing the blessing associated with Abraham, it is no wonder

---

72. Jub 15:26.
73. Bernat, *Sign of the Covenant*, 34; cf. Lev 22:12–13; Num 30:4–17.
74. Delaney, *Abraham on Trial*, 31.
75. Williamson, "Circumcision," 124; cf. Rom 9:24–26.
76. Clements, *Exodus*, 76; cf. Rom 4:16–17.

that Gentiles who desired to join the Jewish community were required to first observe the ritual of circumcision. As Sagi and Zohar further point out, for a

> Gentile to become a Jew, he must be without foreskin. Once he has attained this state, by whatever procedure, he has become a Jew ... A foreskin is a physical imperfection ... a Gentile cannot become a Jew if his foreskin has not been removed. But the removal of the foreskin is not enough. There must be a positive ritual that confers Jewishness upon the proselyte ... this positive ritual is the letting of covenantal blood. In a standard ritual of circumcision, the foreskin is removed and by that very act, covenantal blood comes forth.[77]

The ritual of [PASSOVER] is also activated whenever the concept ΠΕΡΙΤΟΜΗ is invoked. This is as a result of the association of ritual of circumcision as a requirement for partaking of the Passover feast and bearing the circumcision mark is crucial in marking one's obedience to God's commands.[78] The association of the ritual of circumcision with the Passover is one of the reasons given why the Israelites underwent the ritual of circumcision in Joshua 5:2–7. This interpretation is as a result of the Passover feast being recorded as the next event following that of the male members undergoing the circumcision ritual.[79] Though this interpretation tends to make sense since it is only circumcised males who were supposed to partake of the Passover, it is not made explicit in the text that the reason why the Israelites underwent the ritual of circumcision was that they could celebrate the feast of the Passover.

Another reason that is given as to why the Israelites observed the ritual of circumcision in Joshua 5 is that of preparation for war. Hamlin argues that the circumcision ritual that the new generation underwent in Joshua 5 was both an education opportunity as well an initiation ritual into adulthood status intended to make them ready for war.[80] His argument is problematic since it is derived from the Theravada Buddhist society's rite of passage which he says is held to indicate that the initiates are ready to embark on military

---

77. Sagi and Zohar, *Transforming Identity*, 119.
78. Durham, *Exodus*, 173; Exod 12:44–49.
79. Goslinga, *Joshua, Judges, Ruth*, 62; Bratcher and Newman, *Translator's Handbook*, 60; cf. Josh 5:10.
80. Hamlin, *Inheriting the Land*, 31.

service/conquest. This same line of argument is pursued by Gray who also interprets the circumcision ritual as signaling fitness, following the mention of the phrases הַמִּלְחָמָה אַנְשֵׁי "men of war" or "men of military service" in verses 4 and 6 of the same chapter.[81] The entire Joshua narrative has a warlike theme, which makes it possible to interpret the above phrase in light of this military theme. Again, it is important to point out that this interpretation is more of an influence from other neighboring nations who seemed to have observed this ritual as a means of recruiting men for military duty.[82]

The view argued for in this work, as will be further discussed at the end of this chapter, is that the traditional circumcision ritual in Joshua 5 is that of a purging or purification ritual with the goal of removing that which was conceptualized as being filthy or dirty.[83] In Genesis 34 account, where the sons of Jacob required the Shechemites to be circumcised, there is a connection between the ritual of circumcision and that of purity and uncleanness since the sons of Jacob "are implicitly accusing Hamor, Shechem, and all the community of being too unclean for Jacob's family to mingle with," meaning that they had the option of "cleansing" themselves up by undergoing the ritual of circumcision.[84] This interpretation is hinted further by the OG rendering of the Hebrew verb מוּל "he circumcised" with the Greek verb περιεκάθαρεν "he purged/purified," and not with any of the expected Greek cognates of the concept ΠΕΡΙΤΟΜΗ.[85]

The traditional ritual of circumcision within the [OLD COVENANT] frame can also be conceptualized as an ethnic marker or as a sign of identity. This can be found especially in the context where the people of Israel are contrasted to their Philistine neighbors who were referred to as "uncircumcised."[86] The Israelites saw themselves as possessing something that the Philistines did not have, which underlines the emotive attachment that was connected with the ritual of circumcision. Such emotions include the fact that an Israelite would consider it as shameful to die by the hand of the "uncircumcised" and also to

---

81. Gray, *Joshua, Judges and Ruth*, 68.
82. Butler, *Joshua*, 58; Gray, *Joshua, Judges and Ruth*, 72; cf. Josh 5:1, 13–15.
83. Schneider, *Judges*, 204.
84. Cotter, *Genesis*, 255–256.
85. Josh 5:4; Deut 30:6.
86. cf. Judg 14:3; 15:18; 1 Sam 14:6.

share meals with them.[87] Hence the term "uncircumcised" adequately served as reference to the Philistines since most of the local population in the region did practice circumcision.[88]

Among the Jewish people, the ritual of [ΠΕΡΙΤΟΜΗ] also tended to activate a feeling of superior ethnic consciousness. Those who are uncircumcised were viewed as being inferior, unclean, and to an extent sub-human, for this ritual "signified inferiority because of personal impurity."[89] In a way, the association of inferiority with "uncircumcision" should also be understood as being figurative in the sense that circumcision had to do with partaking in the covenant made between God and Abraham and his descendants. As a consequence, even though other nations might undergo the same physical ritual, they do so outside the context of this covenantal obligation and therefore are still perceived as inferior since they have no access to the privilege of observing the biblical laws associated with ritual purity.[90]

In the inter-testamental period, the concept ΠΕΡΙΤΟΜΗ seemed to have also evoked the feelings of trial or persecution.[91] In this period, which was during the reign of King Antiochus IV between 176/5–163 BC, after conquering the Israelites, the king had ordered that the Israelites should not circumcise their sons. The prohibition seems to have been a collision of views; on the one hand the Greeks "saw perfection in the human body and therefore abhorred any form of mutilation" and on the other the insistence by the Jews "upon a bodily mark that was a permanent sign of their difference from other people."[92] This prohibition also took place during the days of Antiochus Epiphanes which led to political and cultural pressures being brought against the Jew, for as deSilva points out, the Jews

> . . . were eager to blend in with the Greeks and other gentiles around them and to participate (naked, as was the custom) in Greek cultural practices and networking opportunities such as the athletic games in the gymnasium (2 Mac 4:13–15) even

---

87. 1 Sam 31:4; Acts 11:3.
88. Faust, *Israel's Ethnogenesis*, 91.
89. Naylor, *Ezekiel*, 426; cf. Gen 34; Ezek 28:10; 31:18; 32:19–31.
90. Hayes, *Gentiles Impurities and Jewish Identities*, 19, 37.
91. 1 Macc 1:10–61.
92. Goldberg, *Jewish Passages*, 39.

performed epispasm in order to reverse the effects of circumcision (1 Mac 1:14–15). A ban on circumcision was rigidly enforced during the most fevered period of Hellenization (1 Mac 1:44–61).[93]

The ritual of circumcision can be said to have also evoked the feeling of "shame" and "indifference" among some Jews. This is supported by the fact that some of them tried to hide or obscure their circumcision marks with the goal of acquiring social and economic status with the Greeks said to have referred to the circumcised Jews as "harlots" as they mingled in bath places.[94] On the hand, the ritual of circumcision evoked the feeling of bravery and commitment since the Jewish population continued to practice it in spite of such threats. Shying away from performing the ritual was considered in itself a violation of the Jewish faith and practice.[95] Those who succumbed to this pressure and went ahead to remove the mark of circumcision on their bodies were accused of abandoning the holy covenant. There are instances where circumcision seems to have been enforced as a move towards hellenization, in view of the fact that as the Maccabean revolt broke out, the followers of Mattathias forcefully circumcised many Jews who were not circumcised.[96] Moreover, after the success of the revolt, several Hasmonean rulers also forced circumcision as a step towards Judaizing ethnic groups such as the Idumeans and the Itureans.[97]

3.1.1.4 Purity Rituals

As mentioned above, the ritual frame of [ΠΕΡΙΤΟΜΗ] activates that of the related concept ΚΑΘΑΡΟΣ "pure/clean." Purity is generally defined "as a rule tacitly, as the norm, qualifying one to take part in the cultus; impurity is inimical to Yahweh and separates one from worship and from God's people, so that it must be opposed and purged out as an abomination."[98] It is beyond the scope of this work to give detailed description of all the rituals that are

---

93. deSilva, "Circumcision," 139.
94. Buchanan, "Circumcision," 123.
95. cf. 1 Macc 1:15, 48, 63; 2 Macc 6:10.
96. Livesey, *Circumcision as a Malleable Symbol*, 15; cf. 1 Macc 2:46.
97. Soards, *New Interpreter's Dictionary*, 669.
98. Link and Schattenmann, "καθαρός," 104.

activated in the Bible by the concept of ΚΑΘΑΡΟΣ, but only a few. The first one is that of the birth ritual given that it is strongly activated when the [ΠΕΡΙΤΟΜΗ] frame is evoked. Since as mentioned above circumcision is observed on the eighth day after birth, it is obvious that this ritual has some connection with the uncleanness of the mother.[99] Giving birth is said to have resulted in ritual impurity and as a result a mother had to undergo a purification process.[100] She was considered unclean for a week if she gave birth to a baby boy, a period which was followed by thirty-three days of impurity. If she gave birth to a baby girl, she was considered to be unclean for two weeks, followed by sixty-six days of impurity, after which she brought both a sin and a burned offerings so as to be cleansed.

It is important to note that most of the rituals associated with purity activate the sub-ritual frame of [SACRIFICE]. This is because sacrifices associated with purity sought to restore one's initial position or equilibrium, which in one way or another seemed to have been compromised or endangered.[101] Some of these ritual sacrifices took a substitution component, with an example being that of the holocaust sacrifices which were wholly burned.[102] A person who was in a state of ritual impurity was expected to offer a holocaust sacrifice of a male animal without blemish. He was supposed to lay his hand on the head of the animal and cut its throat, after which the animal was to be cut up and put on the altar with its blood poured around the altar. Every part of the animal, its head, intestines, and feet, were washed and then burned on the altar. The [SACRIFICE] frame also semi-activates other kinds of sacrifices which include communion sacrifices, expiatory sacrifices including those for sin, for reparation or compensation, and incense offerings.[103] Another purification ritual that might be activated is that of the restoration of a leper.[104] In performing this ritual, a priest was expected to confirm that the former leper was cured by using the so-called declaratory formula, after which he

---

99. Skinner, *Critical and Exegetical Commentary on Genesis*, 294.

100. cf. Lev 12.

101. Gruenwald, *Rituals and Ritual Theory*, 16.

102. de Vaux, *Ancient Israel*, 415; cf. Lev 1–7.

103. cf. Exod 30:34–38; Lev 7:12–17; 22:18–23, 29–30; 4:1–5:13; 6:17–23; 5:14–26; 7:1–6; 1 Sam 2:28; Isa 1:13.

104. Lev 13–14.

went ahead and performed the ritual of purification to restore the former leper back to the community.[105]

3.1.2 The Heart

The other associated concept in the metaphor περιτομὴ καρδίας is that of ΚΑΡΔΙΑ which means "heart," "mind," "chest," and "conscience."[106] The use of the Greek concept ΚΑΡΔΙΑ coincides with that of the OT use of the term לֵבָב (short form לֵב) where the heart is equated to the inner life and as being the centre of personality and the place where God reveals himself.[107] As Derouchie further points out "In Israelite understanding, the human heart was the locus of the LORD'S influence, and thus 'heart' language frequently occurs in contexts that express the LORD's claim to human allegiance."[108] Since the heart is a physical organ, it falls under the [BODY] frame within the body parts domain for it is conceptualized as an inner body organ that sustains life and an organ that is central to man's psychological make-up.[109] It is also conceptualized as a metonymy representing a person (i.e. a person in his totality). This means that when the Bible says in Psalm 22:26 "may your hearts live forever," it is to be understood as a prayer that "the people may live forever."[110]

The heart is also conceptualized as a seat of emotions, or that which makes a person to be human. We find a number of instances where it is used metaphorically as the seat of the deepest spiritual emotions/motives and intellect.[111] It is the seat of such emotions as pain, joy, gladness, desire, tranquility, excitement, weakness, faintness, grief, sorrow, anger, fear, hate, etc.[112]

The heart is also the seat of understanding and knowledge. It is conceptualized as having a rational capacity with a discerning heart said to seek

---

105. cf. Lev 13:44.

106. Luc, "לֵב," 749; Brown, Driver, and Briggs, *Brown-Driver-Briggs Hebrew and English*, 523–525.

107. Sorg, "Heart," 182.

108. Derouchie, "Circumcision in the Hebrew Bible," 196.

109. Ryken, Wilhoit, and Longman III, *Dictionary of Biblical Imagery*, 369; cf. Ps 38:10; Isa 1:5; Luke 21:34; Jas 5:5.

110. cf. Ps 73:26; 84:2; Rom 9:1–2.

111. Ryken, Wilhoit, and Longman III, *Dictionary of Biblical Imagery*, 369; Ps 7:9; 26:2; Jer 17:10; 20:12; Rev 2:23.

112. Gen 6:6; Isa 30:29; Jer 4:19; cf. Lev 19:16; 26:36; Deut 15:10; 19:6; 28:47, 67; Ps 13:3; Prov 6:25; 14:30; John 16:5–6; Acts 14:17.

knowledge and guide one's mouth.[113] It is the place where thinking and reflection is done and the place where memory is found.[114] It is also associated as being the source of will, an example that of King David where he is said to have had a heart to build a temple for the God of Israel.[115] The heart is also conceptualized as a seat of morality, and thus allowing one to have an "uprightness" of heart, "integrity" of heart, a "perfect" heart, and a "pure" heart.[116]

The heart can also be disobedient or adamant, to the extent that those who are disobedient or harbor hard feelings said to have a "hardened" hearts.[117] A broken or crushed heart is symbolic of humility and penitence.[118] One can also have a foolish heart in the sense that their heart is darkened, and on the other hand, one can have a listening or obedient heart.[119] The heart is also conceptualized using the [CONTAINER] schema, in that it can contain the writings of the law, integrity, evil thoughts, sexual immorality, theft, murder, adultery, greed, malice, deceit, lewdness, envy, slander, arrogance, and folly.[120] Since the heart is the seat of immorality, it becomes the target where conversion takes place.[121] As a result, it becomes the center of spiritual life and faith and is subsequently used to evaluate people's spiritual states.[122] Since the motives of the heart are hidden from a human perspective, it is only God who is said to have the power to reveal what is hidden in the hearts of men.[123]

Other related body parts that are associated with emotions include the mind and the kidneys. The functions of the mind are generally associated with those of the heart. The mind is evoked as "the seat and function of the reason" and therefore attributed with functions that include the "power of perception, reason, understanding, insight, consciousness, memory, knowledge,

---

113. Soggin, *Israel in the Biblical Period*, 73; Prov 15:14; 16:23; cf. Deut 8:5; 1 Kings 2:44.
114. 1 Chron 29:18; Hag 2:15; 1 Sam 21:13; Job 22:22.
115. 1 Kings 8:17; cf. Exod 36:2; Deut 6:5.
116. Gen 20:5, 6; Deut 9:5; 1 Kings 8:61; Ps 24:4.
117. 1 Sam 6:6; cf. Exod 7:13, 14, 22; 8:19; 9:12, 35; Rom 2:5.
118. Banwell, "Heart," 626.
119. Rom 1:21, 24; 1 Kings 3:9.
120. 1 Kings 9:4; Rom 2:15; cf. Gen 20:5; Ps 101:2; Matt 15:19; Mark 7:21–22; Acts 5:3.
121. Ps 51:10, 17; cf. Joel 2:12; Acts 2:37; 5:33; 7:54; Eph 3:17.
122. 1 Sam 12:24; Ps 28:7; 112:7; Jer 32:40; Rom 10:6–10.
123. Ryken, Wilhoit, and Longman III, *Dictionary of Biblical Imagery*, 554; Ps 7:9; 26:2; cf. Rom 2:16; 1 Cor 4:5; 8:27; 1 Thess 2:4.

reflection, judgment, sense of direction, discernment."[124] Therefore one can conclude that in the OT the heart is associated as being the "centre of consciousness, thought or will."[125] In the NT, the Greek concept νους is "usually is used in reference to the cognitive, rational and purposive aspects of a person as well as the less concrete aspects such as heart, soul, opinion and understanding or reflection."[126] The concepts ΚΑΡΔΙΑ "heart" and that of ΝΟΥΣ "mind" are used as parallels and as synonyms.[127]

The kidneys, כליה in Hebrew, were a choice portion in the sacrificial beasts for they were perceived as containing life.[128] In the OT, they are also used metaphorically together with the heart as the seat of the deepest spiritual emotions/motives and intellect.[129] In the NT, the Greek concept νεπρος (lit. kidneys) is also rendered as "mind" which points to its associated function as that of being part of the intellect.[130] As Banwell rightly observes, in the Bible the heart is "essentially the whole man, with all his attributes, physical, intellectual and psychological."[131] In the next section, an analysis is done of instances where the concept ΠΕΡΙΤΟΜΗ, in Hebrew מוּלָה, is embedded in metaphorical expressions within the [OLD COVENANT] frame with the goal of finding out the other elements that it tends to be associated with.

3.1.3 Metaphorical Use of the Associated Concepts

The language of circumcision and uncircumcision has been metaphorically applied in the Bible to other parts of the body as well. One of them is the lips in the phrase שְׂפָתַיִם עָרֵל "uncircumcised of lips" which is translated in the LXX as ἐγώ δέ ἄλογός εἰμι "and I am not eloquent." Not only do lips speak but they also shout for joy, offer praise, quiver with fear, guard knowledge, and plead.[132] They are also associated with ethical qualities such as truthfulness,

---

124. Wolff, *Anthropology of the Old Testament*, 51.
125. Banwell, "Heart," 625.
126. Ryken, Wilhoit, and Longman III, *Dictionary of Biblical Imagery*, 554.
127. 2 Cor 3:14–15; Phil 4:7.
128. Banwell, "Kidneys," 850; cf. Lev 3:4; 4:9; 7:4; Deut 32:14.
129. Ryken, Wilhoit, and Longman III, *Dictionary of Biblical Imagery*, 369; Ps 7:9; 26:2; Jer 17:10; 20:12.
130. cf. Rev 2:23
131. Banwell, "Heart," 625.
132. Exod 6:12, 30; Job 13:6; 27:4; Ps 71:23; 63:3; Prov 5:2; Hab 3:16.

righteousness, sinning such as that of speaking lies.¹³³ The connection between the heart and the lips lies in the fact that words are conceptualized as coming directly from the heart.¹³⁴ This association of the ritual of circumcision to the lips in a metaphorical relationship points to the difficulty with which Moses was speaking with the possibility that he might have had faltering lips which led to slow speech.¹³⁵ The meaning of this metaphor is that Moses's mouth was immature or uninitiated, and as a result, he considered his speaking abilities as not good being enough to be used on behalf of God.

Another body part that is associated with the ritual of circumcision in a metaphorical relationship is the "ears." In Jeremiah 6:10, the phrase הָאָזְנָם עֲרֵל "foreskinned of ears," which is translated in the LXX as ἀπερίτμητα τά ὦτα αὐτῶν "thine ears are uncircumcised" is used and in Acts 7:51 we also find the phrase ἀπερίτμητοι . . . ὠσίν "uncircumcised of ears" being used. Ears, just as the mind and the heart, are generally conceptualized as organs of cognition.¹³⁶ They are associated with hearing and understanding, seeking knowledge, and testing words.¹³⁷ One is expected to hear the voice of God primarily through the ear and respond in obedience.¹³⁸ The association of the ears with circumcision in a metaphorical relationship points to the failure of people to listen and obey the voice of God as well as to treat the word of God as offensive as a result of their rebellion.¹³⁹ The context of the passage in Jeremiah 6:10 is that of the prophet trying to warn the people of the coming judgment with the hope that the coming disaster will be averted. But the people paid no attention to the words of the prophet and as Thompson points out, "to the closed ear all admonitions were in vain, the people were insensitive and lacked the insight or understanding to comprehend the divine word . . . Yahweh's word was, in fact, a *reproach (ḥerpâ)* in which they found no pleasure."¹⁴⁰

---

133. cf. Job 2:10; Prov 12:19; 16:13.
134. Ryken, Wilhoit, and Longman III, *Dictionary of Biblical Imagery*, 515; cf. Matt 12:34.
135. Hyatt, *Exodus*, 95.
136. Prov 2:2; Isa 6:9–10.
137. Job 12:11; 13:1; Prov 18:15.
138. Isa 50:4–5; Jas 1:22–25.
139. Huey, Jr., *Jeremiah, Lamentations*, 98.
140. Thompson, "Mercy upon All," 257.

Fruits are also associated with ritual of circumcision in the phrase מַאֲכָל וַעֲרַלְתֶּם "and you will regard its food as foreskin."[141] The LXX translators use a synonymous Greek verb form περικαθαριεῖτε "purge away" with the object of this verb being τὴν ἀκαθαρσίαν αὐτοῦ "its uncleanness."[142] The context of this passage had to do with how the Israelites were to behave after they entered the promised land. For the first three years, the yields from the fruits trees were to be regarded as unclean, and it is only the fourth year's crop which was to be dedicated to God.[143] The MT does not outrightly state how the Israelites were to go about it, but the LXX translators clearly gave further instructions that they were to purge or remove its uncleanness by plucking them off the trees as a practical expression of holiness.[144]

Another foreskinned metaphor which is commonly used is the association of ΠΕΡΙΤΟΜΗ with the heart. One of the instances is found in Leviticus 26:41 in the phrase לְבָבָם הֶעָרֵל "their uncircumcised heart." This metaphor denotes an insensitive and thickened heart that cannot hear God's word.[145] The context of this passage is the assurance of restoration to the people of Israel if they repented of their sins. Another instance where the ritual of circumcision is associated with the heart is in Deuteronomy 10:16 in the phrase וּמַלְתֶּם אֵת עָרְלַת לְבַבְכֶם "and you will circumcise the foreskin of your heart," which is translated in the LXX as περιτεμεῖσθε τήν σκληρο καρδίαν ὑμων "circumcise the hardness of your heart." This passage uses the verb form περτεμεισθε "you circumcise" with τὴν σκληρο καρδίαν "stubbornness" or "stiff-neckedness" as its direct object. A person who is stiff-necked is one who is not submissive "like an ox that refuses to bow its head to the yoke and to turn at the command of its owner."[146] Such an individual is called upon to take the necessary steps towards fearing, loving, serving God, and walking in his ways.[147]

Another passage where the metaphor of the heart is associated with the ritual of [ΠΕΡΙΤΟΜΗ] is in Deuteronomy 30:6 in the phrase

---

141. Lev 19:23.
142. Lampe, *Patristic Greek Lexicon*, 1066a; Muraoka, *Greek-English Lexicon*, 549.
143. Wenham, *Book of Leviticus*, 271.
144. Milgrom, *Leviticus 17–22*, 1679.
145. Milgrom, *Leviticus 23–27*, 2332–2333.
146. Merrill, *Deuteronomy*, 203.
147. cf. Deut 10:12–13.

אֶת־לְבָבְךָ אֱלֹהֶיךָ יְהוָה וּמָל "and Yahweh your God will circumcise your heart" which is translated in the LXX as καί περικαθαριει κύριος τήν καρδίαν σου "and the Lord will purge/purify your heart." The context of this passage is again that of the restoration of the people of Israel. The idea behind the LXX rendering seems to be that of presenting God as the agent who purges people's hearts by removing whatever prevents them from following his teachings.[148] From the perspective of the LXX translators, this rendering just as the ones discussed above, call for moral uprightness and obedience to the terms of the covenant. They also point to the fact that physical circumcision alone is insufficient to put an individual in a right relationship with God.

In Jeremiah 4:4 we find the use of the phrase לְבַבְכֶם עָרְלוֹת וְהָסִרוּ . . . הִמֹּלוּ "circumcise yourselves . . . and remove the foreskins of your heart," which is translated in the LXX as περιτέμεσθε τήν σκληρο καρδίαν ὑμων "circumcise the hardness of heart." The people of Israel are once more called upon to get rid of everything that hinders their commitment to God, failure to which they would arouse God's anger which would burn against them and consequently no one will be able to extinguish it. They are reminded that true circumcision is an act of the heart and as Allen points out

> In the metaphor of circumcision, which also occurs in Deut 10:16, foreskins correspond to the thorns in the earlier image, as a barrier that stands in the way of . . . belonging exclusively to Yahweh. Repetition of the verb "remove" suggests that pagan worship constitutes the barrier. The positive implications of the circumcision metaphor are openness to Yahweh's influence and obedience to the divine will.[149]

Again in Jeremiah 9:25 we find the phrase עַרְלֵי־לֵב "uncircumcised of heart," which is translated in the LXX as ἀπερίτμητοι καρδίας αὐτων "our uncircumcised heart." Since the context of this passage has to do with the people of Israel, we find the possibility for one to be circumcised on the outside yet remain uncircumcised in the heart with such a person not being bound to God's covenant. We are told that the people of Judah failed to live up to the expectation of being circumcised since they lacked the spiritual

---

148. Christensen, *Deuteronomy 21:10–34:12*, 739.
149. Allen, *Jeremiah*, 62.

commitment or attitude that was meant to accompany their physical mark of circumcision.[150] We find a clear contrast being drawn between circumcision as a mere external cutting of the flesh and the cutting that symbolizes a sign of commitment to the covenant and to the God of the covenant. The fact that they did not show obedience to the covenant means that the ritual failed to achieve its purpose, in view of the fact that it did not remind them of their commitment to God. They became just like the people of other nations, notably those who practiced circumcision, since the sign did not identify them as covenant people.[151]

Another instance where we find the heart metaphor used is in Ezekiel 44:7, 9 where we also find the use of the phrase עַרְלֵי־לֵב "foreskinned of heart," which is translated in the LXX as ἀπεριμήτους καρδίᾳ "uncircumcised in heart." The context of this passage is describing those who were supposed to enter God's sanctuary, with the foreigners forbidden to do so. The reason given for this rejection is because they were not circumcised. If for any reason they happen to be allowed in, then such an act could have led to the desecration of the temple, with the Levites being held responsible for such a sin.

Within the [OLD COVENANT] frame, we find that the metaphorical use of circumcision generally highlights a difficulty that in one way or another needs to be removed. In correcting the difficulty of having uncircumcised lips, God appointed Aaron to be Moses's mouth piece.[152] Also in Isaiah 6:7, we are told that a seraph touched the lips of the prophet so as to take his guilt away after confessing that he was of unclean lips. The need for the cleansing of lips makes sense since they are associated with ethical qualities such as truthfulness, righteousness, sinning such as speaking lies.[153] Again the removal of "uncircumcised fruits" symbolizes the purging away of the uncleanness of fruits, which was an expression of holiness. The call to circumcise the "ears" is corrected by the removal of hindrances that make people not listen to the voice of God. Since the heart is the center of all the attributes of man, be they physical, intellectual, or psychological, it needs to be in tune with God and circumcising it symbolizes cleansing/purifying it from all that hinders one

---

150. Allen, *Jeremiah*, 121.
151. Huey, Jr., *Jeremiah, Lamentations*, 122.
152. Exod 7:1.
153. cf. Job 2:10; Prov 12:19; 16:13.

to submit to God appropriately. Luc rightly sums up the metaphorical use of the heart by pointing out that it is used "in reference to the centre of human psychical and spiritual life, to the entire inner life of a person."[154]

Since the old covenant is associated with spiritual hardening, which tended to prevent people from believing God, we find Paul redefining this metaphor within the context of the [NEW COVENANT] frame.[155] Even though the contrast between circumcision as a mere external cutting of the flesh and that of the heart symbolizing a sign of commitment to the covenant and to the God of the covenant is retained within the [NEW COVENANT] frame, there are new elements that are introduced as well as others that are modified within this new frame, a process which is discussed in the following section.

3.2 The Modified Frame

The metaphor περιτομὴ καρδίας takes on a modified meaning in the context of early Christianity in light of Paul's argument in the book of Romans. Given that Israel had failed to keep the old covenant, a new one had become necessary.[156] In this section, I will argue that Paul was modifying both the traditional connotations associated with the generic [COVENANT] frame as well as that of the specific [RITUAL] frame associated with the understanding that circumcision was a qualification in accessing the covenantal blessings. In so doing, Paul exploits what Coulson refers to as the nonstandard meanings of words with old aspects being replaced with new ones.[157] By the use of the complementary approach between CIT and RT, I will demonstrate how the relative prominence of the [OLD COVENANT] frame has been changed and how it is assigned to a more relevant frame, namely, that of the [NEW COVENANT] and at the same time address controversies that arise in this process. I will be demonstrating how a new or modified meaning is constructed from the existing knowledge and in the process highlight the new inputs/prompts that Paul profiles within the relevant DS. My thesis is that Paul modifies/changes the traditional elements associated with the [OLD COVENANT] frame by ascribing

---

154. Luc, "לֵב," 749.
155. Garland, *2 Corinthians*, 191.
156. Jer 31:31–33.
157. Coulson, *Semantic Leaps*, 62.

new meaning to these old aspects, while at the same time, deliberately avoids downplaying the value of Jewish circumcision.[158]

The new frame that results from the process of frame-shifting and which Paul is modifying in the mind of his hearers is that of [ΚΑΙΝΗ ΔΙΑΘΗΚΗ] "new covenant" frame which, unlike its old counterpart, is inscribed in the heart.[159] The Greek concept ΔΙΑΘΗΚΗ means "last will and testament."[160] Jobes and Silva point out that the rendering of the Hebrew term בְּרִית with the Greek term συνθηκη "agreement" could have been adequate, but the fact that God is involved in the making of the covenant means that the use of συνθηκη would have been misleading, since this term does not highlight the role of the divine in the making of the covenant.[161] Other instances where the concept ΔΙΑΘΗΚΗ is used in the book of Romans include instances in Romans 9:4 and 11:27 where it refers to the different covenants made with Israel and also to the renewed covenant which has a more transforming character.[162] Other uses of the concept ΔΙΑΘΗΚΗ in Pauline writings include the ones in 1 Corinthians 11:25 where it refers to the new covenant which was foretold by Jeremiah and now stands ratified, 2 Corinthians 3:6 where the focus is on the renewed covenant being written on human hearts which results in obedience through the agency of the Spirit, 2 Corinthians 3:14 where the term is used to refer to the old covenant associated with spiritual hardening and which prevents people from believing God, Galatians 3:15 where the common understanding or the secular use of the term as a "testament" or "will" is used with a contrast found in verse 17 of the same chapter, and in Galatians 4:24 where the term is given some theological connotations.[163]

These instances point to the fact that not all occurrences of the use of the Greek word διαθηκη in the NT fall under the common theological use of a covenant made between a deity, on the one hand, and a person or group of persons, on the other. We also find the more common use of the term διαθηκη where it is used as reference to an agreement made between two individuals

---

158. Elliot, *Rhetoric of Romans*, 198.
159. Garland, *2 Corinthians*, 159.
160. Danker, *Greek-English Lexicon*, 228.
161. Jobes and Silva, *Invitation to the Septuagint*, 200.
162. Dunn, *Romans 9–16*, 534, 683.
163. Bruce, *I & II Corinthians*, 112; Garland, *2 Corinthians*, 166, 191; Longenecker, *Galatians*, 128.

or nations.[164] The use of the concept ΔΙΑΘΗΚΗ by Paul can be said to be "shaped by its use in the LXX rather than by the current legal usage" with its use in Romans 9:4 being a good instance where this concept is used to denote its saving disposition.[165] In comparing the use of the concept ΔΙΑΘΗΚΗ from both the [OLD COVENANT] and [NEW COVENANT] perspective, Behm further points out that

> In both form and content the NT usage of διαθηκη follows that of the OT. The only difference is to be found in the step from prophecy to fulfillment. One can hardly say that the NT takes the same course as the LXX and introduces religious thoughts into the legal word, so that it is "a testament and yet not a testament." Nor can one refer to a transformation of the covenant concept to include that of a testament. Neither "covenant" nor "testament" reproduces the true religious sense of the religious term διαθηκη in the Greek Bible. διαθηκη is from first to last the "disposition" of God, the mighty declaration of the sovereign will of God in history, by which He orders the relation between Himself and men according to His own saving purpose, and which carries with it the authoritative divine ordering, the one order of things which is in accordance with it.[166]

Within the [NEW COVENANT] frame, the established covenantal relationship is a bilateral one, which, on the one hand is initiated by God through his son the Lord Jesus Christ, and on the other hand, has a believer who responds by faith and seeks to live a new life characterized by obedience to God.[167] In interpreting afresh the covenantal relationship between God and his people, Paul relies on other references from the OT to interpret the Abrahamic covenant of Genesis 17.[168] One such reference is Ezekiel 18:30–31, which lays emphasis on the creation of a new heart and a new spirit that results from an individual's repentance and/or conversion. The other one is Jeremiah 31:31–34, where the two covenants are basically compared to one

---

164. Porter, "Concept of Covenant," 279; Gal 3:15.
165. Behm, "Greek Term διαθήκη," 129–130.
166. Behm, 134.
167. Schreiner, *Romans*, 138.
168. Berkley, *From a Broken Covenant*, 11.

another, with the promise by God to initiate a new covenantal relationship with his people. The change that the prophet Jeremiah seems to emphasize is that of the relationship between God and the people, which would go through a dynamic alteration in terms of the content of God's self-revelation. This is indicated by the use of the Hebrew adjective חדש "new" to describe this nuance of "renewal" or that of something that is "brand new."[169] As Gräbe further points out, "The *newness* of the new covenant consists in God's initiative in the life, death and resurrection of Jesus Christ."[170] Therefore as far as the new covenant is concerned, there are both aspects of renewal as well as that of creating something new, for as Freedman and Miano point out

> On the one hand, Jeremiah is clearly looking forward to something radically different from past reforms. He witnessed the attempts of Josiah to reestablish a working relationship with the Deity and saw them fail. Conversely, he could see no other law but one. To him God did not change his standards; his Law was his Law. The newness was in the manner the Law would be transmitted and implemented, and it is thoroughly visionary. The new covenant was a symbol and a hope which he did not expect to experience in his own time.[171]

In pointing out these two aspects of "renewal" and "newness" of the covenantal relationship between God and his people, Paul states that this new covenant is built upon the foundations of the Abrahamic covenant with a singular recipient in mind (i.e. the Lord Jesus Christ).[172] The distinguishing element in this new covenant is the fact that other communities are included as beneficiaries as well.[173] The new covenant is also described as being greater and better than the old one since it involves the ministry of the Spirit and of righteousness, and also because of the fact that it is intended to last forever.[174] In reinterpreting the traditional frame associated with the ritual of

---

169. Gräbe, *New Covenant, New Community*, 97; Jer 31:31; cf. Exod 1:8; Deut 32:17; 1 Sam 6:7; Lam 3:22–23.
170. Gräbe, 190.
171. Freedman and Miano, "People of the New Covenant," 23.
172. Longenecker, *Galatians*, 126; cf. Gal 3:15–18.
173. Schreiner, *Romans*, 35–37; cf. Rom 1:16; 9:6–8.
174. 2 Cor 3:4–6; Heb 7:20–22; 2 Cor 3:8, 9; 2 Cor 3:11.

circumcision, Paul activates his audiences' contextual framework by quoting from the OT to help them recall some main elements of the Abrahamic covenant. As Stanley points out

> Paul normally embeds his quotations in an interpretive framework that signals to the audience how he intends the biblical text to be understood. In these cases little or no knowledge of the original context is required; the quotation achieves its rhetorical effect as long as the audience acknowledges the authority of the Jewish Scriptures and accepts Paul's reputation as a reliable interpreter of the holy text. In some cases Paul may have purposely targeted the more literate members of the congregation (especially those with more exposure to Judaism) on the assumption that they would explain to the illiterate majority the significance of the verses that he cites. In still other cases he might have gotten caught up in the flow of an argument and failed to consider whether his mostly Gentile audience would be able to comprehend his references to the Jewish Scriptures. No single answer can be posited for every passage, each text must be evaluated on its own merit.[175]

As pointed above, Paul uses intertextual allusions from some OT texts from prophetic literature to interpret Deuteronomy 29–30 and Genesis 17, texts which have common vocabulary with that of Romans 2:17–29. As Berkley points out

> these texts are *linked to one another* by vocabulary and *theme*. All provide *explication* of Paul's conclusions in Rom 2:17–29, both individually and as mutually interpretive texts. These texts also meet the confirmatory criteria. They *recur* in Pauline literature, have *themes in common* with Paul's argument, and in some cases even have a *common linear development* with Rom 2:17–29.[176]

One such prophetic text is Jeremiah 9:23–26, where the nation of Israel is rebuked for being no better than the uncircumcised nations because of her disobedience. As a consequence, God promised to punish the Israelites for

---

175. Stanley, *Arguing with Scripture*, 60–61.
176. Berkley, *From a Broken Covenant*, 107 (emphasis his).

being circumcised in the flesh and not in the heart. Another prophetic text with common vocabulary with the Romans text is Jeremiah 7:2–11, which accuses the Israelites of believing deceptive words. As far as the role of circumcision as a covenant sign was concerned, the text points out that the covenant sign they bore is an unworthy mark since they continually broke the law. A further prophetic text is that of Ezekiel 36:16–27 where God promises a spiritual renewal through a cleansing process. This process was intended to result in the people having a responsive heart (i.e. a heart of flesh), which is a result of the Spirit's work. All these prophetic texts underline the fact that Abraham's covenant with God was intended to be a spiritual circumcision with the focus being that of obeying its stipulations.

In the book of Romans, Paul argues that this renewal is centered on an individual's inward response through faith.[177] He underlines the traditional role of περιτομὴ as a ΣΗΜΕΙΟΝ "sign" or a ΣΨΡΑΓΙΣ "seal" of the covenant but goes further to state that circumcision played the role of sealing the faith which Abraham already possessed.[178] According to Paul, observing the ritual of circumcision in itself does not bring righteousness, for circumcision is a secondary development in the making of the covenant and "had nothing to do with . . . status of uprightness before Yahweh."[179] Different from the traditional understanding of the role of περιτομὴ, this ritual no longer acts as a means of passing-on of privileges and obligations, given that as far as the new covenantal dispensation is concerned, it is through faith that one enters into a relationship with God. Therefore, we can conclude that the relationship between the concepts of ΔΙΑΘΗΚΗ with that of ΠΕΡΙΤΟΜΗ is somehow redefined with ΠΕΡΙΤΟΜΗ not being necessarily an instance of ΔΙΑΘΗΚΗ.

In this [NEW COVENANT] frame, the concept ΠΕΡΙΤΟΜΗ can no longer be used to refer only to Jews since Gentiles are also included in the covenantal blessing.[180] This strengthens Paul's argument that within the [NEW COVENANT] frame, the ritual of circumcision is no longer *the* means by which one is assimilated into the privileges and obligations that are stipulated within the Abrahamic covenant, in view of the fact that the ritual of [ΠΕΡΙΤΟΜΗ] is

---

177. Dunn, *Romans 9–16*, 48.
178. Rom 4:11.
179. Fitzmyer, *Romans*, 379.
180. Titus 1:10.

insufficient to put an individual in a right relationship with God.[181] He points out that the stipulations of the old order are not consistent with those of the new one, for both Jews and Gentiles can now stand before an impartial God and seek justification by grace through faith and not from their deeds emanating from the law.[182] The new frame that Paul is arguing for requires both the inclusion of new elements as well as the modification of old ones, for whenever a new space is set up there is a tendency to find some aspects of the background structure being maintained from the previous space.[183] In the following subsection, elements in this [NEW COVENANT] frame are discussed, especially those that are fundamental in steering the shift of frames. In the process, specific instances are pointed out where the new frame changes as well as how some of the previously encountered concepts activated within this new frame need to be reinterpreted in light of the new vital relations that are cultivated within the integration process.

3.2.1 Frame Elements

There are new elements associated with the concept ΠΕΡΙΤΟΜΗ within the [NEW COVENANT] frame that are profiled within the DS of Romans 2 as well as some old ones from the traditional [OLD COVENANT] frame that are retained within this new frame with others being modified in the process. As far as beneficiaries are concerned, it is no longer restricted to eight-day-old Jewish males. All people from all nations can be beneficiaries as long as they are willing to receive the gift of eternity by accepting the forgiveness of sins. In this new frame, both the "circumcised" and the "uncircumcised" can become Abraham's true descendants since Abraham himself was justified long before he received the ordinance of circumcision and hence he is the spiritual father to the Gentiles as well.[184]

The concept ΙΟΥΔΑΙΟΣ* "Jew," as one of the concepts profiled in Paul's argument, has undergone the process of adjustment to acquire a new meaning.[185] This concept is traditionally associated with those who are from the

---

181. cf. Rom 4.
182. Fitzmyer, *Romans*, 379.
183. Coulson, *Semantic Leaps*, 23.
184. Godet, *Commentary on Romans*, 173; Rom 4:9–12.
185. The asterisk is used with concepts to indicate that the word has gone either through the process of narrowing or broadening; cf. Rom 2:17–29.

tribe of Judah. This tribe was the most honored of the twelve tribes since it is said to have been "chosen, blessed, and exalted by God . . . from whom came the Saviour."[186] In the [OLD COVENANT] frame, the concept ΙΟΥΔΑΙΟΣ evoked the feeling of pride for Jews who thought of themselves as instructed in the law, guides to the blind, light to those in darkness, instructors of fools, and as teachers of infants.[187] This understanding is redefined so that one's "Jewishness (=Praiseworthiness) is dependent not on what spectators can see and approve, but on what God alone can see and approve (the hidden secrets of the heart – 2:16)."[188] Within this [NEW COVENANT] frame, the concept ΙΟΥΔΑΙΟΣ* is on the one hand broadened to include anyone who keeps the just requirements of the law, whether circumcised or not, and on the other, narrowed to exclude born Jews who do not keep the law.[189] This means that by extension, the concept ΠΕΡΙΤΟΜΗ acquires a new meaning in that those who are uncircumcised and walk in righteousness before God, can be referred to as circumcised, and vice versa, since circumcision is associated with obeying the covenant.[190] The old aspects that have to do with nationality and blood relations are replaced with new ones which include people of all nations and based on an inward spiritual response through faith, and not by a physical mark on the body, for all those who believe and belong to the family of God.[191] As a result, Jewish identity is now redefined in a way such that the reference "people of God" also includes Gentiles who are now included in God's salvation.[192]

The new profiled agent in this [NEW COVENANT] frame is the Lord Jesus Christ who is primarily its mediator.[193] The title "Christ" is normally placed before the name "Jesus" so as to emphasize his mediatorial office.[194] He is the one who established this new covenant through his substitutionary atoning death on Calvary, a death which redeems believers from transgressions

---

186. Robinson, *Studies in Romans*, 162.
187. Rom 2:17–20.
188. Dunn, *Romans 9–16*, 128.
189. Rom 2:26.
190. Ironside, *Lectures on the Epistle to the Romans*, 41.
191. Thompson, "Mercy upon All," 208.
192. Berkley, *From a Broken Covenant*, 16.
193. Rom 3:24; cf. Col 2:11; Heb 1:1–2; 9:11–15.
194. Godet, *Commentary on Romans*, 149; cf. Rom 3:24.

resulting from the old covenant, thus making a new life possible for them.[195] As Toews further points out

> the center of the gospel, the driving force of his mission, the hallmark of the church's confession is Messiah Jesus . . . The gospel is first and foremost about a person, Messiah Jesus manifesting God's reign. It is the good news that "God is with us" in and through Messiah Jesus . . . The gospel that Jesus is Messiah always involves fulfillment, new beginnings, new definitions of identity, and new obligations . . . It is about God keeping promises to bring redemption to humanity and to the world.[196]

The Holy Spirit, the third member of the Trinity, also has a crucial role in this [NEW COVENANT] frame. The dative ἐν πνεύματι "in Spirit" in Romans 2:29, which is employed in contrast to ἐν σάρκί "in the flesh," underlines the role of the Spirit as both the agent as well as the means/instrument by which people are recruited into this new relationship.[197] The Holy Spirit is the one who also empowers the members of the new covenant community to be obedient to all the covenant requirements and not violate its stipulations assuring one of not falling short of fulfilling the new covenant standard.[198] This is made possible by the fact that the new covenant relationship is a spiritual process and therefore the covenant members have to depend on spiritual means to maintain this relationship.

In this new frame, the significance of circumcision is being re-evaluated. Its significance no longer lies in the outward mark made on the body but in the inward consecration of the heart.[199] For one to be in Christ, one does not necessarily have to undergo the ritual of circumcision, for the physical sign of the covenant is no longer the means by which people are ushered into a covenantal relationship with God.[200] This means that one can now remain the same way they were outwardly when they came to faith in Jesus Christ.[201]

---

195. Rom 1:8.
196. Toews, *Romans*, 49.
197. Shedd, *Critical and Doctrinal Commentary*, 60–61; cf. 2 Cor 3:6.
198. Freedman and Miano, "People of the New Covenant," 25.
199. Rom 2:28–29.
200. Gal 2:7; 5:2, 6; Eph 3:3.
201. 1 Cor 7:18–19; cf. Gal 5:6.

We also find a new definition as to who a true Israelite is, with Christians being referred to as *the* true Israelites.[202] It is important to point out that Paul is not suggesting a replacement of ancient Israel with the institution of the church, but rather is arguing that the church as an institution is a continuity of the realization of the covenant God made with ancient Israel.[203] The crucifixion of Jesus Christ rendered the physical sign of circumcision done on the flesh unnecessary in accessing the divine blessings leading to Paul's argument that circumcision should not to be imposed on the Gentiles.[204] The emphasis within the [NEW COVENANT] frame is that of "belief," which has to do with the "Spirit" and not "works" of the law, which are driven by the sphere of "flesh."[205] The temporal nature of the old covenant, which was supposed to be authoritative until the time of John the Baptist, is replaced by the eternal nature of the new one and thus makes unnecessary the continuation of observing the Jewish law.[206]

The concept ΝΟΜΟΣ "law" is evoked within the [NEW COVENANT] frame but with a different nuance from that of the [OLD COVENANT] frame. This concept could either specifically refer to a body of nominative rules derived from God or generally to the law which has to do with binding regulations and rules.[207] Within the [NEW COVENANT] frame, the law does not bring salvation and is even associated with leading to the abounding of sin and bringing the wrath of God on the sinner.[208] The role of the law is redefined as not intended to justify but to give knowledge of sin.[209] Paul points out that God has spoken to all men, either through the Jewish law or through the law of conscience, and therefore all, namely Jews and Gentiles, must be answerable before him.[210] The concept ΓΡΑΜΜΑΤΟΣ "the written code," which is also evoked in Romans 2:29, refers to the external ritual of circumcision as compared to the spiritual

---

202. Phil 3:3.
203. McConville, "בְּרִית," 754; cf. Rom 9–11.
204. Rom 3, 4, 15; cf. John 7:22; Acts 15; Gal 5; Phil 3:3; Col 2:11.
205. Gruenwald, *Rituals and Ritual Theory*, 231.
206. Luke 16:16; Rom 10:4; Heb 9:15.
207. Muraoka, *Greek-English Lexicon: Chiefly of the Pentateuch*, 388.
208. Morris, *Epistle to the Romans*, 144; cf. Rom 4:15; 5:20.
209. Rom 3:20; 7:7.
210. Rom 2:17–3:20.

one.²¹¹ This means that as far as the [NEW COVENANT] frame is concerned, possession of the law is of no advantage to the Jews, to whom there was nothing higher than the law, unless they obey it.²¹² It is through ΠΙΣΤΙΣ "faith," an important concept that is also activated in this new frame, that all men are made right with God as the example of Abraham indicates.²¹³ The promise to Abraham was given as a result of his faith not as a reward of legal works.²¹⁴ Christians are said to have been set free from the power of law since they have died to it through the body of Christ.²¹⁵

An important instrument in this [NEW COVENANT] frame is that of the good news, also referred to as the word of faith.²¹⁶ Paul's use of the term εὐαγγέλιον "in light of the use of this term of emperors at their births or when they accomplished something dramatic" to refer to the proclamation of a positive message which brings forth salvation to those who believe.²¹⁷ The good news brings transformation when adhered to and when acted on as an object of belief. The one who proclaims this word of faith also takes a central role within this [NEW COVENANT] frame. This is because in that time, which of course was before the advent of the mass media, the role of a herald was vital and without him there could not have been hearers.²¹⁸ The concept "FAMILY" also takes a new meaning from the traditional one within the [NEW COVENANT] frame. One can now have a "spiritual father" figure who not only introduces one to faith in Christ but also comforts and encourages them to live a life worthy of the gospel.²¹⁹ Other elements in this [FAMILY] sub-frame which are activated include that of brothers and sisters who one becomes connected to because of the blood of Jesus Christ. Christians can now enjoy being joint heirs with God and co-heirs with Jesus Christ as members of the family of God which "implies a right to inherit, even if that right is acquired

---

211. Garland, *2 Corinthians*, 165.
212. Black, *Romans*, 94.
213. Rom 4:1–25.
214. Black, *Romans*, 70.
215. Morris, *Epistle to the Romans*, 145; Rom 7:4.
216. Rom 10:16–17.
217. Witherington III, *Paul's Letter to the Romans*, 31.
218. Stott, *Romans*, 286.
219. Godet, *Commentary on Romans*, 173; cf. 1 Cor 4:15; Phil 2:22; 1 Tim 2:11–12.

by adoption."[220] The concept translated as "brother" and "sister" within this [NEW COVENANT] frame might include or exclude one's siblings based on whether they have also put their faith in Christ.

3.2.2 Other Associated Rituals

The [NEW COVENANT] frame does not totally annul the [RITUAL] frame but rather tends to replace it with new models and forms. Even though within the [NEW COVENANT] frame works done in the flesh are discouraged, the [RITUAL] frame still seems to play a role within this new frame, only that such rituals are defined in the framework of belief.[221] I will briefly demonstrate this by discussing two rituals, that of baptism and that of the Lord's Supper.

There is an attempt to link the role of the ritual of baptism within the [NEW COVENANT] frame with that of circumcision from the [OLD COVENANT] frame, with baptism being referred to as the "circumcision" within the [NEW COVENANT] frame of understanding.[222] Baptism, in this attempt, is understood as the first step of initiation as far as the [NEW COVENANT] frame is concerned, just as circumcision is understood within the [OLD COVENANT] frame.[223] Colossians 2:11–13 is an important text that is used to advance this argument. The kind of circumcision described in the passage is said to be that which is done "with no hands" symbolizing the removal of the body of flesh, which is figuratively represented by baptism and results in freedom from the power of the sinful self. In this view, the role of the baptism ritual can be closely related to van Gennep's notion of rite of passage, since it facilitates religious conversion by signifying a believer's change of status as well as their life condition.[224] This interpretation has some historical connection with the ritual of baptism practiced within the old covenantal law, for a person who had become impure was expected to take a bath and wait until evening before

---

220. Black, *Romans*, 114.
221. Gruenwald, *Rituals and Ritual Theory*, 233.
222. Zee, *Christ, Baptism and the Lord's Supper*, 96.
223. Gruenwald, *Rituals and Ritual Theory*, 237; cf. Kline, *By Oath Consigned*.
224. A rite of passage is defined as having three stages, namely, the pre-liminal, the liminal and the post-liminal stages (van Gennep, *Rites of Passage*; Turner, *Ritual Process*; La Fontaine, *Initiation*). The pre-liminal stage has to do with separation from the old situation, the liminal period with the period between the old and new situation where there is state of transition from one status to another, and the post-liminal period with reincorporation of the individuals who have undergone the rite of passage into the social order with a new status.

they could be declared pure.²²⁵ This kind of baptism is also said to have been accompanied by a sacrifice in the same manner that a Jewish person who had been purified from any uncleanness would offer a sacrifice. There is also a possibility that the historical basis for Christian baptism has some connection with the baptism ritual that was performed in the adoption of the proselytes as members of the Jewish community. If a non-Jew, who by default was perceived as being unclean, desired to join the Jewish community of faith, they had to be purified and therefore undergo both the rituals of circumcision and baptism.²²⁶ As Zee further points out

> In these rituals the images of death and resurrection were often used. The proselyte's conversion to Judaism marked the end of a life of slavery to the pagan gods and the beginning of a new life of obedience to Yahweh, the one true God. Two rituals were especially associated with this conversion: circumcision, and the ritual birth or baptism. It is clear that circumcision was the most important of these rituals, and the one that really marked the passage from death to life. The baptism was a ritual that took place one week after the "death" of circumcision. It marked the point at which the proselyte was ritually clean and was therefore permitted to engage in Jewish worship.²²⁷

The attempt to equate the ritual of baptism in the [NEW COVENANT] frame with that of circumcision from the [OLD COVENANT] frame is opposed to Paul's understanding of the role of baptism. According to him, baptism signifies the union of the believer with Christ in his death as well as their death to sin.²²⁸ Baptism, being a once-for-all event, symbolizes a number of things within the NT understanding. It demonstrates to others that one has received forgiveness of sins and is therefore cleansed, belongs to Jesus Christ, shares in the death and resurrection of Jesus Christ, has experienced the new birth, and also is now a member within the body of Christ, namely the church.²²⁹ The ritual of baptism purges believers from being enjoined to the original

---

225. Lev 15:6, 12, 17, 19, 22, 27; Num 19:10, 22; Deut 23:12.
226. Zeitlin, "Who Is a Jew?," 251.
227. Zee, *Christ, Baptism and the Lord's Supper*, 77.
228. Murray, *Epistle to the Romans*, 214, 215; cf. Rom 6:3–11.
229. Acts 2:38; 22:16; Rom 6:3–5; cf. Col 2:12; Titus 3:5–15; cf. 1 Cor 12:13; Gal 3:26–29.

sin of Adam and Eve and hence becomes a sign that people who have gone through it can now enter into the life of the age to come.²³⁰

The ritual of the Lord's Supper, in Greek κυριακὸν δεῖπνον, is also an important ritual observed within the [NEW COVENANT] frame.²³¹ In all the occurrences of this institution in the NT (i.e. Matthew 26:26–29; Mark 14:22–25; Luke 22:15–20, and 1 Corinthians 11:23–26), there are occurrences of the phrases ἡ καινή διαθήκη "the new covenant" and [τὸ αἷμά μου] τῆς διαθήκης "[the blood of] the covenant."²³² The apostle Paul seems to have modified the ritual of the Lord's Supper out of that of the feast of Passover, which is associated with the [OLD COVENANT] frame, for as Gruenwald points out

> Paul takes the event out of its Passover context and turns it into the "Lord's Supper," that is, into a communal meal that can take place in any circumstance . . . In its new formatting, it has transformative goals that are completely different to those of the Jewish Passover ritual. The New ritual is no longer set in the framework of enacting the memory of the Exodus, but in the framework of the Passover Supper that Jesus and his disciples celebrated, with its new redemptive functions.²³³

Even as the ritual of Passover in the OT provides the foundation of the Lord's Supper, there are some important elements associated with the ritual of Passover that are lost. Such include the specific timing as to when it was supposed to be observed, given that it was traditionally observed once per year and in a specific location, while that of the Lord's Supper is observed more regularly and in different locations. Within the institution of the Lord's Supper, Jesus is equated with "the Passover lamb that was slain for the salvation of God's people."²³⁴ The taking of wine becomes central in the observation of the ritual of the Lord's Supper, symbolizing the salvific effects of the blood that Jesus shed on Calvary and bread symbolizing partaking of the body of Christ with the goal of bringing transformation of individuals into a

---

230. Gruenwald, *Rituals and Ritual Theory*, 248; Eller, *Place of Sacraments*, 48.
231. 1 Cor 11:20.
232. cf. Matt 26:28; Mark 14:24; Luke 22:20; 1 Cor 11:25.
233. Gruenwald, *Rituals and Ritual Theory*, 251.
234. Janzen, *Exodus*, 169.

community of believers.²³⁵ Again the institution of the Lord's Supper gains a new meaning within the [NEW COVENANT] frame since it looks forward and anticipates the liberated life that is to come.²³⁶ After looking at the modified frame and related institutions, which serves as the background framing of the associated concepts in the metaphor περιτομὴ καρδίας "circumcision of heart," the next section analyzes the conceptual integration process behind its interpretation.²³⁷

3.3 The Conceptual Integration Process

In this section, I will demonstrate how the meaning of the metaphor περιτομὴ καρδίας "circumcision of heart" is mentally constructed within the context of Romans 2. Since what is represented by this metaphor is a prepackaged blend, so to speak, using the complementary approach between CIT and RT, I will seek to identify the various mental spaces, trace the links between them, and draw the intended inferences within the integration process. Some of the issues discussed in this section include that of frame blending and the specific elements that are activated within the suggested six interrelated mental spaces in the integration network, namely, the two outer spaces (i.e. the DS and the RS), and the inner space (i.e. the GS, the two input spaces, and the BS), in an endeavor to derive the meaning of this metaphor.

3.3.1 Frame Blending

The operation that is involved in the construction of the meaning of the metaphor περιτομὴ καρδίας is that of double-scope integration network. In this form of integration network, both inputs have distinct frames with each frame contributing towards the structure of the blend. The two organizing frames have to do with entering a covenantal relationship with God, on the one hand by observing the law and on the other by believing in Jesus Christ. According to Paul, these two frames are incompatible since it is not possible to get right with God by observing the law.²³⁸ The double-scope network also

---

235. Gräbe, *New covenant, New Community*, 73; Gruenwald, *Rituals and Ritual Theory*, 249.
236. Janzen, *Exodus*, 170.
237. Rom 2:29.
238. Bray, *Romans*, 72.

permits the use of the vocabulary and grammar from one frame to talk about the other inputs. An example is in the book of Hebrews where concepts associated with the [OLD COVENANT] frame such as ΜΩΥΣΗΣ "Moses," ΣΑΒΒΤΙΣΜΟΣ "Sabbath rest," ΑΡΞΙΕΡΕΑ "high priest," ΑΓΙΟΝ ΣΚΗΝΗ "Sanctuary/Tabernacle," ΘΥΣΙΑΣ "sacrifices" and ΠΡΟΣΨΟΡΑΣ "offerings" are used to explain the superiority of the new covenant over the old.[239] Though such aspects of the old frame are maintained within the new one, they are interpreted differently to fit within the new frame. The act of contrasting the role of Moses, whose ministry within the old covenant, with that of Jesus Christ within the new covenant frame, leads to the derivation of new contextual implications shedding more light into the ministry of Christ, and as Lane further points out

> The figure of Moses as the mediator of Israel's covenant and cult is of critical importance in Hebrews. The writer contrasts the Mosaic era, the Mosaic covenant, and the Mosaic cult with the new situation introduced by God through Jesus. This is intimated in the opening lines of the homily, in the contrasts of the word spoken to the fathers through the prophets with the word spoken through the divine Son . . . The extended comparison of the old and new cult . . . with its focus upon access to God in the Mosaic era and in Christian worship, develops the parallel between Moses as the mediator of the old cult and Jesus as the mediator of the new.[240]

This double-scope integration network also involves the blending of the two frames, namely that of the [OLD COVENANT] and that of the [NEW COVENANT], with some aspects of continuation leading to new contextual implications as well as some that are incompatible between the two leading to the elimination of such assumptions in light of the new evidence provided. It is on the basis of the [OLD COVENANT] framework, mainly through the prophets in the holy Scriptures, that the new one was laid, with Paul anchoring his theological argument in Romans 2:17–29 in OT truth.[241] An example is the

---

239. Heb 3:1–6.
240. Lane, *Hebrews 1–8*, 73.
241. Rom 1:2; Osborne, *Romans*, 29.

Lord Jesus Christ, who is the mediator of the new covenant. From the old covenant perspective, he is said to have been the σπέρματος "seed" of David, while in the new one he is said to have been the "son of God."[242] As far as the cross-space mapping between the elements is concerned, we find that the beneficiaries in the [OLD COVENANT] frame were primarily the people of Israel. In the [NEW COVENANT] frame, there is both a clash in that other nations are included as beneficiaries, as well as a continuation in view of the fact that after the adoption of the Gentiles is complete, God will accomplish his plan over the people of Israel.[243] The word translated as "everyone," which is used more than seventy-one times in the book of Romans, is a central theme pointing out that God's salvation is universal in its scope.[244] Another clash is that the old covenant was based on the law, while the new one is based on a righteousness that is apart from the law, with the former assumption being eliminated in the context of the new evidence provided in the current DS of Romans 2.[245]

There is also a clash between the two covenants as far as the role of circumcision is concerned. In the [OLD COVENANT] frame, every male had to undergo circumcision to be counted as one of its beneficiaries. In the [NEW COVENANT] frame, we see the elimination of this existing assumption since within this frame, circumcision is no longer the means by which privileges and obligations of the covenant made to the patriarchs are passed from one generation to another. The benefits within the [NEW COVENANT] frame are more than just that of a child of Abraham and inheriting promises such as that of the land, since it primarily involves being a child of God and receiving the forgiveness of sins. There is also a clash across the two domains as far as the object of circumcision is concerned as the sexual organ in the [OLD COVENANT] frame is eliminated and replaced by that of the heart within the [NEW COVENANT] frame.

We find new rituals emerging as well as others taking on new significance within the [NEW COVENANT] frame through the derivation of new contextual implications. Such include the rituals of baptism and that of the Lord's Table,

---

242. Rom 1:3.
243. Rom 1:16; 11:2.
244. Toews, *Romans*, 53.
245. Rom 2:17; 3:21.

which are discussed above, as well as the creation of new institutions, which include offices such as those of bishops and deacons. The false assumption within the old framework that women can only be included through their relationship with their fathers and husbands is eliminated in light of the new evidence thus they can now experience the ritual of the second birth on their own. We also find the institution of the family being redefined within this [NEW COVENANT] frame through derivation of new contextual implications, with concepts in the family domain as FATHER*, BROTHER*, SISTER*, etc. being extended to incorporate a new spiritual meaning. In this new meaning, these terms include more than sharing of blood bonds, with believers expected to demonstrate absolute devotion to one another, just as is expected in the family setting.[246] The specific timing of the eighth day within the [OLD COVENANT] frame is eliminated with the experiencing of the new birth left open to anytime that one responds in faith and accepts the stipulations of the new covenant. Again, we find the temporal nature of the old covenant frame giving way to the eternal nature on the new one.[247] One of the distinctive elements that is profiled in the [NEW COVENANT] frame is the role of the Holy Spirit who is the agent of this inner process.[248]

3.3.2 The Outer Spaces

In the integration network, I have included two outer spaces, namely the DS and the RS, relations that connect the mental spaces within the network as well as determine which elements are projected to the blend (see figure 4 below). Within the DS, we find the structure and function of the text contributing towards the argument that Paul is making. The RS is central in providing the framing that guides further mapping between the inputs as well as in driving the process behind the selection of projections. It is important to note that the two are connected, with the argument in the DS forming the basis which determines the background knowledge or framing which is activated within the RS.

The source language discourse space (SLDS) within which the communication takes place is specifically that of the book of Romans, but focusing

---

246. Osborne, *Romans*, 331.
247. Barnett, *Second Epistle to the Corinthians*, 187–188; cf. 2 Cor 3:11.
248. Rom 2:29.

primarily on Romans 2:17–29.[249] Some of the factors to be addressed which occur within the DS is that of the setting of the discourse, which include its participants and its stylistic or rhetorical nature, which go a long way in influencing the interpretation of the metaphor περιτομὴ καρδίας.[250] Since the background framing of this metaphor is dependent on both the structure and purpose or function of the text, the DS will assist in pointing out how this metaphor contributes towards the bigger argument that Paul is making, especially within the first four chapters of his letter.

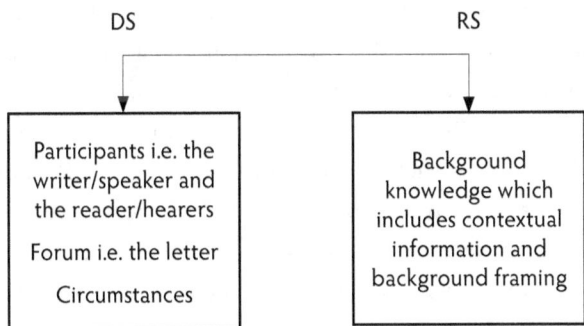

Figure 4: The source language discourse and relevance spaces

3.3.2.1 The Source Language Discourse Space

Paul, as expected of any upcoming Jewish scholar of the time, was educated in rhetorical skills. This means that the epistle to the Romans belongs to the domain of rhetoric, rather than that of a mere letter, due to the substantial

---

249. The book of Romans has been traditionally treated as a "theological treatise" par excellence which gives "a systematic exposition of Paul's own theological position" (Barclay, *Letter to the Romans*, 1). In this book, Paul also aims "to assert, and logically develop, an organic whole, the good news of salvation announced by Christ, especially in view of the distinction of Jew and Gentile; to show that this good news is in harmony with God's declarations and conduct as recorded in the Old Testament; and to apply it to matters of secular and of church life" (Beet, *Commentary on St. Paul's Epistle*, 25). Apart from Paul having an apologetic purpose in mind in the writing of this letter, he also had a missionary and pastoral purpose, all of which hang together and reinforce one another when taken in totality (Dunn, *Romans 9–16*, lv–lviii). This book has had an impact that is "radical and far-reaching" which has continued to influence the church over the centuries (Barrett, *Commentary on the Epistle to the Romans*, 1).

250. Cameron, *Metaphor in Educational Discourse*, 27; Wikberg, "Studying Metaphors," 109.

amount of argumentation found in it.[251] Due to its argumentative nature, I will be analyzing the DS by using what is referred to as rhetorical criticism given the fact that Paul is making use of this genre to influence his audience to adhere to a given position or thesis.[252] Rhetorical criticism "focuses on the communication between an author and a reader by analyzing the strategies an author employs to influence a reader's view or shape a reader's response," which is exactly what Paul is doing in his letter to the Romans.[253] According to the above definition, the practice of rhetorical criticism does not stop by analyzing the strategy the author uses, but also focuses on the role of the recipient. In emphasizing the role of the recipient, Mitchell points out that this criticism has to do with "how readers participate in that reality as they read a text which is meant to elicit certain responses."[254]

The epistle to the Romans is said to contain discursive traits following the principles of Greek rhetoric for in this epistle we see Paul defending a number of theses.[255] The three types of ancient rhetoric that were practiced by the ancient Greeks were judicial, deliberative, and epideictic.[256] The judicial type, which was mostly used in law courts, had the goal of convincing hearers on whether a past action that was taken was right or wrong, whether it was just or unjust.[257] According to Kennedy, the second letter to the Corinthians is a good example, except for chapters 8 and 9, which are deliberative.[258] The deliberative type, which was mostly used in the assembly, sought to persuade

---

251. Witherington III, *Paul Quest*, 116; Keener, *Romans*, 3.

252. Rhetorical criticism has been used to analyze NT texts such as the teachings of Jesus (Kennedy, *New Testament Interpretation*, 39–72), the book of Acts as a unit (Kennedy, 97–156) as well as the speeches in the book of Acts (Kennedy, 114–139), the gospels both as a unit (Black, *Rhetoric of the Gospel*) and as individual books (Kennedy, *New Testament Interpretation*, 101–113), the epistles of Paul (Harvey, *Listening to the Text*, 22–23) including Thessalonians (Kennedy, *New Testament Interpretation*, 141–144), Galatians (Smit, "Letter of Paul to the Galatians"; Witherington III, *Paul Quest*, 119–122; Kennedy, *New Testament Interpretation*, 144–152), Romans (Kennedy, 152–156), and Titus (Classen, *Rhetorical Criticism of the New Testament*, 45–67). It has also being used to analyze the book of Revelation (Kennedy, *New History of Classical Rhetoric*, 258–259; Wuellner, "Paul's Rhetoric of Argumentation," 128).

253. Tate, *Biblical Interpretation*, 286.

254. Mitchell, "Rhetorical and New Literary Criticism," 617.

255. Aletti, *God's Justice in Romans*, 33.

256. Klein, Blomberg, and Hubbard, Jr., *Introduction to Biblical Interpretation*, 431–432; Watson, "Contributions and Limitations," 133.

257. Witherington III, *Paul Quest*, 116.

258. Kennedy, *New Testament Interpretation*, 86.

or dissuade an audience concerning an action in the future on whether it will be possible, advantageous, or necessary.[259] According to Kennedy the Sermon on the Mount and that of the plain can be classified as deliberative.[260] This is because these texts give advice to the disciples on how they are expected to conduct their lives and also invite them to consider how they should live that life with the focus being in the immediate future. The epideictic type, also referred to as the oratory of praise or blame, arose from the need to secure a favorable hearing and was used to urge the people to affirm or resist a given view or a set of values in the present.[261] Examples include the Magnificat in Luke 1:46–55 and Jesus rebuking the Pharisees in Matthew 23.[262] It is important to note that even though there could be an overlap between these three types of ancient rhetoric in the NT, there is one which will always stand out as dominant in a given passage. The rhetorical goal of Paul in Romans 1:18—3:20 is to point out that both Jews and Gentiles are under the power of sin and that both need the saving power of God's justice. In order to "arrive at this goal, Paul must convince his audience that even Israel, which has the benefit of God's law and the covenant sign of circumcision, has failed to observe the law."[263]

In order to analyze the DS and determine the logical argument that Paul is making in this DS, I will use a five stage methodology suggested by Kennedy.[264] The first one is to determine the rhetorical unit, the second is to determine the rhetoric situation, the third is to identify the rhetorical problem addressed in the passage, the fourth is to see how the author arranges his argument, and the last one is to review whether the rhetorical exigence (i.e. the problem that caused him to write) has been met. As has been suggested above, the DS where the metaphor seems applicable in forwarding the argument that Paul is making is Romans 2:17–29.[265] In the text before it (i.e. verses 1–16) Paul seeks to eliminate the Jewish exception by warning that those who pass judgment on others are not exempted from the same judgment since they also commit

---

259. Witherington III, *Paul Quest*, 116.
260. Kennedy, *New Testament Interpretation*, 39–63; Matt 5–7; Luke 6:17–49.
261. Kennedy, 73–74.
262. Kennedy, 77–78.
263. Keener, *Romans*, 71.
264. Kennedy, *New Testament Interpretation*, 33–38.
265. Aichele, et al., *Postmodern Bible*, 150.

the same sins. The coordinating conjunction διό in 2:1 makes a deduction or a conclusion to the foregoing argument in 1:18–31.[266] There is an alternation of the use of pronouns in 2:1–16, with verses 1–5 using the second person singular form, while in verses 6–16 use the third person pronoun form.

Romans 2:17–24 is a sub-unit different from the preceding one given that in verse 17 the conjunction δέ is used which signals the start of another section.[267] There is also the change of personal references as well as a change of the delivery style from that of giving a series of statements to that of a dialogue between the first and second person.[268] The change of personal pronouns is from the third person form, in the previous section, to that of the second singular form, previously used in 2:1–5. This indicates that the subject has changed, with this section focusing mainly on the Jews, unlike the previous one which focuses on the Gentiles. Verses 25–29 are linked to verses 17–24 by sharing the use of the second person references as well as by the shared theme of obeying the law, though to an extent it also advances the argument by addressing a new topic, namely, that of περιτομή.[269] Paul is not just making an argument for or against the rite of circumcision, but rather he is employing a rhetorical argument to "turn the tables" on his enemies using the very rite that they held dearly.[270] The end of the discourse section is marked by a series of rhetorical questions in 3:1. These questions introduce a new line of argument by pointing out that despite having such advantages including that of circumcision, the Jews continued in their transgression against the law.[271]

The second stage is to determine the rhetorical situation that gave birth to the writing of the letter to the Romans. This letter was written a few years after the Jews were evicted from Rome by Emperor Claudius in 49 AD.[272] The circumstances that led to Paul writing the letter to the Romans had to do with his plans to visit them on the way to do missionary work in Spain, with the journey to Spain prompting an opportunity to fulfill his long time desire to meet the Roman Christians whom he invites to support him on his Spanish

---

266. Wallace, *Greek Grammar Beyond the Basics*, 605, 673.
267. Wallace, 674.
268. Lee, *Paul's Gospel in Romans*, 177.
269. Lee, 183.
270. Fredriksen, "Judaism," 235.
271. Schreiner, *Romans*, 139.
272. Miller, *Obedience of Faith*, 110; cf. Acts 18:2.

mission.²⁷³ The church in Rome seems to have been predominantly Gentile, though the letter also addresses issues affecting the Jewish constituency of the congregation with the letter assuming that the readers have a certain degree of familiarity with the Jewish Scriptures and Christian traditions.²⁷⁴ In substantiating his position of the dual composition of the Roman church, Stanley argues that

> The fact that Paul quotes so often from the Jewish Scriptures in Romans, far more than in any of his other letters, is sometimes cited as evidence for a maximalist reading of the letter. Supporters of this view point out that Paul seems to assume that his Roman audience will know the original context of many of his quotations and be able to supply the links needed to make sense of his argument. From this they conclude that Paul must have known that the church in Rome was composed primarily of Jews and/or Gentiles sympathetic to Judaism who had learned the Jewish Scriptures from regular participation in the synagogue.²⁷⁵

In an attempt to come to terms with the proposal that both Jewish and Gentile constituencies were assumed in the writing of this letter, there has been an attempt to argue of the possibility of two separate documents being composed as one in the body of Romans.²⁷⁶ The position taken here is that the audience in Rome

> consisted of believers from both Jewish and gentile backgrounds. Romans 16:3–16 offers concrete evidence of Jewish believers while Paul's direct address to gentile believers provides solid evidence for the presence of Christians from gentile backgrounds. The available evidence does not permit a definite decision as to which group was in the minority or majority, though Paul's statements to those of gentile birth indicate that they were likely the majority or at least exerted strong influence among the Christian

---

273. Miller, 101, 103; cf. Rom 1:10–13; 15:23, 24, 28.
274. Miller, 108; cf. Rom 1:5–6, 13; 11:13; 15:16, 18.
275. Stanley, *Arguing with Scripture*, 137.
276. cf. Kinoshita, "Romans – Two Writings Combined."

groups. In light of the organization of Christians into house churches and the large number of Christians in the city, it can be assumed that the make-up of different house churches varied.[277]

This is demonstrated by the fact that Paul seems to direct his statements to either of the parties as well as to emphasize the place of both parties under God by encouraging them to welcome one another for mutual edification.[278] He sought to unite them by pointing out that both groups stand equally judged before God and that neither ethnic descent nor following the law could save Israel.[279] He also points out that the Gentiles were not supposed to despise the Jewish believers, and as Wedderburn rightly argues

> The Roman church was *originally strongly Judaizing in character*, and the form of Christianity which was originally established in that city was one which combined belief in Christ with adherence to the Jewish Law. That version of Christianity may have been espoused by some gentiles as well as Jews, particularly by gentiles who had already been in contact with the Jewish synagogues. *Into that situation had come Christians proclaiming a different version of Christian message, one which dispensed with the need for obedience to the Jewish Law as such.* This latter group gained in numbers and strength with the passage of time – it was, after all, far more attractive to non-Jews for whom keeping the Law was a considerable disincentive – whereas the strength of the Judaizing stream within the Roman church had been seriously weakened by Claudius' disciplinary measures against members of the Jewish community . . . By the time that Paul wrote, however, Claudius was dead, and his edict of expulsion, if it had not been repealed, may at least have lapsed, so the Jews could freely move back to Rome . . . it was also to be expected that the strength of the Judaizing tradition in the church there would be increasing again, as well as the non-Christian Jewish community in the capital city, bringing with it the risk of further

---

277. Miller, *Obedience of Faith*, 109–110.
278. Rom 2:17; 11:13; 1:16–17; 14:1, 19; 15:2, 7.
279. Rom 3:11; 4:16; 7:22–23; 9:6–8; 10:2–4.

troubles in the form of friction between the proponents of the Law-free gospel and their Jewish and Judaizing neighbours. Part of that danger, the risk of friction between Judaizing Christians and supporters of the Law-free gospel, Paul seeks to avert by appealing for mutual tolerance and esteem.[280]

Paul's main purpose of writing this letter is to do a self-introduction and to make known to the church at Rome the content of the gospel he was preaching among the Gentiles.[281] This letter makes a threefold prayer request. First that his ministry to Jerusalem will be accepted, second that the Roman Christians will help him on his journey to Spain, and third that they would receive him on his way to Spain.[282] He was also better situated to advise the Christians at Rome because he had a taste of both sides. On the one hand, he draws from conventional Jewish wisdom since he was acquainted with the Jewish laws and customs after being thoroughly taught and having committed himself to the traditions of his fathers, and on the other, he was a convert as well as a legitimate apostle of Jesus Christ.[283]

The third stage is that of identifying the rhetorical problem that necessitated the discourse or the verbal response given. The circumstances of this letter seemed to have been occasioned by the different values and perspectives between the Jewish and Gentile followers of Christ. There was tension between these two groups, especially as it came to matters related to observing the Jewish law "regarding clean and unclean foods as well as observance of special days."[284] Romans 2:17–29 addresses itself to the Jewish constituency in the church who seemed to have been boasting about their national and religious heritage, especially the fact that they were the ones who had been given the law. They also seemed to have boasted of their place as God's special people and that is why they bore the mark of the covenant. Paul pointed out that such human boasting has no place in the kingdom of God and argues that the bigger agenda should be that of both divides being united in the body

---

280. Wedderburn, *Reasons for Romans*, 64–65 (emphasis his).
281. Kümmel, *Introduction to the New Testament*, 309, 312–313.
282. Stott, *Message of Romans*, 34.
283. Miller, *Obedience of Faith*, 117; Acts 9; 22:3; Rom 15:16; Gal 1:4.
284. Miller, 121.

of Christ.[285] Paul seems to have written this letter to also address some issues that had risen between him and the Jewish Christians at Rome. He wanted to "persuade them of the truth of his gospel and to dispel the deep misgivings they were bound to have about him and his gospel. More broadly, Paul needed to do this if he and his communities were not to be isolated from the growing Christian community at the centre of the Roman Empire."[286]

The fourth stage is to look closely at how the author arranges the material in the text, taking stock of how the individual sections of the argument work together towards a unified rhetorical situation in the discourse. According to Elliott, the first eight chapters of the book of Romans give a theological exposition of the Christian gospel in opposition to Judaism.[287] In this section, Paul was aiming "not to declare the election of Israel simply null and void, but to direct the Jews to the reality of the coming God, who indeed demands more from his chosen people than merely external obedience."[288] The portion 1:18–3:20 has been widely considered as Paul's offensive against "the Jew" pointing to the fact that the Jews, just like the Gentiles counterparts are also sinners, because they do not keep the law and thus they cannot be justified before God by their works. In 1:18 we find the *propositio* thesis which states that "the wrath of God is revealed from heaven against all ungodliness and wickedness of men. . ." (RSV). According to Aletti, this thesis is followed by proof through facts,[289] proof based on principles,[290] a response to possible misunderstanding,[291] and proof from recourse to authority[292] which ends with a *(sub) peroraritio*,[293] stating that "Now we know that whatever the law says, it says to those who are under the law, so that every mouth may be silenced and the whole world held accountable to God."[294] As Tobin further points out

---

285. cf. Rom 10:5–13; 11:17–24.
286. Tobin, *Paul's Rhetoric*, 99.
287. Elliot, *Rhetoric of Romans*, 59.
288. Stuhlmacher, *Paul's Letter to the Romans*, 50.
289. Rom 1:19–32.
290. Rom 2:1–29.
291. Rom 3:1–8.
292. Rom 3:9–18.
293. Rom 3:19–20.
294. Aletti, *God's Justice in Romans*, 63–64.

What Paul has done in 2:12–29 is to argue that the conduct of Jews must be judged on the same basis as the conduct of the Gentiles. He demonstrates this, however, through the use of quotations from the Jewish scriptures as well as through the use of other traditional Jewish viewpoints. Where Paul moves beyond those viewpoints is in juxtaposing them in a conservatively oriented argument from previous judgments on similar cases. This juxtaposition itself is rooted in what Paul claims is a scripturally grounded, traditional Jewish argument, that is, the impartiality of God. In reality, Paul has argued for untraditional conclusions on what he hopes his audience would regard as traditional assumptions and viewpoints.[295]

The focus of Romans 2:17–29 is on the relation of the Jews to the law, with the law being the major theme in verses 17–24, addressing the contradiction of the Jews who knew the law yet dishonored God by not obeying its requirements. The question of religious identity is also addressed in verses 25–29 with the section condemning the conduct of those who think they are exempted from the consequences of their sins. The difference between the Jews and non-Jews is non-existent before God with the ritual of circumcision used to illustrate this view.[296] As Aletti further points out

> If vv. 17–24 insist on the clear identity of the Jew, in vv. 25–29 Paul returns to the differences and the fluid boundaries. The vocabulary of circumcision and uncircumcision, which serves to determine the differences between Jew and non-Jew, is intentionally used, for as is known, since the prophets, circumcision of the heart permits the determination of what is just and what is not. And Paul is really going to arrive at an ultimate reversal of the status when he affirms that, if the non-Jew has a circumcised heart and the Jew an uncircumcised, God, by virtue of his impartiality, will treat the Jew as a pagan and the pagan as a Jew.[297]

---

295. Tobin, *Paul's Rhetoric*, 118.
296. Tobin, 117.
297. Aletti, *God's Justice in Romans*, 80.

In order to understand the argument Paul is making in this section, one is expected to understand traditional Jewish viewpoints and how Paul uses them to his own purposes.[298] In verses 23–24, he alludes to a citation in LXX of Isaiah 52:5 to support his claim that the very ones who claim to have the law do dishonor God by breaking the same law. In verses 17–20, the apostle Paul mentions ways through which the Jews boasted about God and how they depended on the law for justification. In verses 21–24, he points out that even though the Jews were boasting about the law, they were guilty of the same sins that they were accusing the Gentiles of committing, and in so doing ended up dishonoring God.

The conjunction γάρ at the beginning of verse 25 points to an implied proposition among the Jews that circumcision functions as protection against God's wrath due to their special covenant relationship with God.[299] Verses 25–29 begin by a discussion of the value of circumcision, with Paul arguing that the law, the covenant, and circumcision belong together. The explanatory conjunction γάρ in verse 28 is used as an inferential particle that introduces an independent sentence and provides additional information to substantiate the argument Paul has been making from the beginning of the chapter. In making his argument, Paul appeals to Jewish thought that perceived circumcision as of symbolic importance in the cutting of sensual pleasures and other passions and also having value only if one obeys the demands of the covenant which are set forth in the law.[300] The Jewish people treated those who were uncircumcised with abhorrence and thus the issue of circumcision was crucial in arresting the attention of the Jews since it was their distinguishing national rite.[301] As Moo further argues "Paul goes beyond any first-century Jewish viewpoint in suggesting that physical circumcision is no longer required and in implicitly applying the term 'Jew' to those who were not ethnically Jews."[302] Therefore the use of the metaphor περιτομὴ καρδίας in verse 29 is stylistic and serves as a rhetorical device to give further proof to the argument that Paul is making in Romans 2:17–29.

---

298. Tobin, *Paul's Rhetoric*, 116
299. Nygren, *Commentary on Romans*, 132.
300. Tobin, *Paul's Rhetoric*, 116; Schreiner, *Romans*, 138.
301. Haldane, *Exposition of the Epistle to the Romans*, 105.
302. Moo, *Epistle to the Romans*, 175.

The last stage is that of reviewing whether the rhetorical exigence has been met. It is hard to know how the church reacted to Paul's rhetoric, for there are no records to that effect. But as far as his rhetoric skills are concerned, Paul was successful in arguing for the "non-divisiveness" of the gospel that he preached. In the frame of the current DS, he redefines the understanding associated with the concept ΠΕΡΙΟΤΜΗ by modifying the traditional frame to create a new one. He argues that the old frame is not consistent with the covenant stipulations, and in the modified frame he excludes physical circumcision as a requirement. In the course of his argument, he argues for a new construal of other related concepts that are evoked in the interpretation of the conventional metaphor περιτομὴ καρδίας by modifying the traditional meaning attached to these elements. One such concept is that of ΑΚΡΟΒΥΣΤΙΑ "uncircumcision," the antithesis of ΠΕΡΙΤΟΜΗ, which is activated as a contrasting mental space.[303] This concept, which both refers to the state of being uncircumcised as well as a referent to the Gentiles, is traditionally accompanied by the understanding that those who are uncircumcised stand outside the covenant with YHWH.[304] This is substantiated by the fact that the concepts translated as ΑΠΕΡΙΤΜΗΤΟΣ and ΑΚΑΘΡΤΟΣ in the LXX are used together in Isaiah 52:1 to declare that in the age of restoration such people will never again enter into the holy city of Jerusalem. This understanding is now challenged in the current DS through the derivation of new contextual implications, for as long as the uncircumcised keep the just requirements of the law, they are also to be regarded as being circumcised.[305] Therefore, by use of what Fauconnier and Turner refer to as the use of counterfactuality, Paul challenges the traditional association of unbelief/ungodliness with uncircumcision.[306] This means that those concepts which are evoked when the concept ΑΚΡΟΒΥΣΤΙΑ was evoked, such as ΕΛΛΗΝ "Greek" and ΕΘΝΟΣ "Gentile" should be re-interpreted in light of this new profiled meaning within this DS.[307]

The traditional divide between a Jew and a Gentile (i.e. that of inclusion and exclusion respectively) is now eliminated and abandoned within this

---

303. cf. Rom 2:25–27.
304. Rom 3:30; 4:10; Keil, "Books of Samuel," 485.
305. Rom 2:26.
306. Fauconnier and Turner, *Way We Think*, 87.
307. cf. Rom 2:10, 11, 14.

new frame since all nations are now included in the covenant relationship with YHWH as long as they submit to its terms. Again, excluding terms as "unclean" and "unprivileged" should be construed afresh through the process of derivation of new contextual implications as referring to all those who refuse to obey the new covenant stipulations, regardless of whether they are circumcised or not. Therefore, as the discourse continues to unfold in chapter two, there are related concepts within the DS that have been modified from their traditional meaning necessitating the readers to adjust their cognitive models in order to make sense of Paul's argument.[308]

3.3.2.2 The Source Language Relevance Space

The RS is central in providing the framing that guides further mapping between the inputs as well as in driving the process behind the selection of projections and dictating the emergent factor in the blend. There is much that can be attributed to both Paul and his audience as being part of their vast background knowledge which could be activated by the associated concepts in the metaphor περιτομὴ καρδίας. This poses the challenge of discerning the specific knowledge that is activated as well as that which is ignored or discarded in the process of meaning construction. According the RT, the lexical meaning of an utterance involves a fine-tuning process as the encoded concepts interact, with the expectation of relevance driving the selection of the relevant contextual information.[309] The RS provides the selective thought content that goes into the framing of the mental spaces as well as in the construction of reasonable inferences that are allowed in the integration network. In the process of coming up with elements and relations for the right network connections, I will be demonstrating how the relevance theoretic framework impacts the content of the mental spaces as well as how the integration process works.

I will also use the framework of RT to address the textual issues that arise, both in the interpretation of the associated concepts in this metaphor (i.e. ΠΕΡΙΤΟΜΗ and ΚΑΡΔΙΑΣ), as well as the other related concepts that are evoked within the selected DS. These textual issues include those of lexical adjustment

---

308. Larson, *Meaning-Based Translation*, 249; Richards, *Philosophy of Rhetoric*, 47–65.
309. Wilson, "Parallels and Differences," 43; Wilson and Carlson, "Unitary Approach to Lexical Pragmatics," 230.

processes by either narrowing or broadening, solving cases of ambiguity, assigning referents to referential expressions, supplying contextual assumptions, derivation of explicatures and implicatures, deriving cognitive effects, as well as arriving at completely new assumptions from existing ones. The solutions to these textual issues should be based on expectations of relevance since the cognitive system seeks to achieve the greatest number of cognitive effects for the least processing effort in order to achieve optimal relevance.

An example of lexical adjustment in terms of narrowing or broadening a concept and/or that of solving ambiguity relates to the concept ΠΝΕΥΜΑ evoked in Romans 2:29. This concept has a vast background knowledge with a number of terms been used to translate it. Such include "wind,"[310] "breath [of life],"[311] "human spirit,"[312] seat of emotion and will,[313] seat of consciousness and intelligence.[314] It is also associated with the "Spirit of God" who is attributed as the cause of extraordinary phenomena such as that of giving gifts,[315] conception of children,[316] and the production of ethical results.[317] This concept is also translated as the "mind" of Christ,[318] the one who is operative in the external world,[319] as a ministering spirit or angel,[320] and as a demon or evil spirit.[321] Within Paul's writings, we find the Spirit being associated with a number of roles which include marking one as belonging to Christ, enabling a believer to live a new life, uniting believers into the body of Christ, as well as being the medium of the union between Christ and the believer.[322] And as Osborne points out, "this is a salvation-historical switch – the Old Testament

---

310. John 3:8; Heb 1:7.
311. 2 Thess 2:8; Rev 11:11; 13:15.
312. Osborne, *Romans*, 78; Luke 8:55; Matt 27:50; Luke 23:46; John 19:30; Jas 2:26.
313. Matt 26:41; Mark 14:38; Luke 1:47; John 4:23.
314. Matt 5:3; Mark 2:8; 1 Cor 2:11.
315. Matt 10:20; 12:31, 32; Mark 3:29; 13:11; 1 Cor 12:4.
316. Matt 1:18, 20; Luke 1:35.
317. Matt 3:11; Mark 1:8; Luke 3:16; Rom 5:5; 8:2, 4–6, 9, 13, 14, 23, 26, 27; 9:1; 14:17; 15:13, 16, 30; 1 Cor 2:4; 3:16; Gal 4:6: 5:5.
318. 1 Cor 2:11.
319. Acts 8:39.
320. Heb 1:14.
321. Acts 8:7, 16; 10:1; 16:16.
322. Dunn, "Spirit," 700–703.

covenant centering on the law has now given way to the New Testament covenant centering on the age of the Spirit."[323]

The question must be raised as to whether the specific role of the Spirit in Romans 2:29 is that of an agent or to a reference to the ritual of circumcision as being a spiritual or inner process. Though both options drive home Paul's point that an outward conformity to the requirement of the law is contrary to the expectation of the gospel, the context seems to narrow to the Spirit who is the divine being by whom men are transformed.[324] The Holy Spirit here takes the role of the "indwelling power that can transform believers into the image of God" enabling them to obey God's commands, a thing they could not do before.[325] This interpretation is arrived at in the blend through the process of completion by means of strengthening of the existing assumption by drawing from the background knowledge given that the agency of the Spirit is promised to be an integral part of the promised renewal which would result in the people having a "new heart."[326] Furthermore, the option of human agency is eliminated on the grounds that it is inconsistent with commonsense knowledge when it comes to addressing matters of spirituality. Therefore, the agent that is projected in the blend is that of the Spirit, which may be interpreted as a dative of agent, instrument, or means. As Bertone rightly points out

> Paul perceived a decisive point of discontinuity between the former covenant and the new era of the Spirit, where the Spirit displaces the Law and functions exclusively as the principle of new life; i.e., the Spirit's role is comprehensive in that he secures a familial relationship with God and sustains this relationship by fashioning the practical and behavioural dimensions of the believer's life.[327]

---

323. Osborne, *Romans*, 78.
324. Dunn, *Romans 9–16*, 142.
325. Garland, *2 Corinthians*, 165.
326. Ezek 36:27.
327. Bertone, "The Law of the Spirit", 205–206.

3.3.3 The Source Language Inner Spaces

The inner spaces in a network have to do with relations that lie within the integration network. Discussed below are the generic space, the two input spaces, and the blended space within the SL integration network.

3.3.3.1 *The Source Language Generic and Input Spaces*

The properties in the GS that apply to the general structure of the integration process, namely, those of agency, goal, recipients, object, time, instrument, and means, have corresponding elements in the input spaces as demonstrated on figure 5 below. The two input spaces are that of the physical ritual of [ΠΕΡΙΤΟΜΗ] from the [OLD COVENANT] frame in IS_1 and that of the spiritual process of ΕΥΑΓΓΕΛΙΟΝ "gospel" from the [NEW COVENANT] frame in IS_2. The Jewish ritual of circumcision in IS_1 has to be understood first in order to understand the spiritual process that takes place in the other mental spaces. IS_1 also serves as the organizing frame or the scenario that structures the content of the virtual world in the BS. IS_1 in itself is a blend that results from two other input spaces. On the one hand is that of a baby boy being circumcised and on the other is that of an adult member of the society benefiting from the covenantal blessing promised to the patriarchs and their descendants.[328] In the blend, now IS_1, the performative function of circumcision represents access to God's blessings which is the desired state of reality. This process happens through the compression of vital relations of time, change, identity, cause-effect, and representation. As far as time is concerned, we find that though the two input spaces are separated in time, the entire life of benefiting from the patriarchal blessing is condensed to match the few minutes that the child undergoes the ritual of circumcision. As far as the vital relation of change is concerned, we find that the male child in IS_1 is automatically transformed to be one of God's chosen people. The whole event of a lifetime of experiencing God's blessings can be said to have been compressed to that of making a mark on the sexual organ of the male child. In this respect, the mental space with the male child can be said to be "identical" to that of the adult member in the other input space, despite the manifest differences in terms of age, experiences, etc. IS_1 also integrates the vital relation of cause and effect, the cause being undergoing the ritual and the effect that of partaking the patriarchal

---

328. cf. Gen 12:1–3.

blessings. We also find a representative role, in that it is the boy child, not the girl child, who is expected to undergo the ritual of circumcision, with the girl child being enjoined as a beneficiary as well. This can also be attributed to the role relation in the blend, since the male is perceived to be the representative head of the household unit and therefore the women under his household become automatic beneficiaries.

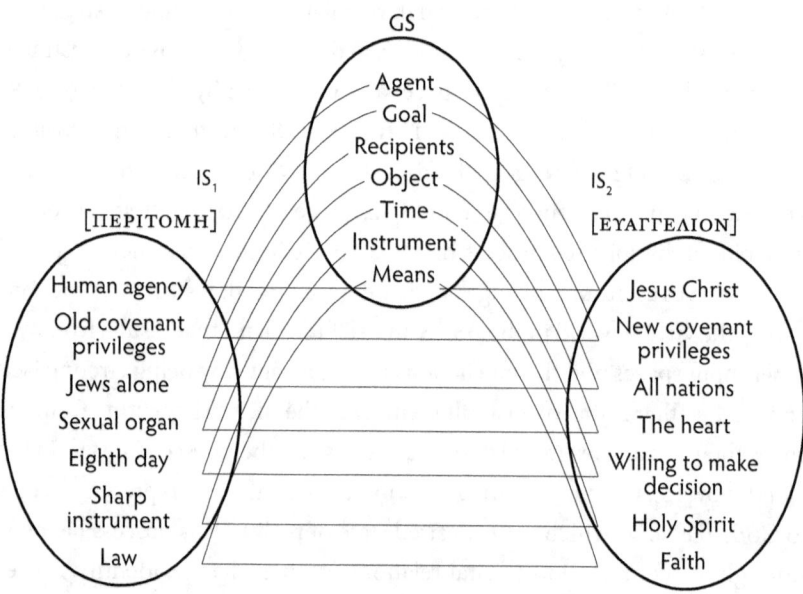

Figure 5: The source language generic and input spaces

IS₂ is that of the abstract scenario represented by the application of the ritual of περιτομή to καρδία "heart," referred to as εὐαγγέλιον [θεου] (i.e. "the gospel [of/about/from God]").[329] This has to do with the act of believing in Jesus Christ, which makes one an inheritor of his kingdom, which is referred to elsewhere in the book of Romans as ὑπακοὴν πίστεως "the obedience that comes from faith," κλητοί Ιησου "belonging to Jesus Christ," and πίστεως Ιησου Χριστου "having faith in Jesus Christ."[330] The good news is the one which brings transformation when adhered to as well as acts as the object of belief.[331]

---

329. Rom 1:3, 16.
330. Rom 1:5; 1:6; 3:22.
331. Rom 10:16–17.

One of the cross-space mappings between the elements of these two inputs is from the general property of agency in the GS which is filled in IS₁ by human agency (i.e. that of family members), which is mapped in IS₂ to that of the person of Jesus Christ who is the mediator of the new covenant.[332] The general property of goal is filled by old covenant privileges and responsibilities, which include land and progeny in IS₁ that are mapped in IS₂ by a redefined notion of covenant privileges and responsibilities, which include that of the forgiveness of sin. For the general property of recipients, the elements in the two input spaces are that of Jews in IS₁ who are mapped with people of all nations in IS₂. This is as a result of the concept ΙΟΥΔΑΙΟΣ "Jew" acquiring a new meaning within the [NEW COVENANT] frame through the process of derivation of new contextual implication to include all those who embrace this inward spiritual process. The slot of object projected from the GS is filled by the sexual organ in IS₁ which is mapped to that of the heart in IS₂. Since the heart is conceptualized as the seat of immorality, it becomes an object which needs cleansing and/or renewal. The timing of the ritual in IS₁ is that of the eighth day after birth while in IS₂ it is left open since one is recruited anytime they respond in faith and accepts the stipulations of the new covenant. The slot of instrument from the GS is filled by a sharp instrument in IS₁ that is mapped to that of the Holy Spirit in IS₂. The general property of means from the GS is filled by the law of circumcision in IS₁ which is the only way to access the privileges promised in the old covenant, while in IS₂ it is filled by the element faith which is only means by which men are put right with God.

3.3.3.2 The Source Language Blended Space

It is only a limited number of entities/elements from the input spaces that end up being projected to the BS as indicated in figure 6 below. Since the two input spaces are incompatible, the relevance theoretic framework directs and constrains how the respective salient elements are projected or fused as well as which inferences are brought to bear in the BS. The blend takes its organizing frame from IS₁, namely, that of the ritual of [ΠΕΡΙΤΟΜΗ] from the background framing of the [OLD COVENANT]. Human agency from IS₁ is eliminated as false in light of the new evidence that the underlying process

---

332. Rom 1:8; 3:24.

is spiritual, with the element Jesus Christ in IS₂ being strengthened and projected into the blend as background framings from OT prophesies are brought to bear though the process of completion. From the background framing, Jesus fulfills the two requirements of the promised Messiah, that of being a descendant of David fulfilling the requirement of his royal origin, and at the same time that of being the son of God, roles that were essential for the anticipated messianic liberation.[333] The concept ΙΗΣΟΥ ΧΡΙΣΤΟΥ "Jesus Christ" thus activates the background knowledge of his role as the mediator of the new covenant which he established through his substitutionary atoning death on Calvary.[334]

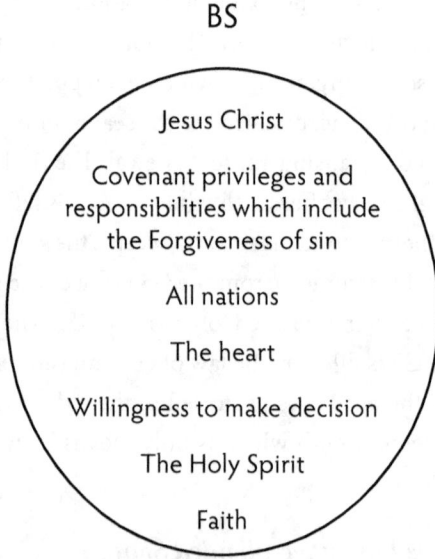

Figure 6: The source language blended space

There is another kind of HUMAN AGENCY* that emerges in the blend through the derivation of new contextual implications which has to do with the concept ΔΟΥΛΟΣ "slave/servant" referring to a person who is called to partner with God in preaching the good news.[335] This concept has undergone

---

333. Byrne, *Romans*, 39; cf. Rom 1:3–4.
334. Robinson, *Studies in Romans*, 7; cf. Rom 3:24.
335. Moo, *Epistle to the Romans*, 41; cf. Rom 1:1.

the lexical process of narrowing to mean a servant of the gospel, a description that seems to have been derived from the OT through the process of completion, since prophets are referred to as "servants of God" and given new application within the NT.[336] This concept, through the process of elaboration by derivation of new contextual implications, evokes the feeling of humility and suppresses that of pride/boasting, with the latter being associated with the teachers of the law.[337]

The goal that is projected to the blend, through the process of composition by derivation of new contextual implications, is that of accessing the covenant blessings and privileges as well as that of the forgiveness of sins. The existing assumption from IS_1 is strengthened so as to allow the beneficiaries to partake the covenant blessings and privileges. The concept COVENANT* has undergone lexical modification in the blend by both restricting and broadening its category. It is narrowed to exclude benefits such as "physical land" for this is a spiritual process and commonsense dictates that all nations cannot physically fit into the small country called Israel. It also excludes the element "law" by eliminating it as a false assumption in light of the new evidence that the coming of Jesus Christ made unnecessary the continuation of the Jewish law, and as Witherington III points out

> Paul believes that no longer being under the Law does not mean no longer being required to behave in a righteous manner. On the other end of the spectrum, it is not true that Paul is simply talking about badges or marks of righteousness such as Sabbath-keeping and circumcision when he says that Christ is the end or termination of the Law. Something more profound is going on . . . in Paul's writings *telos* seems always to include the notion of termination . . . righteousness for those who believe is available now through *another* means – not through the Law but through faith . . . Righteousness is not attained nor maintained by means of the Law but by another means. Christ has put an end to the Law as a way of pursuing righteousness.[338]

---

336. cf. Josh 1:1; Jude 2:8; 2 Sam 3:18; Neh 1:6; Job 1:8; Amos 3:7.
337. Rom 1:1; 2:17–20; 3:27; 4:2.
338. Witherington III, *Paul's Letter to the Romans*, 260–261.

The concept of COVENANT* has also undergone broadening to include additional elements such as that of the forgiveness of sins.[339] Paul, quoting from Isaiah 27:9, interprets the covenant in light of the forgiveness of sins which is "integral to the fulfillment of God's covenant with Israel."[340] The process of completion in the blend is driven by the strengthening of existing assumptions since forgiveness of sins had already been previously prophesied.[341] Paul argues that both Jews and Gentiles stand guilty before God's judgment and that they will receive the same condemnation for their sins. In order to access the blessings of God, one needs to confess his sins and submit to the righteousness that comes from God. This righteousness is imputed by God's sovereign grace to the sinner on the basis of the substitutionary atoning death of Christ.[342]

The element "all nations" is projected into the blend as beneficiaries through the process of elimination of the existing assumption that only Jews are to benefit in the RS of the [NEW COVENANT] frame. The Greek concept ΕΘΝΟΣ in IS_2 can be understood in its narrower sense as a reference term to the "Gentiles" or the "heathen." This understanding allows for the process of composition to take place in the blend with elements "Jews" and "nations" being projected as single elements into the blend. This also allows for the vital relation of an event structure for Paul argues for the historical order of salvation with the Jews who had been given the first opportunity having another opportunity in the coming of the Messiah at the end of time following the "grafting" of Gentiles.[343] Again from the background framing through the process of completion, we find that other nations are already included in the promised covenant resulting in the strengthening of the existing assumption.[344] The coming together of the nations as one can also be explained as resulting from the process of compression in the blend. This is as a result of the independent elements from the inputs (i.e. "Jewish" and "other nations") being projected separately as beneficiaries which gives an equal footing to *all* as far as the gospel is concerned.[345] As Morris further points out

---

339. Rom 11:27.
340. Moo, *Epistle to the Romans*, 729.
341. cf. Ps 19:4, Isa 59:20, 21; 27:9; Jer 31:33, 34; Hos 2:23.
342. Hendriksen, *Romans*, 62–63.
343. Hendriksen, 61; cf. Rom 1:16; 9–11.
344. cf. Ps 19:4; Isa 59:20, 21; 27:9; Jer 31:33, 34; Hos 2:23.
345. Moo, *Epistle to the Romans*, 659.

> The scope of salvation is universal . . . The gospel is for all and knows no limitation by race. In the matter of salvation God puts no difference between one nation and another. Paul assigns a certain priority to the Jew but immediately balances it with his reference to the Greek . . . there is not one gospel for the Jews and another for the Gentiles. All who are saved are saved by the one gospel and are brothers and sisters in Christ.[346]

The heart is the object of this renewal that is projected to the blend on the basis that this process is spiritual and hence what counts is the inward process which God esteems of greater significance.[347] It is projected by the fact that it is naturally the first interpretation that is arrived at in the context of a spiritual process and thus, unlike the sexual organ, it is the one requiring the least processing effort. The concept ΚΑΡΔΙΑ in the blend has also undergone the process of lexical adjustment as the seat where all kinds of vices reside, vices that are recorded in detail in Romans 1:8–3:20, strengthening the assumption that it is the object of conversion. The process of conversion is open for all those who make the decision to follow Christ regardless of their age.[348] From the [OLD COVENANT] frame, a further inference can be drawn that since it is an eight-day-old child undergoing the physical ritual of circumcision, he is not in a position to personally consent or dissent to the ritual. This inference is hindered from making it to the blend given the fact that there exists the vital relation of intentionality within the [NEW COVENANT] frame hence only those who exercise their faith can undergo this spiritual process.[349] We also find the process of de-compression in that, unlike the old framing where the boy child undergoing the ritual represents the female counterpart, within the new frame, each individual is expected to make their own decision which results in either embracing or rejecting the new covenant.

The Holy Spirit is projected to the blend from IS_2 as the one who transforms the believer so as to conform to the image of God. The sharp object from IS_1 is eliminated on the basis that it is inconsistent with commonsense knowledge since the underlying process is spiritual. The concept ΠΝΕΥΜΑ

---

346. Morris, *Epistle to the Romans*, 68.
347. Morris, 143.
348. Morris, 68.
349. Rom 1:16, 17.

"spirit" in the blend has undergone the process of lexical adjustment and narrowed down to the spirit of God who is the divine being by whom men are transformed. The agency of the Spirit in the blend can also be arrived at through the process of completion with the strengthening of the existing background knowledge. We find instances in the OT where the agency of the Spirit is made salient as he is promised to be an integral part of the promised renewal which would result in the people having a "new heart."[350] Faith is the means of accessing this new covenantal blessing, for it is through faith with any attempt of achieving righteousness through observing the law (of Moses) being suppressed from being projected to the blend.[351] The cleansing or renewal process remains a matter of an individual's inward response through faith. Paul claims that the traditional role of περιτομὴ as a σημεῖον "sign" or a σφραγῖδα "seal" of the covenant, is primarily to seal the faith that Abraham already possessed.[352]

In the virtue or the imaginative world of the BS through the process of derivation of new contextual implications, those who are circumcised are referred to as uncircumcised, and vice versa. One of the inferences drawn in the blend is that the ritual of circumcision no longer determines ones spiritual response to the covenant.[353] It is only to those who do the will of God that circumcision can be said to be a true sign of the covenant with those who break the law, even though circumcised, being regarded as "uncircumcised." We also find the vital relation of compression in the blend in that the whole event of recruitment as a member of the new covenant is compressed to the making of a confession, for it is by the act of confessing that one is saved.[354] In the blend, we also find the vital relation of change in that a condemned sinner can now live a holy life reflecting the newly acquired status. In the blend, through the process of elaboration, we also find the integration of cause and effect with the new member who was recruited through the Holy Spirit continuing to experience his ministry.[355]

---

350. cf. Ezek 36:27.
351. Byrne, *Romans*, 124; Rom 3:21.
352. Rom 4:11.
353. Hendriksen, *Romans*, 107; cf. Rom 2:25.
354. Rom 10:9.
355. Plumer, *Commentary on Romans*, 196.

3.4 Meaning of the Metaphor Περιτομὴ Καρδίας

In the context of Romans 2, the additional inputs from the discourse and relevance spaces in the blending process point towards a more specific meaning of the metaphor περιτομὴ καρδίας. This meaning narrows to that of a cleansing or purging ritual, a meaning arrived at in the blend through the process of completion by derivation of contextual implications from already existing information, as the relevant background knowledge is brought to bear in the conceptual integration process. In building my argument, I will argue that the ritual of circumcision is perceived as fulfilling the role of a cleaning or purging ritual, a view mostly derived from the perspective of the LXX translators. I will first give a bit of historical background on the role of the LXX in the context of the first church since I will be claiming that the use of the LXX then informs the meaning of the metaphor περιτομὴ καρδίας in Romans 2:29.

At the dawn of the NT era, Greek and Aramaic had replaced Hebrew as everyday languages of communication of the people of Palestine. Greek was also the lingua franca among the diaspora Jews, and as an attempt to preserve their religious legacy, the Jews in Egypt translated the Bible into Greek at around 250 BC.[356] Since then, the LXX has undergone numerous subsequent re-translation and revision processes meaning that it should be viewed as a collection of many translations.[357] As Jobes and Silva point out

> there is really no such thing as *the* Septuagint . . . Because the Greek translation of the Hebrew Bible has such a long and complicated history, the name *Septuagint* is used to refer to several quite different things. In its most general sense, the term refers to any or all ancient Greek translations of the Hebrew Bible, just as one might now refer in general to the "English Bible," with no particular translation in mind. . . . Often, the term is also used to refer to a particular printed edition of the Greek text, whether that edition reproduces the text of a particular manuscript or prints a reconstructed text . . . one might understandably, though mistakenly, infer that the Greek translation found in a given ancient manuscript or modern edition is a homogeneous text produced in its entirety at one point

---

356. Marcos, *Septuagint in Context*, 19.
357. Marcos, xi.

in time. In fact, no such homogeneity exists in any collection of the Greek books of the Old Testament . . . The books of the Hebrew were originally translated independently into Greek by different translators over several centuries . . . In fact there was no one uniform Greek version of the entire Hebrew Bible – just individual scrolls that had been copied from other scrolls through the ages . . . The particular collection of Greek texts of the biblical books that comprise the earliest one-volume Bibles, such as Codex Sinaiticus and Codex Vaticanus, usually came to be by the historical happenstance of whatever texts were at hand, irrespective of their origin and character.[358]

The LXX is important since it was the Scriptures of the OT and therefore it is from the LXX that we find many of the OT citations in the NT being taken from.[359] As Jobes and Silva further point out

> The Septuagint, not the Hebrew Bible, was the primary theological and literary context within which the writers of the New Testament and most early Christians worked. This does not mean that the New Testament writers were ignorant of the Hebrew Bible or that they did not use it. But since the New Testament authors were writing in Greek, they would naturally quote, allude to, and otherwise use the Greek version of the Hebrew Bible.[360]

The renderings by the LXX translators of MT concepts reflects on how those concepts were understood in their context which includes the influence of theology at the time that the translators were translating this document.[361] As a result of this quoting, the LXX has far-reaching implications since it informed foundational Christian interpretation of given concepts in the NT. One such rendering is the deliberate choice to render the Hebrew verb מול "he circumcised" with the Greek verb περιεκάθαρεν "he cleansed/purged/purified," and not with the expected Greek cognates of the concept ΠΕΡΙΤΟΜΗ

---

358. Jobes and Silva, *Invitation to the Septuagint*, 30–31.
359. Dines, *Septuagint*, 142–143.
360. Jobes and Silva, *Invitation to the Septuagint*, 23.
361. Jobes and Silva, 22.

"circumcision" with this meaning bringing on board a different nuance to the meaning and purpose of the ritual of circumcision.[362] By the use of this rendering the LXX translators underline the conceptualization of this ritual as a spiritual process with the nuance of "getting-rid-of-something-unwanted," so to speak, as its salient factor with the change of morality as its salient goal. As Winter rightly points out

> A secondary and subsidiary meaning of circumcision is that it signifies an excision of impurity, a removal of the defilement of sin with which even infants are born. This sinful nature is transmitted from one generation to another by sexual intercourse and by the generation of each new life. Circumcision signifies the cleansing that we all need to fit us for the presence of the living God . . . This is an amazing concept and later we will see more clearly its relationship to baptism and the immersion of our whole body in water.[363]

Looking critically at such a rendering in Joshua 5:4 where the physical ritual is associated with the cleansing/purification process, the rendering of the Hebrew verb מול "he circumcised" with the Greek verb περιεκάθαρεν "he cleansed/purged/purified" could be attributed to the possibility of the translators using a different Hebrew *vorlage* behind the MT which was different from that of the OG. Among the eight times that the concept translated as "circumcision" or "uncircumcision" is used in the Greek text of Joshua 5:2–9, it is rendered using the Greek cognates of the concept ΠΕΡΙΤΟΜΗ (see appendix C for a detailed comparison between the MT and the LXX of Joshua 5:2–9). Since Joshua 5:4 is the only rendering in the Greek text of Joshua 5:2–9, it rules out the possibilities of stylistic variation as well as that of the use of euphemism. It is most likely that the OG translator deliberately chose to use another nuance of the meaning of this concept, to help the readers focus more on the role of circumcision as a "purifying" or "purging" ritual.

What exactly were the initiates being purged from? One of the places to look for an answer is in Joshua 5:9 which talks of "the reproach of Egypt" as that which the Lord removed from them. This reproach could be a reference to

---

362. Liddell and Scott, *Greek-English Lexicon*, 1375c; Muraoka, *Greek-English Lexicon*, 549a.

363. Winter, "Cutting and Washing," 73.

the shame of being slaves in Egypt which could have resulted in the Israelites being disgraced by other nations.[364] Hamlin agrees with this view and states that this ritual should be understood as having restored the Israelites freedom and dignity.[365] Another suggestion that has been given is that this reproach refers to the uncircumcised state of the Israelites.[366] I find this view reasonable, since according to Genesis 34:14, the state of uncircumcision is a reproach which was supposed to be removed by performing a "cultic ritual in obedience to Yahweh."[367] The same association of the reproach with uncircumcision is given by Neusner and Green, who in quoting M. Nedarim 3:11, points out that the Rabbis described "the foreskin as a disgusting imperfection, the removal of which renders the body perfect."[368] We also find the existence of a ritual script as an accompaniment to the physical operation of circumcision from the second to the fourth centuries AD, which contained five liturgical parts with the first two being prayers of sanctification.[369] This must have been as a result of the understanding of the ritual of circumcision as having a cleansing role as well. Another proof of the association of the concepts ΠΕΡΙΤΟΜΗ and ΚΑΘΑΡΟΣ is found in Isaiah 52:1 where the uncircumcised are said never to again enter the holy city of Jerusalem with uncircumcised males conceptualized as being unclean needing to be purified through the ritual of circumcision.[370]

As far as extra-biblical sources are concerned, they are divided between the MT and the OG renderings. Even though the fragments of 4QJosh[a] seem to represent an independent Hebrew tradition from that of the MT, for this specific rendering in Joshua 5:4, it follows the MT tradition.[371] Other early translations such as the Syriac, the Targum, and the Vulgate also follow the MT tradition.[372] There is a notable difference which is distinctive of the

---

364. cf. Zeph 2:8–9; Ezek 36:15.
365. Hamlin, *Inheriting the Land*, 34.
366. van der Meer, *Formation and Reformulation*, 353.
367. Butler, *Joshua*, 59.
368. Neusner and Green, *Dictionary of Judaism*, 121.
369. Hoffman, "Circumcision," 91.
370. van der Meer, *Formation and Reformulation*, 347.
371. De Troyer, *Rewriting the Sacred Text*, 35; Woudstra, *Book of Joshua*, 40; van der Meer, *Formation and Reformulation*, 94, 96.
372. Soggin, *Joshua*, 68.

Vulgate in that it keeps an ambiguity as far as the reference "they" in 5:6 is concerned (see appendix D). This ambiguity could open the possibility of the interpretation that the generation that was born in the desert was consumed and therefore it was a third generation that Joshua circumcised. In his discussion of this passage, Auld points out that Josephus does not mention the ritual of circumcision but only discusses the Passover ritual in verses 10–12, an oversight which is attributed to the possibility that he was embarrassed to admit before his Roman, non-Semitic readership that the Israelites failed to keep the covenant of circumcision.[373] The act of circumcision as fulfilling the role of a cleansing ritual is also found in the Codex Vaticanus (B), the oldest Greek manuscript of Joshua dated in the fourth century AD, which uses the same concept as that used by the OG translator.[374] Philo in his writing, *The Special Laws* I.1–11, is also said to have indicated that circumcision is "an act of purification that sanctifies the whole body as befits the consecrated order."[375]

The choice by the OG translator to render Joshua 5:4 as an act of purification could also have resulted from an influence from the Greek translation of the Pentateuch, for as Olofsson points out

> One major contribution to the study of the Septuagint is the theory that the Pentateuch, the first translated part of the LXX, has served as a sort of a text-book for the rest of the translators. It is only natural that the Greek Pentateuch should influence the translation of the subsequent books, because this translation not only preceded that of the other books; the Pentateuch is also without doubt the most important part of the Holy Writ in Jewish tradition.[376]

There are three potential LXX Pentateuch passages that could have influenced the choice by the Joshua OG translator(s). In LXX Deuteronomy 18:10, we find the use of the Greek verb περιεκάθαρεν "he purged/purified." The context of this passage is that of a parent sacrificing their child to the god Molech through fire, a practice which was used as a means of turning away the wrath

---

373. Auld, *Joshua*, 124.
374. Auld, 12.
375. van der Meer, *Formation and Reformulation*, 349.
376. Olofsson, *LXX Version*, 26.

of the divinity or as part of the cult of the dead.³⁷⁷ The MT concept מַעֲבִיר "one who makes to pass [through fire]" is rendered in the LXX as περικαθαίρων "one who purifies or purges [their child with fire]." The purification process is conducted by means of fire which is "calculated to absorb defilement or contagion" and has the metaphorical meaning of "purifying completely."³⁷⁸ The use of the concept ΚΑΘΑΡΟΣ in this passage is quite close to that of Joshua 5:4 since the ritual of circumcision is portrayed also as a means of purification, with reproach being the object to be removed. The main difference is that in the context of Deuteronomy 18:10 the divine being is supposed to grant favor after receiving the sacrifice, while in Joshua 5:4 the divine being is the agent making the process possible.

Another passage where the concept ΚΑΘΑΡΟΣ is used is in the LXX of Deuteronomy 30:6, with the context of this passage being that of the restoration of the people of Israel. The MT phrase דְּבָבְל־תָּא דִּיהֵלָא הֲוִהי לְמוֹ "and Yahweh your God will circumcise your heart" is translated in the LXX as καὶ περικαθαριεῖ κύριος τὴν καρδίαν σου "and the Lord will purge/purify your heart." The idea behind the LXX rendering has to do with the conceptualization of God as the only agent who is able to purge people's hearts by removing whatever prevents them from following his teachings.³⁷⁹ According to this passage, some of the vices that need to be purged include rebellion and iniquities. The same metaphor is used, though with a different object in LXX of Deuteronomy 10:16, where the verb περιτεμεῖσθε "you circumcise" has τὴν σκληροκαρδίαν "stubbornness" as its direct object. These two different renderings of the same metaphor in Deuteronomy 30:6 and 10:16 acts as a hint that the LXX Pentateuch translators used the two concepts ΠΕΡΙΤΟΜΗ and ΚΑΘΑΠΟΣ interchangeably. Both of these renderings call for moral uprightness and obedience to the terms of the covenant by getting rid of everything that hinders commitment to God. The individual themself is called upon to take the necessary steps towards fearing, loving, serving God, and walking in his ways.³⁸⁰ These renderings point out to the fact that

---

377. Chingota, "Leviticus," 1601; Nelson, *Deuteronomy*, 233.

378. Lampe, *Patristic Greek Lexicon*, 1066a; Liddell and Scott, *Greek-English Lexicon*, 1375c; Muraoka, *Greek-English Lexicon*, 549a.

379. Christensen, *Deuteronomy 21:10–34:12*, 739.

380. cf. Deut 10:12–13.

the physical ritual of circumcision is insufficient to put an individual in a right relationship with God.

Another LXX Pentateuch passage that has rendered the concept ΠΕΡΙΤΟΜΗ as a cleansing process is Leviticus 19:23. Here the translators have used the verb περικαθαριεῖτε "purge away" with the object τὴν ἀκαθαρσίαν αὐτοῦ "its uncleanness." The context of this passage has to do with how the Israelites were to behave when they entered the promised landPromised Land. For the first three years, they were expected to regard the yields from the fruit trees as unclean and therefore avoid eating them. The MT uses the phrase וַעֲרַלְתֶּם "and you will regard its [fruit as] foreskin [as] uncircumcised." This means that they were supposed to consider the fruit as something to be removed. The MT does not state this practical act as something the Israelites were expected to be involved in but the Pentateuch LXX OG translators gave further instructions as to how the Israelites were supposed to go about in dealing with such fruits. They were supposed to "purge" or remove such uncleanness by plucking off the fruits as a practical expression of holiness.[381] Since the context of this passage is that of pruning fruit trees, the literal rendering of the Hebrew verb מול with the cognates of the concept ΠΕΡΙΤΟΜΗ would not have been a good choice.[382] Again just as in Joshua 5:4, the context of this passage has to do with the act of purging or removing uncleanness, thus the rendering by the OG translators. By the use of the cognates of the concept ΚΑΘΑΡΟΣ, the OG translator again underlines the conceptualization of the ritual of circumcision as being first and foremost a spiritual process with cultic purity as its salient factor.

In these passages, we find the ritual of ΠΕΡΙΤΟΜΗ being associated with objects such as guilt and sin. The LXX of Deuteronomy 30:6 discussed above, which is the most probable Scripture that Paul quoted the metaphor in Romans 2:29 from, has the context of the restoration of the people of Israel.[383] We find here the process of completion in the blend taking place since the idea behind the Pentateuch LXX rendering is that peoples' hearts need to be purged or cleansed by removing whatever prevents them from following God's teachings, with the same teaching being underlined elsewhere

---

381. Milgrom, *Leviticus 17–22*, 1679.
382. van der Meer, *Formation and Reformulation*, 346.
383. Noh, *Metarepresentation*, 18.

in the OT.[384] We find the continuation of this teaching also in the context of the [NEW COVENANT] frame. Jesus himself taught that it is not that which comes from outside which defiles a person but that which comes from the inside.[385] We also find a call for the purity of heart as a requirement to enter God's presence.[386] Just as in the [OLD COVENANT] frame, it is God who makes possible this spiritual purity in the hearts of men, be they Jews or Gentiles, as long as they put their faith in him.[387]

Since, as we have established above that NT writers borrowed heavily from the Greek version of the OT, it is very likely that Paul must have borrowed this sense as well in quoting this conventional metaphor since the LXX was his Bible, and as Stanley further points out

> All modern investigators are agreed in viewing the Greek Septuagint as a primary Vorlage for Paul's citations from the Jewish Scriptures. The reasons for this consensus are not far to seek. Of the roughly eighty-three biblical texts adduced by Paul in his undisputed quotations, thirty-four come from places where the Septuagint is closely allied with the Masoretic text. These texts offer no evidence one way or the other as to the nature of Paul's Vorlage. Of the remaining forty-nine texts, however, fully forty-four follow the Septuagint at points where it diverges from the Masoretic text. Included here are passages that agree verbatim with the Septuagint as well as verses that show signs of significant editorial activity. The results are the same across every book of Scripture, and extend to the questionably Pauline materials as well. Only five Pauline quotations show a measure of agreement with the Masoretic text over against the Septuagint tradition, but even these five are accompanied by deviations from the Masoretic tradition that makes direct resort to the Hebrew unlikely. Support is growing for the view that

---

384. cf. Jer 33:8; Ezek 39:24; cf. Ps 24:3–10; 51.
385. Matt 15:11, 16–39; Mark 7:15, 18, 20, 21–23.
386. Matt 5:8.
387. Acts 15:9; Rom 4.

Paul relied on a Hebraizing revision of the Old Greek, or even a different translation altogether, in these cases.[388]

The use of the metaphor περιτομὴ καρδίας in Romans 2:29 is an echo from its use in the OT, especially Deuteronomy 30:6, with the use of this echo pointing out to how his thoughts must have been permeated by the Greek Scriptures.[389] The context of the metaphor περιτομὴ καρδίας in Romans 2:29, just as that of Deuteronomy 30:6, has to do with the restoration of the people of Israel by cleansing or purging or cleansing or removing the uncleanness of their hearts. Through the process of completion in the blend, we find Paul drawing from the background knowledge of the use of the ritual of ΠΕΡΙΤΟΜΗ from the LXX translators' perspective which narrows its meaning to that of a cleansing or purging ritual which all people need to undergo so as to be cleansed of their sins. This interpretation is relevance driven since in the DS of Romans 2 we find the derivation of contextual effects with earlier processing activities being recalled leading to the extension of context "by 'going back in time' and adding to the assumptions used or derived in previous deductive processes."[390] This leads to the derivation of the assumption of the cleansing ritual through which people are cleansed of their sins.

3.5 Summary

In this chapter, I have argued for a modified frame that Paul was leading his audience to construct in their minds. I have mentioned the elements that are activated in the traditional frame as well as those that have been modified or replaced altogether by new ones in the modified frame. Using the complementary approach between CIT and RT, I have argued that the lexical adjusted meaning of the metaphor περιτομὴ καρδίας in the context of Romans chapter two has to do with that of a cleansing or purification ritual. The additional input spaces, namely, the discourse and relevance spaces in the integration process, have been central in making my argument since they play a crucial role in constraining the drawing of author intended inferences that elicit the right responses.

---

388. Stanley, *Paul and the Language of Scripture*, 67.
389. Hays, *Echoes of Scripture*, 157–158.
390. Sperber and Wilson, *Relevance, Communication and Cognition*, 140.

CHAPTER 4

The Conceptualization of
*IRUA**, *HAKIRI* and *NGORO*

4.1 Introduction

In this chapter I will analyze the Kikuyu conceptualization of IRUA* "[male] circumcision" and those of HAKIRI "mind" and NGORO "heart." I will use the suggested complementary approach between CIT and RT to highlight the underlying conceptual structures and background frames that are evoked and show how these concepts are associated in given metaphorical relationships. The concept IRUA has in the recent years undergone lexical adjustment through the processes of narrowing and is consequently more restricted to refer to only [IRUA] *rĩa arũme* "male circumcision," thus the use of the ad hoc concept [IRUA*]. This distinction is made because in its basic form the concept IRUA* refers to both [IRUA] *rĩa arũme* as well as [IRUA] *rĩa irĩgũ* "clitoridectomy," also referred to as female genital mutilation [FGM] by those who are vigorously campaigning against it. There are a number of reasons why the concept [IRUA] *rĩa irĩgũ* is not the focus of this research. The first one is because this rite of passage has almost disappeared, and the few families who practice it do it underground, since it has become a crime punishable under the Kenyan law. The second reason is because in the Jewish culture, which is the source culture that the concept ΠΕΡΙΤΟΜΗ is derived from, the ritual of clitoridectomy is not evoked since this practice was not practiced among women in the Bible (Gross, "Circumcision in the New Testament", 422). The third reason is that the concept [IRUA] *rĩa irĩgũ* evokes anti-Christian and barbaric feelings since Christian missionaries and other Westerners who were against it referred to those practicing it as heathens and mutilators of the woman's body (see Murray, "Kikuyu Female Circumcision"; Gachiri, *Female Circumcision*). This attitude, which has been picked up by a majority of churches today, goes back to the conflict between the missionaries and Africans back to the 1920s and 1930s (Brown, *Christian Response to Change*, 10). The Africans believed that the banning of the [IRUA] *rĩa irĩgũ* had nothing to do with Christianity but that it was an attempt by the missionaries to suppress the African traditions and practices. The disagreement led to the establishment of churches and schools by the Africans, examples being the African Independent Pentecostal Churches of Africa (AIPCA) and the African Christian Churches and Schools (ACC&S), institutions that are still thriving among the Kikuyu today. The controversy over [IRUA] *rĩa irĩgũ* also caused a division between the Kikuyu who embraced Christianity and the Mau Mau, a rebel group that fought for the independence of Kenya. As a result, the *Mau Mau* viewed those who refused to have their girls undergo [IRUA] *rĩa irĩgũ* as enemies of independence and as a result they persecuted such people. The term Kikuyu is used in this study as a reference to both the ethnic people group who go by this name as well as to the language that they speak. According to Grimes, the language has five major dialects including the Southern dialect, which is spoken in the former administrative districts of Kiambu and Maragwa, the Mathira dialect, which is spoken in the former administrative district of Karatina, the Ndia dialect, which is spoken in the former administrative district of South Kirinyaga, the Gichugu dialect, which is spoken in the former administrative district of Northern Kirinyaga, and the Northern Kikuyu dialect, which is spoken in the former administrative district of Nyeri as well as the northern parts of Murang'a.[1] The language is classified as a Bantu language belonging to the Thagicu group of North-East in the interior branch of the Bantu family.[2]

The geographical location of this people group is in the central part of Kenya, which extends from Mount Kenya in the North towards Nairobi in the South and from the Aberdare mountains in the West to Ukambani in the

---

1. Grimes, *Ethnologue*, 138.
2. Grimes, 138; Moseley and Asher, *Atlas of the World's Languages*.

East.³ From this traditional location, the Kikuyu have scattered everywhere in Kenya, especially in the neighboring county of Nairobi, as well as in the former province of the Rift valley, which can be attributed to their aggression in doing business. The speakers of the language are estimated to be around five million, 95 percent of their children are said to be in school, and also to have had Bible portions from 1961.⁴ My research is concentrated on the now administrative counties of Kiambu, Murang'a and Nyeri, which are known to be the traditional strongholds where Kikuyu is spoken. The following section analyzes the main frame elements and any other related sub-events embedded in the IRUA* conceptual substrate that are activated, and where need be, related sub-events will be discussed as if they were isolatable from the main event, though this is not the actual reality.

4.2 Conceptualization of IRUA*

In this section, general information based on the field research concerning the meaning of the concept IRUA* is given. These include its background framing as well its main frame elements that are activated including its deontic status and ethical values. Attention is also drawn to how this concept has undergone the process of frame shifting in recent years. These changes, as will be pointed out, have resulted with some of the related sub-events which are embedded in the conceptual substrate been reduced or abolished altogether, with some elements and related practices being modified in the process.

4.2.1 The Meaning of IRUA*

The concept IRUA* refers to the process, both mental and physical, that boys undergo to become *arũme* "grown-up men." There are three stages that form part of the conceptual network which are activated when the concept IRUA* is evoked. The first one is that of the preliminary preparations before the day when the initiate's *gĩkonde* "foreskin" is removed, the second stage has to do with the events of the actual day when the "cutting" is done, and the third stage, which lasts for two to three weeks, mostly focuses on the seclusion period. In the past, it was mandatory for initiates to undergo all these three

---

3. Fedders and Salvadori, *Peoples and Cultures of Kenya*, 117.
4. Grimes, *Ethnologue*, 138.

stages of [IRUA*] before one was considered to be fully initiated.⁵ Nowadays these stages have been compressed to two, the actual day of performing "the cut" and the seclusion period. The purpose of the elaborate events that accompany the ritual of [IRUA*] is to ascertain that the person undergoing [IRUA*] is well equipped in all areas of life so as to be a productive community member.

Though there have been some compressions of scaling down resulting in some elements dropping out, there are few key moments of the ritual that are left intact meaning that the important aspects of this ritual still remain. The concept IRUA* evokes four main associated meanings that form its conceptual network. The first one has to do with the transition from the stage of participating in *waana* "childish behavior" or *ūhĩĩ* "behavior of one who is uncircumcised" to that of becoming *mũndũ mũgima* "an adult."⁶ This meaning involves scaling as far as the vital relation of change and cause-effect is concerned, for as Fauconnier and Turner point out, "rituals integrate cause and effect, so that any aspect of the performance can be experienced as simultaneously a cause and its effect in both the blend and the future life."⁷ This cause and effect relationship is reflected in the main synonym of the verb form *kũrua* "to circumcise" which is *kũgimara* "to become an adult member of the community," with the ritual being the cause and becoming an adult member the effect. Examples 16 and 17 below illustrate these two words being used interchangeably.

(16) Kĩhĩĩ   kĩrĩa   gĩkũrũ   kĩa
     boy.not.undergone [IRUA*] that.which is.eldest   of
     Njaũ   wa   Nyamang'u   nĩkĩraruire
     Njaũ   of   Nyamang'u   has.under-
                                                gone [IRUA*]

"The eldest son belonging of Njaũ son of Nyamang'u has undergone [IRUA*]."

(17) Kĩhĩĩ   kĩrĩa   gĩkũrũ   kĩa
     boy.not.undergone.[IRUA*] that.which is.eldest   of

---

5. Muriuki, *History of the Kikuyu 1500–1900*, 118–119.
6. Kanogo, *Squatters and Roots*, 77.
7. Fauconnier and Turner, *Way We Think*, 85.

Njaũ	*wa*	*Nyamang'u*	*nĩkĩragimarire*
Njaũ	of	Nyamang'u	has.become. adult

"The eldest son belonging to Njaũ son of Nyamang'u has become an adult."

This rite of passage also fulfills what can be referred to as a purging function since the ritual is the means by which the initiate is expected to get rid of behaviors associated with *ihĩĩ* "uncircumcised boys," that include being irresponsible, naughty, mischievous, as well as playing childish games. From then on, one is expected to take on the behavior of an adult since he has become an adult member of the society.[8]

The act of the cutting of the foreskin symbolizes the act of purging or removing any behavior associated with the *ihĩĩ*. The association of childish behavior with the foreskin is demonstrated in the advice that is normally given to the initiates to leave behind childish behavior just as their foreskins were detached from their bodies and thrown away. In the past, there was an accompanying symbolic ceremony to show that one has left *ũhĩĩ* called *kũruta ũrimũ* "to remove foolishness." This ceremony was performed on the second day of the seclusion period when necklaces were removed from the boys to symbolize the removal of foolishness associated with *ihĩĩ*.[9] The other object that an initiate is purged from is fear, with the initiate automatically acquiring the title *mũndũ mũrũme* "a man of courage."

The second associated meaning which is activated by the concept IRUA* is that of the time when *irui* "initiates" are hardened to become *arũme* "men of courage," meaning that the concept IRUA* activates the sub-concept *ũcamba* "courage." The key moments in this hardening process are when the cut is performed as well as during the seclusion period when the initiates are expected to nurture their courage as well as prove that they have what it takes to become *mũndũ mũrũme* "a man of courage." One of the reasons is that in the past, those who underwent this rite of passage were scheduled to become *njamba cia ita* "warriors" with their main role being that of protecting the community from outside raids. Unlike today, the initiates were expected to

---

8. Kanogo, *Squatters and Roots*, 77.
9. Leakey, *Southern Kikuyu before 1903*, 632.

bear the painful process associated with [IRUA*] since they were not anesthetized and therefore needed to be courageous during the operation. Moreover, since at that time [IRUA*] was a public ceremony, there was much at stake, as those who conducted themselves courageously ended up being applauded, while those who showed signs of fear were labeled as cowards and ended up being teased for the rest of their lives.[10] There are a number of proverbs that are associated with [IRUA*] which underline the necessity of the virtue of *ūcamba* as examples 18 to 20 below illustrate.

(18) *Irī   gwīthamba iticokaga*
     After.they ([IRUA*].candidates) bath   they.do.not.go.back
     guota   mwaki
     to.warm.themselves   with.fire
     "After the candidates for [IRUA*] take a bath they were not expected to go back and warm themselves (in their father's home)."

(19) *Kūrua   nī   kūhīa*
     to.go.through.[IRUA*] is   (like) to.be.burnt
     "Going through [IRUA*] is a few minutes pain (therefore one should bear it)."

(20) *Irī   gwīthamba iticokagia   nguo.*
     When ([IRUA*].candidates) bath   they.do.not.put.back clothes
     "Once the candidates of [IRUA*] has washed themselves they do not put their clothes back."[11]

The third meaning associated with the concept IRUA*, which was also highlighted as a key moment in the process of [IRUA*], is that of *mambura* "a time of celebration and feasting." In the past, there was a form of singing which was held the night before the circumcision day called *marara-nja*, which is a compound word meaning "sleeping-outside." The main participants

---

10. Gatheru, *Child of Two Worlds*, 59; Murray, "Kikuyu Female Circumcision," 22–23; Mugo, *Kikuyu People*, 19.

11. In the former generation *irui* used to wear *cuka* "a cloth sheet" around themselves throughout the seclusion period until the time when their wounds would heal. They abandoned the clothes that they came with to be circumcised as a sign of their abandonment of behaviors associated with the *waana* "childishness" or *ūhīī* 'behavior of the "uncircumcised."

in this celebration were women who celebrated in the homestead of the potential candidate by singing erotic songs throughout the night, a practice which has died over time mostly due to the influence of Christianity. The homestead where an initiate is recuperating is expected to have lots of food as close relatives and friends frequent the home to celebrate during the time that the initiate is recuperating. The most common food during this time is *njũgũ* "cow peas," which are used figuratively to invite other people for such celebrations as the following example demonstrates.

(21) *Nĩndagwĩta   ũke   ũrĩe   njũgũ.*
     I.have.you(sg).invited you.to.come to.eat cowpeas
     "I invite you to come and celebrate with me [because my son has undergone[IRUA*].]"

The fourth meaning associated with the concept [IRUA*] is that it was a time of teaching, without which [IRUA*] loses its meaning. A highlight of this teaching process is during the seclusion period when the teaching referred to as *uumithio* is offered. The content of this teaching is meant to equip an initiate with life skills so as to enable him to live a respectable life, both on an individual and communal level. Such education includes tips on how to conduct oneself before elders, what to do and not to do when faced with various problems, and issues relating to sexuality, to mention a few.[12] Most of the content of *uumithio* has to do with issues of sexuality since parents tend to shy away from uttering words considered to be embarrassing before their children. The common teaching phrase used in *uumithio* is the formula which can be translated as "since you have left the stage of *ũhĩĩ* and now you are a *mũndũ mũgima*, you should not do . . . but do . . ." The mind is generally conceptualized as an object that needs to be continually educated and equipped thus undergoing [IRUA*] is not an end in itself as pointed out in the sayings in examples 22 and 23 point out.

(22) *Kũruithio   nĩ   kũhingũrĩrwo mũrango wa kũgimara*
     to.be.circumcised is   to.be.opened door   of maturing
     hakiri   kana kũheo   kĩrĩra.
     mind   or   to.be.given   traditional teachings

---

12. Kenyatta, *Facing Mount Kenya*, 141.

"To be circumcised is like opening the door to become mature or for one to be given more traditional teachings."

(23) Kūgimara   mwĩrĩ   gũkũhingũragĩra mũrango wa
     to.be.circumcised in.body   opens.for.one   door   of
     kũgimara   hakiri.
     maturing   mind.

"To be physically circumcised opens the door for one to mature in the mind."

Therefore, the concept IRUA* traditionally evokes four main associated meanings, which form the background knowledge that constitutes the conceptual network associated with this concept. The first meaning has to do with the entire process, which marks the transition from the stage of childhood to that of adulthood, the second one with the hardening of initiates to become *arũme* "men of courage," the third as reference to a time of celebration and feasting, and the fourth as a time of teaching the initiates. The next sections underscore the main frame elements that are activated when the concept IRUA* is evoked.

4.2.2 Frame Elements

This sub-section discusses elements as well as links that are activated when the concept IRUA* is evoked. These include participants and their associated roles, the attendant circumstances which include settings of time and place, as well as some of the main instruments that are used.

4.2.2.1 KĨHĨĨ

The concept KĨHĨĨ "an uncircumcised boy" is activated as the beneficiary of this rite of passage. This concept activated other associated sub-concepts such as ŨMARAMARI which means being childish, naughty and mischievous. Some of the childish games associated with this concept include *gũtwara mũbara* "playing with a hoop made of strong bent stick," *kũhũra mbira* "spinning wooden pegs and whipping them with a lash called *kĩgũtha*," *kũhũra nyororoka* "skidding in clay mud using trunks from banana stems," and hunting small animals, such as birds, rats, and squirrels, among other activities. Such boyish activities are also referred to as *mũũmbũro wa ihĩĩ* "the games of uncircumcised boys." In the past, the potential candidates referred to as *ngurū*, were encouraged to indulge in such behavior a few months before the actual date of circumcision as a means of shedding off their boyish nuances before entering manhood.[13] The society could tolerate such notoriety looking forward to the time when the *ihīī* (plural for *kīhīī*) would undergo [IRUA*], after which they were expected not to engage in such behavior anymore. It is believed that if a *kīhīī* does not actively participate in the stage of *waana* or *ūhīī*, there is a likelihood of such behavior re-surfacing long after he has undergone [IRUA*].

As mentioned above, the concept KĪHĪĪ is associated with mischief and bad behavior. It is common to hear members of the society blaming *ihīī* for most of the mischievous behavior in the society, in spite of the fact that they might have not witnessed them doing such. A good example is in the context of a village gathering that has a mixture of people of all ages. One might hear a person make the following complaint.

(24) *Aaai!   Hena   kīhīī   gīathuria!*
     Aaai!   There.is   uncircumcised.boy   he.spoiled.air
     "Aaai! An uncircumcised boy has spoiled the air."

A *kīhīī* is also thought of as one who is undependable as compared to those who have undergone [IRUA*] as the following proverb indicates.

(25) *Mūici   na   kīhīī   atigaga   kīeha*
     Thief   with   uncircumcised.boy.   stops   to.worry
     kīarua.
     when.he.goes.through.[IRUA*].
     "One who steals with an uncircumcised boy stops living in fear when the boy undergoes circumcision."

As a result of the negative connotations associated with the sub-concepts WAANA or ŪHĪĪ, the uncircumcised boys look forward to the day when they would undergo [IRUA*] and have this stage behind them. It was expected of every *kīhīī* to undergo [IRUA*] with no exception, and if one does not do so voluntarily, he might have to be forced to do so. If by any chance one is

---

13. Wambūgū, Ngarariga, and Kariūki, *The Agīkūyū*, 87–88.

discovered later in life not to have undergone [IRUA*], his extended family would disown him, with such a person being excluded from participating in any of the clan and community activities or events. As Wambũgũ, Ngarariga, and Kariũki point out "to be uncircumcised was to be the general laughing stock, a butt for derision and contempt; such a person had either to be a mere child and treated as such, or he was abnormal."[14]

4.2.2.2 KĪRUI

The concept KĪRUI refers to one who is in the process of recuperating from his wound and also undergoing the traditional teaching associated with [IRUA*], since this rite of passage is first and foremost a teaching ritual. One of the sub-concepts activated when the concept KĪRUI is evoked is that of ITĪĪRI, which refers to the place where circumcision used to take place before the introduction of health centers. This place was strategically located near a river so that initiates could dip themselves in its waters early in the morning in order to make their bodies numb. Another sub-concept that is activated by the concept KĪRUI is that of CUKA "sheet," which was tied around the initiate immediately after "the cut" was performed. It became his only clothing throughout the recuperation period. It was tied with the knot on the right shoulder so that the KĪRUI can use the left hand to make sure that the CUKA does not touch the wound. Nowadays, the initiates do not use a CUKA, but they normally make a hole through one of the pockets in their shorts and use one hand to protect the wound from coming in contact with the cloth surface.

Another concept that is activated when that of KĪRUI is evoked is that of MŨTHONGE or KĪGANDA, which refers to a hut which the initiates recuperate in. In the past, this was a temporary hut that was made using branches and banana leaves, and could host often twelve or more initiates. This is where the initiates were instructed on how to handle social and family life issues by members of the senior age-groups. After the initiates recuperated from their wounds, they were to leave the hut, not by the door they entered by, but through the back, by pulling down the wall. This was done to symbolize the fact that they were not the same way they were when they first entered the hut. No one was allowed to return to the hut even if he happened to have left behind a valuable possession, after which the hut was burned down.

---

14. Wambũgũ, Ngarariga, and Kariũki, 85.

Nowadays when the concept MŨTHONGE is evoked, it is normally referred to as ITHŨNŨ and is more of a semi-permanent structure which the initiate continues to live in, since a circumcised man is not supposed to sleep in his mother's hut.

4.2.2.3 KIUMĨRI

Another concept activated by the concept IRUA* is that of KIUMĨRI, which refers to one who has just recuperated from his wound. Though a kiumĩri has earned the title of mwanake "an unmarried man who has undergone [IRUA*]," he is somehow still in the process of getting recruited into waanake "the life of the unmarried men who have undergone [IRUA*]" by other aanake (the plural form of mwaanake) from previous age-groups. Ciumĩri (the plural form of kiumĩri) bribe the aanake from preceding age groups so as to be allowed to dance with girls as well as to perform a ritual known as ngwĩko "sex without penetration." This act of bribing was mostly done to teach the initiates that they have to respect members of the preceding age groups and other senior members of the society. In the past, this bribe took the form of ndũrũme "ram" but with the changing times, it has come to be referred to as giving thigara cia mũrangano "cigarettes to bribe the seniors." This bribe is mandatory and every kiumĩri is forced to comply.

4.2.2.4 MWAANAKE

Another concept that is activated strongly whenever the concept IRUA* is evoked is that of a MWAANAKE "a circumcised [young] man who is unmarried." The concept MWAANAKE is a compound word mwaana-ke which literally means "child-take," symbolizing the act of a father giving his now circumcised son a bow and arrows to go and look for game meat to bring back home for the family to eat. This concept is associated with a new status, both on an individual and societal level, with the now circumcised young man becoming a member of a privileged class called Aanake. The concept MWAANAKE activated that of MŨNDŨ MŨGIMA "an adult member of the community," and to refer to a mwaanake as a kĩhĩĩ "an uncircumcised boy" is considered to be an insult among the Kikuyu. The aanake follow a well-defined code of conduct as well and have defined responsibilities to fulfill. They are conceptualized as people who take delegated responsibilities seriously, more than a kĩhĩĩ does, and also as no longer dependent on their parents. This new expectation is reflected in a phrase that is used as a synonym to the word *mwaanake*, which is *njui hũre* "a chick (that the mother hen) has chased away," a metaphor borrowed from the act of a mother chicken chasing her now grown chicks to go and look for their own food. Thus, the concept MWAANAKE is associated with hard work since one was expected to work hard so as to provide for himself and for his family when the time comes for him to marry. If one was perceived as being lazy, the beautiful and hardworking girls of his village would avoid him and as a consequence he would normally end up marrying an equally lazy and less beautiful girl.

4.2.2.5 MŨTIIRI

The concept MŨTIIRI, which is associated with one who nurses the initiate as he recuperates as well as the person who acts as the initiate's godfather for the rest of the initiate's life, is also activated when the concept IRUA* is evoked. This word is derived from the root *tiira* which means "to give support to something that would otherwise fall if that support is withheld." In the past, circumcision was performed as the candidates were sitting down and the *mũtiiri* would literally help the candidate to stand up after the surgery was performed. The *mũtiiri* also takes the crucial role of a teacher and is expected to know all the traditions of the tribe. He is also expected to be a respectable and a morally upright person since much of the education is taught through observation.[15] The relationship between a *mũtiiri* and the initiate together with the family of the initiate is a lifelong relationship, with the *mũtiiri* being invited as a regular guest at important events/feasts of that family. Since *mũtiiri* is conceptualized to be the "god father" to the initiate, some families would even go to the extent of seeking the assistance of a diviner in choosing a *mũtiiri* because his role was believed to be "a religious duty which should be approved by God and the ancestors."[16] A *mũtiiri* is expected to take his teaching role very seriously, and if by any chance one happens to misbehave, people would enquire who his *mũtiiri* is, since they would naturally associate such behavior with the failure of the *mũtiiri* to provide good teaching to the initiate.[17]

---

15. Muriuki, *History of the Kikuyu*, 9.
16. Gachiri, *Rite of Passage for Christian Boys*, 168.
17. Mugo, *Kikuyu People*, 18.

4.2.2.6 MŨCIARI

As one would expect, the concept MŨCIARI "parent" is strongly activated when the concept IRUA* is evoked. The concept MŨCIARI is more than just one's birth parents. It includes also the brothers of one's father, who are also referred to with the title of *baba* "father," as well as their wives who are referred to as *maitũ* "mothers." The form of the verb used to refer to the role of the parents in the ritual (i.e. *kũruithia* "to circumcise"), though in the passive, points to their important role, as example 26 indicates.

(26) *Ithe   wa   Waceke   nĩararuithirie*
     Father   of   Waceke   cut.his.sons.'foreskin (passive)
     ihĩĩ   iria   ciake   cia   mahatha.
     uncircumcised boys   those   his   of   twins
     "Waceke's father has made the necessary arrangements for his uncircumcised twin boys to be circumcised."

Unlike the other participants in the ritual of [IRUA*], the parents' responsibilities start long before the [IRUA*] ceremony itself. The father figure to the initiate is expected to have taught the potential candidate such values as respect for elders as well as the virtue of working hard. Such training opportunities would include directing the son to accompany him in his daily chores and also inviting the son to join him in his *thingira* "man's hut" in the evenings so that they could interact and talk. The boy child is wholly dependent on such teachings, which take the form of folklore as well as verbal instructions. It is also the father figure's responsibility to evaluate whether the boy is ready for [IRUA*], and after he is convinced that the son is mature both psychologically and physically, he is to send him to his in-laws to seek for permission to be circumcised. The main reason behind this action is to find out whether the in-laws require some of the outstanding dowry to be paid and it is only after any requirement has been met that the preparations for [IRUA*] would start officially.

In the past, it was also the father's responsibility to introduce the boy as a candidate of [IRUA*], which was by then a public affair.[18] He would invite village elders and slaughter for them what is referred to as *ndũrũme ya kũhoya*

---

18. Wambũgũ, Ngarariga, and Kariũki, *The Agĩkũyũ*, 86

[IRUA*] "a ram for requesting permission [for his son] to undergo [IRUA*]." Other gifts that were offered included a gourd full of hydromel, which is a mixture of honey and water left to ferment, as well as several jars of *mūratina* which is a local brew, millet porridge, and a goat, gifts which were regarded as "requisite fee for the circumcision and for the acknowledgment and recording in the annals of the community."[19] The ceremony of *gũitanga njohi* "pouring beer on the ground" was also performed to invite the ancestral spirits to be part of the event and to request them to watch over the potential candidate who was preparing to go through [IRUA*]. It was believed that it was only after this was done that the initiate could recuperate from his wound quickly. In the day that the candidates were to be circumcised, as a sign of their blessing, "the parents sprayed their sons with branches of *mũkenya* dipped in beer, with their lips they also sprinkled a few mouthfuls of the same beer on their bodies, then, they conducted them to the river where they were washed."[20] After the son recuperated, the father would slaughter another goat, referred to as *mbũri ya thubu wa mĩtĩ* "the goat for making soup from herbs." The meat of the goat was prepared using special herbs fetched by experienced elders who knew the exact type of herbs and where to find them. The father figure would also invite elders to come and drink *mũratina*, symbolizing the fact that the son has recovered from his wound and is now a full member of the society.

There are other responsibilities specifically associated with the mother figure to the initiate that are undertaken during this period. In the past, one of these responsibilities was for her to recruit one of her close friends or relatives to shave the head of her son after undergoing [IRUA*]. Such a woman was to take on the role of a second mother to the initiate, with the initiate expected to respect her just as he would do his own mother.[21] The mother to the initiate, together with her *airu* "co-wives," are the ones in charge of making sure that food is always available in the homestead for guests who frequent the home to celebrate, and more specifically for the initiate who is recuperating from his wound. There is an added advantage associated with a woman whose son has undergone [IRUA*] in that she acquires a new title with its

---

19. Wambũgũ, Ngarariga, and Kariũki, 90.
20. Wambũgũ, Ngarariga, and Kariũki, 92.
21. Wambũgũ, Ngarariga, and Kariũki, 95.

accompanying status in the community.[22] She is no longer referred to as *kangʼei* "a mother who does not have a circumcised son" but with a more prestigious title of *nyakīnyua* which means "one whose son(s) has undergone [IRUA*]." The mother to the initiate specifically invites women who have acquired the *nyakīnyua* title to come and celebrate with her and help her to perform what is referred to as *ithinga rīa mūnyū*, which is a ritual of smearing white clay on the walls of her new son's hut as a sign of her son's newly acquired status.

4.2.2.7 MŪRUITHIA

Another concept that is activated within the frame of [IRUA*] is that of MŪRUITHIA "the one who circumcises." In the past, when this concept was activated, it was associated with some people who hailed from certain selected families who were entrusted with this responsibility. It was one of those trades that was passed from one generation to another. The eldest son in that selected family was set apart for this work by offering a *horohio* "sacrifice" of seven goats to make any amendments. After this atoning sacrifice, the *mūruithia* was taken to a river and immersed in its waters by a diviner and it was claimed that when such a person rose from the water, a seed would be found attached in his buttocks, which was a sign that he was set apart for this work. How the seed came to be attached to his buttocks remains a mystery.

The concept MŪRUITHIA also evoked the feeling of fear, since one of his roles was to test the courage of the candidates to make sure that they were brave enough to undergo the ritual. He could come wearing a large skin hat, having painted his face with white chalk. He could jump around to try and scare the candidates to make sure they were ready before performing the surgery from one candidate to the other. He was expected to be thorough in his work and to perform the procedure as quickly as possible, since at that time there was no medicine to anaesthetize the candidates. Nowadays the concept MŪRUITHIA evokes that of a person who has attained the formal qualifications of a surgeon that would allow him to perform the procedure. Unlike the past, it does not matter whether a doctor performing this surgery has undergone [IRUA*] or not, since the doctor might come from a community that does

---

22. Routledge and Routledge, *With a Prehistoric People*, 157.

not practice circumcision. There are occasions where female doctors perform such surgeries, which in the past would have been a taboo.

4.2.2.8 KĨAMA GĨA ATHURI

The concept KĨAMA GĨA ATHURI "council of elders" is also activated within the [IRUA*] frame. One of the roles associated with the elders, especially in the past, had to do with deciding when [IRUA*] was to take place. The elders also took the role of blessing the candidates before they went for "the cut" by sprinkling the traditional beer over each of the candidates as a symbol of blessing and at the same time pour some to the ground so as to appease the ancestral spirits. A mixture of hydromel with bowels from goat's intestines was sprinkled by elders on the heads as well as on the sexual organs of the initiates as a sign of blessing and good wishes.[23] The elders would also make marks on the candidates using a white chalk referred to as *ira* which was obtained from Mount Kenya (also called *Kĩrĩnyaga*) where *Ngai* "God" was believed to have his dwelling. They would pour a brownish powder called *rũthuko* to the ground in order to drive away evil spirits. They would also administer a special liquid called *ũũmũ*, which was a mixture of millet flour, castor oil, milk, and special herbs because it was believed that this mixture had the power to stimulate the candidate's courage and fortitude.[24] This disgusting mixture could also be partaken after the initiates underwent [IRUA*] "without a glimpse to show that from then they were men, superior to such truffles as daintiness of taste."[25] They also undertook the role of advising the candidates during the last day of their coming out of the *mũthonge* "the hut where initiates recuperated" and were the ones entrusted with the responsibility of selecting who among the initiates would join the privileged class of *njamba cia ita* "warriors."

4.2.2.9 NGAI

The concept IRUA* also activates that of NGAI "God" as an agent in the process since [IRUA*] as a social function has some religious significance. In the past, *Ngai* would be appeased through various sacrifices and requested to protect

---

23. Wambũgũ, Ngarariga, and Kariũki, *The Agĩkũyũ*, 95.
24. Routledge and Routledge, *With a Prehistoric People*, 160.
25. Wambũgũ, Ngarariga, and Kariũki, *The Agĩkũyũ*, 95.

and bless the candidates of [IRUA*].[26] An example of such a sacrifice is where goat meat was roasted under a special tree called *mũgumo* and the scent was believed to ascend towards Mount Kĩrĩnyaga where *Ngai* was believed to have his dwelling.[27] The application of the white chalk substance mentioned above called *ira*, which was fetched from Mount Kĩrĩnyaga to make markings on the body prior to the day of "the cut" had some spiritual significance. Since Mount Kĩrĩnyaga is where God was believed to dwell, it was believed that *ira* had his blessings. Again, the markings were done following a pattern that was said to have originated from a divine command.[28] A purification ceremony was also held on the eve of [IRUA*] to cleanse any impediments.

4.2.2.10 *Time of* [IRUA*]

The time of [IRUA*], especially in the years past, was decided by whether the number of potential candidates was substantial enough to form a *riika* "age-group" and also if there were no calamities such as diseases and war in the land.[29] If the candidates were only a few, a period when there is no [IRUA*] taking place referred to as *mũhingo*, would be pronounced. This period could last for three or four years until the number of candidates would build up to be sufficient enough to form a *riika*. Those candidates, who would still undergo [IRUA*] during this period of *mũhingo* by undergoing the ritual in another place where there was no ban, would still be part of the same age-group and share the same name with those who would be circumcised when the ban was lifted. As far as the age of the potential candidates is concerned, the qualification age for boys would be mainly between fifteen and eighteen years, after they developed pubic hair in their private parts and also when they have experienced a change of voice. Nowadays the boys are ready for circumcision after completing primary school in readiness to join post-primary institutions.

In order to avoid the challenge of being scrutinized by the entire community, the ritual of [IRUA*] was held in the early hours of the morning while it was still dark. This was driven by a collective responsibility to hide those

---

26. Murray, "Kikuyu Female Circumcision," 6.
27. Mugo, *Kikuyu People*, 14, 17.
28. Routledge and Routledge, *With a Prehistoric People*, 156.
29. Kirika, "Aspects of the Religion of the Gikuyu," 5.

who might end up being labeled as cowards and risk being laughed at and worse still lack a woman to marry when that time comes. The ceremony of [IRUA*] was mostly held in the months of April and May, just after the planting season, since at this time the least labor was required in the farms.[30] This timing was also appropriate since it was fairly dry, since in the past the initiates had only one *cuka* "sheet" to cover themselves with, which would be able to dry as they went to take a bath in the river. In modern times, [IRUA*] ceremonies are held during school holidays as potential initiates are mostly upper primary school students, with the December holidays being the favorite as they are longer than the other school holidays. It is expected that the boys transiting to secondary schools should first undergo [IRUA*] so as to avoid bullying, since it is considered a *mũgiro* "taboo" for the circumcised and the uncircumcised to share accommodation.

4.2.2.11 RIIKA

The concept RIIKA "age-group" is strongly activated when the [IRUA*] frame is activated. It is composed of initiates who undergo the ritual of [IRUA*] at the same period of time. The sub-concept WAKIINĨ is also activated referring to an inner group of comrades who were "cut" using the same circumcision knife called *rwenji* as well as shared the same hut in their recuperation period. The members of this close group exhibit a very strong sense of comradeship to one another, even stronger than that of brothers born of the same mother share. The *wakiinĩ* colleagues go through most life challenges together and therefore remain close companions for the rest of their lives. In the past, this companionship was so close that they used to share wives, with the children of these comrades referring to their father's *wakiinĩ* colleagues using the title *baba* "father."[31] The following proverb underlines the close comradeship that *riika* members are supposed to share.

(27) *Riika   rĩtihithagwo   gĩathĩ*
    (One's) age group   is.not.hidden   meeting
    "One is not supposed to hide anything from his riika."

---

30. Routledge and Routledge, *With a Prehistoric People*, 157.
31. Muriuki, *History of the Kikuyu*, 119.

Again, just as one belongs to his family for the rest of his life, one also belongs to his *riika* for as long as he lives with the following proverb pointing to this close bond.

(28) *Nyũmba   na   riika   itiumagwo*
One's family and   one's age-set   not.abandon
"One cannot abandon his family or age group."

The concept RIIKA is conceptualized as the basis upon which duties were allocated to the members of the society.[32] One such responsibility has to do with leadership in the community which was passed from one *riika* to another, with the *riika* in power being entrusted with "political, judicial, and religious matters of the whole land."[33] A *riika* would rule until they acquired the title of a *guka* "grandfather," which is around a span of forty years, with the end of each *riika* reign being marked by a social event of handing over power called *itwĩĩka*. Another duty that used to be passed from one *riika* to another, before the coming of the colonial government, is that of providing security against hostile neighboring communities as well as going for raids to these communities.

After undergoing [IRUA*], the members of that *riika* automatically qualified to enter the junior warriors' category with their main occupation being learning how to fight using spears, clubs, machetes, bows and arrows.[34] After serving for a period as junior warriors, the *riika* would then serve under the prestigious category of *njamba cia ita* "warriors" before moving on to serve as junior elders. The members of that *riika* would then move on to serve as elders, for as was mentioned above, the institution of *riika* served as the basis of organizing the government in Kikuyu society.[35] Today there are two groups of *riika* which alternate power among themselves, that of *Irũngũ* (or *Maina*) and that of *Mwangi*, which are a generation apart (See appendix E for a detailed list of respective Kikuyu governments over the years). The following proverb points to the fact that leadership is passed from one *riika* to another.

---

32. Muriuki, 135.
33. Kirika, "Aspects of the Religion of the Gikuyu," 4.
34. Muriuki, *History of the Kikuyu*, 14.
35. Gatheru, *Child of Two Worlds*, 63.

(29) Wa   Mwangi   ndũtogaga   keerĩ/meerĩ.
    (Fire) of Mwangi does.not.burn   twice
    "The riika of Mwangi does not rule twice in a row."

Due to the change in the form of government today, the institution of *njamba cia ita* "warriors" is now defunct. Since then, the institution of *riika* has continued to adapt itself to fit the times as members of *riika* seek for opportunities to foster their unity. One such attempt is referred to as *ngwatio* which means assisting one another to do manual work, especially in doing farm work such as preparing farms, planting, weeding, harvesting, etc. Other forms of *ngwatio* include *ithinga* "mixing mud for making walls," constructing cow pens, looking after livestock together, to mention a few. *Riika* mates are supposed to watch over one another and if a member of a given *riika* misbehaves, his *riika* mates are supposed to correct him and reprimand him, if need be, for putting his *riika* to shame. Administering sanctions on errant members of a *riika* would include denying such a member privileges such as participating in *ngwatio* as well as hindering him from associating with his *riika* mates. They would do so until they were certain that the errant member conforms and would require him to give a fine of a goat which they would eat together to make amends.

The concept RIIKA is also activated when it comes to distinguishing a person's age, for before the age of literacy dawned, birthdates were hard to remember. A person's age can be calculated by knowing what age-group he belongs to and when that group underwent [IRUA*]. Age-groups were named according to major social events or natural occurrences happening in the land around the time that a group was about to undergo [IRUA*]. An example is the time when certain disease outbreaks took place, thus there are age groups known as *gĩthũkũ* "measles" (1871), *rũharo* "dysentery" (1877), *mũtũng'ũ* "small pox" (1894), *gatego* "syphilis" (1903), and *ũhere* "scabies" (1912). See appendix F for a detailed list of age groups and the time when they occurred.

4.2.3 Frame Shifting

Nowadays, there is a parallel attempt to "Christianize," so to speak, the concept IRUA*, which has resulted in most traditional elements which were associated with the traditional rite of passage being modified. The goal of this initiative is to specifically protect initiates who confess the Christian faith from the "un-Christian" influence that is associated with the traditional approach. This program, which normally runs for two to three weeks, aims to blend the traditional approach with the Christian one.[36] To an extent, this initiative has gained favor even among parents who do not necessarily confess the Christian faith, since in comparison with the traditional approach, it saves them money even as they are assured of their sons being equipped with the right teaching. As Gachiri points out this approach includes

> All the good cultural values in the traditional rite. It will also include other modern and Christian values that the parents and the community desire for their children. The boys will be taught what is expected of them as fathers, husbands, sons, sons-in-law and age-set members and their various responsibilities and privileges. They will get comprehensive instruction on the various relationships in the community and how to conduct themselves in the various roles. The mental abilities of the participants will be kept in mind while they are trained to live a disciplined life, especially with regard to sexual behavior, control of desires such as for food and drink, and endurance that accompanies the liminal state of seclusion.[37]

One example of this blending is the borrowing of the institution of age groups, and just as the traditional initiation rite of passage was based on age groups, the program encourages those who go through it to form age groups, which are also expected to last for a long time. The concept MŨTIIRI "sponsor" has also been borrowed from the traditional approach. It has been modified to an extent since such sponsors are provided by the leadership of the church. Some of the qualifications include being a mature Christian, being psychologically and emotionally healthy, well-informed on current affairs and the challenges facing the young people, being friendly and able to work with the youth so as to be able to assist the initiates to whole-heartedly embrace Christianity and to meet their obligations as adult members of society.[38] Another modification has to do with the role of the parents, which is

---

36. Gachiri, *Rite of Passage for Christian Boys*.
37. Gachiri, 114.
38. Gachiri, 170.

now quite minimal with the church addressing the logistical issues involved, with the parents only required to pay the agreed fee. The church-sponsored [IRUA*] is held in a rented facility, mostly a school compound, which has such readily available facilities as dormitories, classrooms, chapel, game and recreation facilities, a kitchen and dining hall. The church also hires staff or recruits volunteers to help in the program and the parents are invited only to attend the graduation ceremony held at the end of the program.

As far as the church sponsored [IRUA*] is concerned, the concept of NGAI is acknowledged every step of the way. In one of the manuals used to run this church-sponsored program, referred to as Rites of Passage Experiences (ROPES) by the Nairobi Chapel, the candidates are encouraged to surrender to God all their fears and pain that they are about to experience.[39] They are also encouraged to join their pain with the redemptive pain that Jesus endured and bore on their behalf and therefore they are encouraged to endure the pain courageously since to do so is a Christian virtue.[40] Again as far as the church-sponsored ritual is concerned, depending on the specific church leadership, *athuri a kanitha* "church elders" are associated with some of the roles that the traditional *kĩama gĩa athuri* executed. The church elders have a say in making decisions such as when the event will take place, where it takes place, as well as giving advice in the time of graduation of the candidates. I will be pointing out some of the conceptual similarities and differences that this "Christianized" approach is likely to have from a traditional approach when it comes to the conceptual integration process, and how given elements have been modified in the process.

4.3 The Conceptual Integration Process

In this section, the conceptual integration process in the interpretation of the associated concepts HAKIRI "mind" and NGORO "heart" as they are associated with that of IRUA* in a metaphorical relationship/blend is discussed. The field findings are used to demonstrate how the conceptual integration process works in the interpretation of the metaphors *kũgimara hakiri* and *kũrua ngoro*.

---

39. Gachiri, 140.
40. Gachiri, 142.

4.3.1 Association of [*IRUA**] and *HAKIRI*

Based on the field research findings, I will first analyze how the concept *HAKIRI* is conceptualized in the metaphorical blend *kũgimara hakiri*. For some of the data from the field research see appendix G. This is because this metaphor is used as background to understanding the metaphorical association of the ritual of [*IRUA**] with that of *NGORO* "heart." Using the complementary approach between CIT and RT, I will reconstruct how the elements in the input spaces are projected, as well as demonstrate how relevant inferences arrived at. The metaphor *kũgimara hakiri* is commonly used in the context of giving advice to initiates on how to behave now that they have become adult members of the society. The concept *KŨGIMARA* "becoming as adult" is in a metonymic relationship with that of *IRUA** "circumcision," with the later being the cause and the former the effect, since as has being pointed out in examples 16 and 17 above, these two concepts are used interchangeably.

4.3.1.1 Conceptualization of *HAKIRI*

The concept *HAKIRI* "mind" is associated with the decision-making process, with this process normally referred to using the verb *gwĩciria*, as examples 30 and 31 below point out.

(30) *Kwaga   gwĩciria.*
     not   thinking
     "Not thinking/reasoning well."

(31) *Gwĩciria   wega.*
     to.think   well
     "To think/reason well."

The mind is also attributed qualities as examples 32 and 34 illustrate and also as object with some actions performed on it, as examples 35 to 36 illustrate.

(32) *Meciria   mega.*
     mind   good
     "Good thoughts."

(33) *Meciria   moru.*
     mind   bad

"Bad thoughts."

(34) *Kũgarũra meciria.*
    change   mind
    "To change one's mind."

(35) *Kwĩnogia meciria.*
    to.tire   mind
    "To make the mind tired."

(36) *Kwerekeria meciria.*
    focus   mind
    "Focus one's mind [on something]."

The mind is conceptualized as having "thinking value" and thus as having human or animal/non-human characteristics. If a person behaves in a way that is considered inhuman, the following statement can be used to describe them.

(37) *Ena   meciria   matũrĩku   ta   ma   nyamũ.*
    he.has thoughts   promiscuous   like of   animal
    "He has promiscuous thoughts [and therefore acts] like an animal."

A "bad" mind is associated with those who engage in actions that are contrary to the set or acceptable norms in the society. Such actions include vices such as rape, adultery, stealing, abusing others, beating one's parents, etc. A mad person is also said to have *hakiri itarĩ njega*, literally "brains that are not good/normal," since mad people are associated with such vices.

4.3.1.2 Reconstruction of the Blend Kũgimara Hakiri

Working backwards from the blend *kũgimara hakiri* "maturity of mind," there are two input spaces from which the content of the blend is projected from as figure 7 indicates. The first is that of [IRUA*], which also provides the organizing frame of the blend, and the second is that of KŨGIMARA HAKIRI, which provides elements in the blend. The projections into the blend are relevant driven and involve relation compressions through scaling and syncopation.

The projected elements into the blend are as a result of some being eliminated as false in light of the evidence that the association allowed within the outer spaces (i.e. the discourse and relevance spaces) are those that have to do with the mind as the object and not the sexual organ. The general property of agent in the GS is filled by the roles of *mūrūithia* "circumciser" IS_1 which is matched to that of *mūtiiri* "godfather" in IS_2. The agency which is projected to the blend is that of *mūtiiri* "godfather" from IS_2 who is entrusted with the teaching process that is expected to result in the maturity of the initiates. The projection of this agency to the blend also involves the process of scaling since there are a number of other agents who are involved in the teaching process in one way or another throughout the initiates' lives. It also involves the relation compression of syncopation in that only one stage of the teaching process is highlighted given that the learning process continues as long as a person is alive. Thus the role of *mūtiiri* is highlighted, since he is the one who is conceptualized as the key agent entrusted with teaching the initiate and consequently he is the one who is projected into the blend.

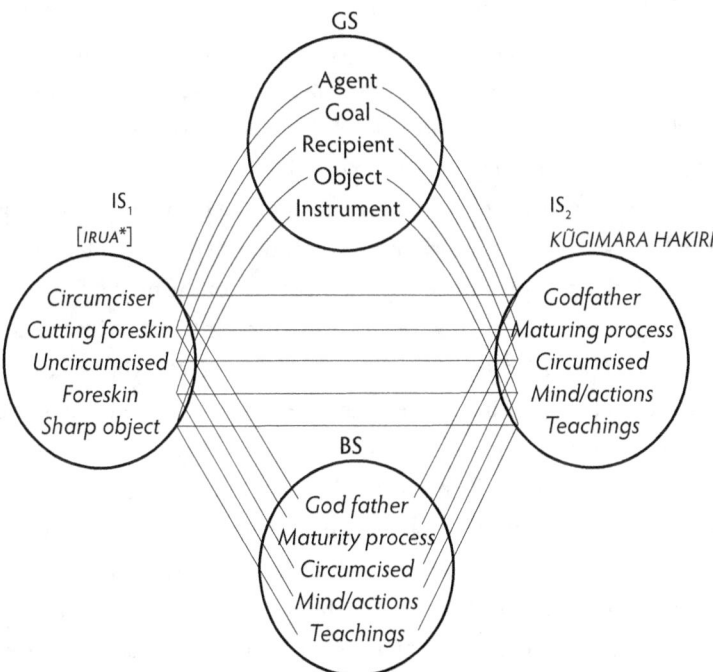

Figure 7: Integration process of the metaphor *kūgimara hakiri*

The goals that are activated in the input spaces are that of *kũrenga gĩkonde* "cutting the foreskin" in IS$_1$ and that of *meciria/ciĩko ng'ima* "minds and actions that are mature" from IS$_2$. The latter, namely, *meciria/ciĩko ng'ima* from IS$_2$ is projected to the blend through the process of composition, since the connections allowed within the outer spaces have to do with the mind being the object and not the sexual organ. The recipients in the integration network involve *kĩhĩĩ* "uncircumcised boy" from IS$_1$ which is matched to that of *mũndũ mũgima* "adult member of the society" from IS$_2$. The one which is projected to the blend is that of *mũndũ mũgima*, through the process of completion since an uncircumcised boy is normally not expected to think or behave maturely.

The objects in the input spaces are that of *gĩkonde* "foreskin" in IS$_1$ which is matched to that of *meciria/ciĩko* from in IS$_2$, with the latter being projected to the blend, following the process of composition allowed within the outer spaces since the problem addressed is that of immaturity of the mind and actions. The generic property "object" in the GS is filled by *rwenji* "sharp object" in IS$_1$, which is highlighted through the process of syncopation since there are many other objects that are involved in the ritual of [IRUA*]. This is matched to that of *uumithio* "teaching offered during the seclusion period" in IS$_2$ which is projected to the blend in light of the context given that what is targeted is one's thinking process and character change.

A number of inferences can be arrived at in the blend by combining new information with known information so as to derive new contextual implications with the goal of completing the structure of the blend. From IS$_2$, the element that one is not born with a mature mind interacts with the content of the blend (i.e. that of an adult member of the society who is expected to behave maturely), resulting in the inference that one has to be taught in order to acquire a mature mind. A further inference that can be derived in the blend is that this teaching is not for *ihĩĩ* "uncircumcised boys" but for those who undergo the ritual of [IRUA*] since this ritual is the one which marks the beginning of such teachings. Another inference that can be arrived at through the process of elaboration in the blend is that of the possibility of one undergoing the ritual of [IRUA*] yet be considered as immature if he happens to exhibit childish or immature behavior. The blend also results with its own emergent logic. An example is that since the one who has undergone [IRUA*] is regarded as a mature person, he is expected to be able to make solid decisions and discern issues, including fulfilling roles such as that of taking care of his family. Another emergent logic is that the person who exhibits mature behavior is likely to be appointed as a leader and hence entrusted with important responsibilities on behalf of the people.

The metaphor *kũgimara hakiri* could be said to describe a person who is able to make mature or concrete decisions, to act and talk maturely, have a deep understanding of issues, be disciplined, among other virtues. The opposite of this is *gũkorwo wĩ mwana hakiri* "to be immature/childish in mind," and includes a circumcised person exhibiting such characteristics as that of harboring the attitude that one knows it all, lack of virtues such as patience, understanding, and respect, refusing to take counsel, lack of the wisdom in addressing basic problems or challenges, associating with the wrong people, to mention a few.

4.3.2 Association of [IRUA*] and NGORO

In this sub-section, I will analyze the conceptualization of the concept NGORO "heart" as well as reconstruct the conceptual integration process that is activated when this concept is associated with that of [IRUA*] in the context of Romans 2. I will point out the underlying frames that are activated, reconstruct the inner and outer spaces as well as the links that are activated in the integration process. I will also point out the specific elements that are projected and/or suppressed and relevant inferences that are allowed to take place. The integration process is based on responses from the field research. Discussed below is the conceptualization of the concept NGORO "heart" in Kikuyu.

4.3.2.1 Conceptualization of NGORO

The Kikuyu concept NGORO "heart" is readily activated within the [BODY] frame. One of the roles of NGORO is that it is used as a compression of identity given that as a body organ it is associated with establishing whether a person is alive or dead as indicated in the example below.

(38) *Nĩmũrwaru   biũ   no   ngoro   no   ĩrahũra.*
     3sg.sick   much   but   heart   is.still beating
     "He/she is very sick but is still alive [since the heart is still pumping blood]."

The concept NGORO is also used in a relation compression in a part-whole relationship (i.e. as a metonymy for the person). As a result, the heart is given personal attributes which point to the character of the person, as examples 39 to 43 indicate.

(39) *Ngoro hūthū.*
 Heart light
 "A person who keeps wrongs."

(40) *Ngoro ndūtū.*
 Heart heavy
 "A person who is difficult to deal with."

(41) *Ngoro theru.*
 Heart clean
 "A person who is good to people."

(42) *Ngoro njega.*
 Heart good
 "A good person."

(43) *Ngoro ngirīrīria.*
 Heart patient
 "A person who exercises patience."

The concept NGORO is also conceptualized as a container pointing to a compression of the vital relation of space. As a result, it is associated as the place where emotions and feelings are stored as examples 44 to 46 illustrate.

(44) *Ngoro ya tha.*
 Heart of mercy
 "A merciful person."

(45) *Ngoro īkīnyiria.*
 Heart allergic
 "A heart that does not like [something]."

(46) Ngoro   njītīi.
    Heart   proud
    "A proud heart."

The concept NGORO is also used as the compression of the vital relation of intentionality since it is conceptualized as the hub where emotions are expressed as examples 47 to 51 indicate.

(47) Ngoro   yakwa   ndīmwendete.
    Heart   mine   not.like.him/her
    "My heart does not like him/her."

(48) Ngoro   yakwa   īraigua   o   kūmuona.
    Heart   mine   feeling   like seeing.him/her
    "My heart desires to see him/her."

(49) Ngoro   yakwa   īiguaga   īmūhūnīte   mūno.
    Heart   mine   it.feels satisfied.by.him/her very.much
    "My heart does not like him/her very much."

(50) Ngoro   yakwa   nī   īratumatuma.
    Heart   mine   is   jumping.jumping
    "I am excited."

(51) E   ngoro   njūru   mūno.
    He/she.has heart   bad   very.much
    "He/she does not have a welcoming heart."

The concept NGORO has also acquired a "Christianized" meaning in that it is the place where conversion takes place. This can be demonstrated by the following phrase which is commonly used to indicate that one has given their life to Christ.

(52) Ngoro   yakwa   nī   honoku
    Heart   mine   is   saved
    "I am saved/born again."

In summary, the concept NGORO is conceptualized as a compression for a number of vital relations. These include that of a living organ, which indicates whether a person is alive or not, as a metonymy for a person, as a container or storage of qualities, emotions and feelings, and also as the place feelings or emotions are expressed. It is important to note that emotions are also associated with other parts of the body as well which include the intestines (*gũtuĩka mara* "to fear" [literally "to be cut in the intestines"]), the body (*gwĩthithimũkwo mwĩrĩ* "to shiver" [literally "to be shaken in the body"]), the hair (*kwambarara njuĩri* "to be scared" [literally "hair stood up"]), the feet (*kũinaina magũrũ* "to be frightened" [literally "legs shook"]), among others. The concept NGORO* in the context of Romans 2:29 is narrowed as a reference to that of a container or storage of qualities, characteristics, or feelings whether good or bad and also as the place where feelings or emotions emerge from as well as the place where they are expressed.

4.3.2.2 Field Findings on *"Kũrua Ngoro"*

In this sub-section, an overview is given of the findings of the research on how Kikuyu Christians understood the metaphor translated as "*kũrua ngoro*" "circumcision of heart" in Romans 2:29. Most of the interviewees used overtones from their background framing of the ritual of [IRUA*], specifically that of the metaphor *kũgimara hakiri* "maturity of mind" to explain the spiritual process implied by the metaphor "*kũrua ngoro*," as the following sample from their responses point out. For more examples from the field research see appendix H.

(53) *Mũndũ ũgimarĩte na thĩinĩ.*
Person matured on inside
"A person who has spiritually matured."

(54) *Kũgimara meciria na gwĩtigĩra Ngai.*
Maturing in.mind and fearing God
"Maturing in mind and also fearing God."

(55) *Nĩ kũgimara na gũtigana na maũndũ ma tene*
It.is to.mature and leaving the things of past
"It is maturing and leaving behind [bad] things that one used to do in the past."

(56) Nĩ   mwĩto   wa   kũgimara   kĩroho   na   gũtigana   na
    It.is   calling   to   be.mature spiritually   and leaving   the
    mĩtugo   ĩtarĩ   ya   kĩũngai.
    traditions which.not of   God
    "It is being called/separated so as to become spiritually mature and leaving traditions that are not Godly."

(57) Nĩ   kũgimara   mũndũ agatiga gũkorwa   arĩ   mwana wa
    It.is   maturing   person   abandons to.be a   child of
    kĩroho   agatuĩka   mũgima   kĩroho.
    spiritual he.becomes mature   spiritually
    "It is [the process of] maturing [so that] a person abandons being a spiritual child and becomes mature spiritually."

(58) Gũtinio   kana kweheria ũmũndũ wa kĩmwĩrĩ.
    to.be.cut   or   remove   self   of flesh
    "To be cut or to remove acts of flesh."

(59) Ciĩko   ciaku   cikonania   ũgima.
    Actions   yours   to.demonstrate   maturity
    "It is when one's actions demonstrate that one is mature [spiritually]."

(60) Kũgimara   na   kwĩheana   mũno   kũrĩ Ngai na
    to.mature and   to.surrender   very.much to   God   and
    ũthamaki   wake.
    Kingdom   his
    "To mature and [as a result] surrender more to God and his kingdom."

(61) Nĩ   kũgimara   mũndũ   agatuĩka   mũgima   kĩroho.
    it.is   to.mature   person becomes   mature   spiritually
    "It is to mature [so that] a person becomes mature spiritually."

According to the above field findings, it is clear that this spiritual process is interpreted using the frame of [IRUA*] as a rite of passage into maturity status. It is only the object of association in the process which changes from that of HAKIRI "mind" to that of NGORO* "heart." The next section looks at the underlying background frames that inform this association.

4.3.2.3 The Receptor Language Outer Spaces

The interpretation of the metaphor translated as *kūrua ngoro* "circumcision of heart" is influenced by the two outer spaces (i.e. the discourse and relevance spaces). The DS refers to how the metaphor interpreted as "*kūrua ngoro*" is interpreted within the context of Romans 2 as per the field findings. The RS provides the background knowledge that shapes the frames that guide further mapping between the integration spaces since it is the force that constrains the selection or suppression of projections and inferences to and from the blend.

4.3.2.3.1 The Receptor Language discourse space

In discussing the DS, which informs the interpretation of the metaphor translated as "*kūrua ngoro*" "circumcision of heart," it is important to point out how the associated concepts in this metaphor have been rendered in previous discourse spaces. The old Kikuyu translation leans towards a literal rendering of this metaphor. Leviticus 26:41 talks of "*ngoro cikariite ta itaruite*" meaning "hearts that seem uncircumcised," Deuteronomy 10:16 calls people to "*wīruithie gīkonde kīa ngoro cianyu*" "circumcise the foreskin of their hearts," Deuteronomy 30:6 talks of "*Ngai waku akūruithie ngoro*" that is "your God circumcising your heart," Jeremiah 4:4 of the act of "*kwīruithia ngoro cianyu*" "circumcising your hearts." This literal translation is rendered in association with other parts of the body as well. Exodus 6:12, 30 talks "*mūndū wī mīromo ītari mīruu*" "a person who lips are not circumcised," and Acts 7:51 "*ta andū maruīte arīa maregaga kūigua na . . . matu manyu*" meaning "like people who are uncircumcised in the way you refuse to listen with your ears." In Jeremiah 6:10, the old Kikuyu bible renders the metaphor of circumcised ears with an equivalent metaphor, "*matū mao me njiika na matinjiguaga*" meaning "their ears have a swelling and their do not listen to me." The tendency to render this metaphor literally leads to the activation of the inference of maturity associated with the traditional ritual of [IRUA*] discussed in detail in the next section.

On the other hand, the new Kikuyu translation sometimes leaves the heart metaphor implicit, and thus untranslated, and in other places it paraphrases it. In Leviticus 26:41 the metaphor is translated as "*. . . njiarwa icio cianyu ingīkenyihia . . .*" "if your descendants humble themselves"; Deuteronomy

10:16 "... *tūūraai mwathĩkagĩra MWATHANI*..." "continue to be obedient to the Lord"; Deuteronomy 30:6 "*Mwathani... nīakaamūhe... ngoro njathĩki*..." "The Lord... will give you... obedient hearts"; and Acts 7:51 where it is translated as "... *inyuĩ ngoro cianyu iteetĩkĩĩtĩe*..." "... you whose hearts do not believe..." This also goes for the rendering of other body parts. The "uncircumcised lips" in Exodus 6:12, 30 are rendered as "*mūndū utooĩ kwaria*" "a person who does not know how to speak (well)" and "uncircumcised lips" in Acts 7:51 rendered as "*andū mataiguaga ūhoro wa Ngai*" "people who do not listen to the message of God." The translation decision to do away with the metaphor is in line with the proposal by Nida and Taber to get rid of expressions that are "hard to understand," a decision which denies the readers the achievement of contextual effects which cannot be achieved through explicating or getting rid of the metaphor.[41]

4.3.2.3.2 The Receptor Language relevance space

The RS which is recruited in the interpretation of the metaphor "*kūrua ngoro*" is echoed in form of the genre formula translated as "since you have left one stage behind and now have entered another stage you should not do... but do..." This hortatory saying is normally used in the teachings referred to as *uumithio* which is activated within the traditional frame of [IRUA*]. The fact that the interpretation of the metaphor *kūrua ngoro* deals with a different object within the [KIROHO] frame, (i.e. that of NGORO "heart" and not that of HAKIRI "mind") leads to a different RS being set up. One of the aspects that is maintained from the [IRUA*] frame is the conceptualization of this spiritual process as that of leaving behind some behaviors associated with one stage and taking on those associated with the new acquired status as indicated by the following sample of responses from the field research.

(62) Nĩ   kũgimara   na   gũtigana   na   maũndũ   ma   tene.
     It.is   to.mature   and   leaving   the   things   of   past
     "It is maturing and leaving behind [bad] things that one used to do in the past."

(63) Nĩ   mwĩto   wa   kũgimara   kĩroho   na   gũtigana   na
     It.is   calling   to   be.mature   spiritually   and   leaving   the

---

41. Nida and Taber, *Theory and Practice of Translation*, 7–8.

mĩtugo ĩtarĩ   ya kĩũngai.
actions which.not of God
"It is being called/separated so as to become spiritually mature and leave behind traditions that are not Godly."

(64) Gũtinio   kana kweheria ũmũndũ wa kĩmwĩrĩ.
to.be.cut or   remove   self   of flesh
"To be cut or to remove acts of self."

(65) Nĩ   kũgimara   mũndũ agatiga gũkorwa arĩ   mwana wa
It.is maturing   person   abandons to.be a   child of
kĩroho   agatuĩka   mũgima   kĩroho.
spiritual he.becomes mature   spiritually
"It is [the process of] maturing [so that] a person abandons being a spiritual child and becomes mature spiritually."

(66) Kũgimara   na   kwĩheana mũno   kũrĩ Ngai na
to.mature   and to.surrender very.much to God and
ũthamaki   wake.
Kingdom   his
"To mature and [as a result] surrender more to God and his kingdom."

(67) Nĩ   kwĩruta   kũrĩ Jesũ na   gwĩka wendi wake.
it.is surrender to Jesus and to.do will   his
"It is to surrender to Jesus and to do his will."

(68) Nĩ   kũgarũrwo   mũndũ agatiga   gũkorwo arĩ   mwĩhia
it.is   to.be.changed person   abandons being   a   sinner
agatuĩka mũndũ   mũthingu.
becomes person   holy
"It is to be changed [so that] a person abandons being a sinner and becomes a holy person."

Some of the things that one is expected to leave behind, as the examples above point out, include *maũndũ ma tene* "[evil] things that one was doing before [he got saved]," *mĩtugo ĩtarĩ ya kĩũngai* "behavior/actions that do not glorify God," *ũmũndũ wa kĩmwĩrĩ* "acts of self," *mwana wa kĩroho* "spiritual babe," *wĩhia* "sin," etc. The new actions or behaviors that an initiate is expected to embrace include *kwĩheana mũno kũrĩ Ngai na ũthamaki wake* "to surrender completely to God and [to] his kingdom," *gwĩka wendi wake* "to do his will," *ũthingu* "holiness," among others. Just like the content of this teaching in the traditional frame of [IRUA*] is meant to equip initiates with life skills now that they have become adult members of the society, the new way of life activated within the [KIROHO] frame is intended to equip Christians with values, beliefs and attitudes that would enable them to live fruitful lives and stop living as immature Christians.

The setting up of the [KIROHO] "spiritual realm" as the new background framing leads to the broadening of the concept IRUA* with all its related concepts being redefined within this new RS. An example is the concept MAŨNDŨ MA TENE "former things/actions," which one needs to get rid of since they belong to the former stage/age which is redefined in light of what would be considered as sinful or evil from a biblical perspective. Such would include rituals such as that of [GWĨKO] which refers to fondling with girls, that of [KWĨHURA MBIRO] involving sex which is meant to remove the marks left after the wound is healed, that of bullying of initiates during the seclusion period, singing and dancing to immoral songs, etc., are eliminated as false assumptions in the context of the new [KIROHO] frame which is basically informed by a Christian world view.

Another example has to do with the understanding of the concepts MWAANA "child" and MŨNDŨ MŨGIMA "an adult." The concept MWAANA when activated within the traditional [IRUA*] frame refers to one who engages in childish behavior referred to as *waana* or *ũhĩĩ*. Such behavior includes *gũtwara mũbara* "playing with a hoop made of a strong bent stick," *kũhũra mbira* "spinning wooden pegs and whipping them with a lash called *kĩgũtha*," and *kũhũra nyororoka* "skidding in clay mud using trunks from banana stems," among others. Within the context of the new [KIROHO] frame, the concept MWAANA* is redefined as a reference to those who are immature in faith and are likely to participate in sinful behavior condemned from the biblical perspective. On the same note, the concept MŨNDŨ MŨGIMA is also redefined within this new RS to refer to a person who is spiritually mature and can be entrusted with church responsibilities, including that of teaching others. Within this new RS, the concepts MWAANA* and MŬNDŪ MŬGIMA* are not necessarily defined by one's age, given that a mature person can be young in age and yet be mature in faith, and vice versa.

4.3.2.4 The Receptor Language Inner Spaces

The RS context of the [KIROHO] "spiritual" frame affects the formulation of the inner spaces in the interpretation of the metaphor translated as *kŭrua ngoro* "circumcision of heart" in the DS of Romans 2:29. In highlighting these inner spaces, I will be pointing out links between these mental spaces as well as how the notion of the achievement of cognitive effects is achieved.

4.3.2.4.1 The receptor language generic and input spaces

The type of integration network that is recruited in the construction of the meaning of the metaphorical blend "*kŭrua ngoro*" "circumcision of heart" in Romans 2:29 is that of a single-scope network. The input spaces are that of [IRUA*] in IS_1 with the organizing frame of [KŬGIMARA] "entering adulthood status" and that of KŬHONOKA "being born again," which is activated within the [KĪROHO] "spiritual realm" in IS_2. The source frame of [KŬGIMARA] is selected to organize the blend. The properties in the GS that apply to the general structure in the integration process include agency, goal, recipient, age, object, and instrument, which have corresponding elements in the input spaces as demonstrated in figure 8.

IS_1 itself is a blend resulting from two other input spaces through the compressions of time, cause-effect, and change. As far as the vital relations of time and change are concerned, we find that though the two input spaces resulting in IS_1 are separated in time and status they have been brought together with the boy undergoing the ritual being perceived as an adult member of the society. There is the integration of a cause and its effects in that the performance of the ritual is experienced simultaneously in both the blend and in the future life of the individual. This is demonstrated in the fact that the lifetime of an adult member of the society is compressed to that of undergoing the ritual of [IRUA*]. In the performative function of the ritual, we find the vital relation of change since the teenage boy undergoing the ritual is automatically transformed into an adult member of the society.

A number of elements are activated under the category of human agency in IS_1 due to the different roles attributed to them within the ritual frame of

[IRUA*]. These include *mūruithia* "the one who circumcises," *mūtiiri* "one who nurses the initiate as he recuperates or the initiate's godfather," *aciari* "parents," and *Ngai* "God," whose blessings are sought for the success of the ritual, among others. The goal of this ritual is on the one hand to mark that one has left the stage of *waana* or *ũhĩĩ* and on the other to usher one into adulthood status. This stage activates other related concepts such as *riika* "age group" together with its accompanying responsibilities. The recipients or beneficiaries in IS_1 are *ihĩĩ* "uncircumcised boys" in their teenage years. The object is the prepuce of the sexual organ which is symbolic of the removal of childhood behavior and the instruments are both that of a sharp object as well as that of teachings, since [IRUA*] is first and foremost a teaching ritual with the goal of shaping the mind and behavior of the initiates.

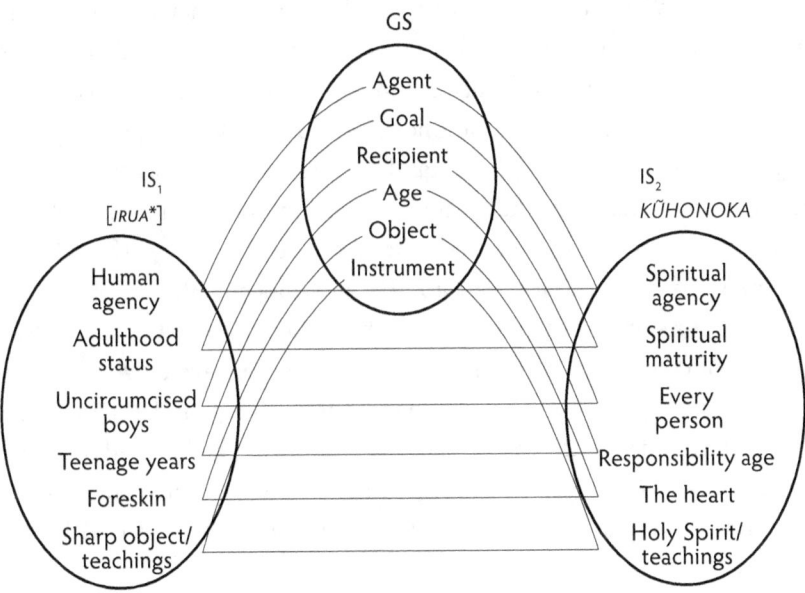

Figure 8: The receptor language generic and input spaces

In IS_2, the spiritual agency that is activated strongly is that of NGAI* with this concept undergoing change over the years due to the influence of Christianity mostly through the process of derivation of new contextual implications through interaction with existing information. The concept *Ngai* has been equated as being the same as that of the God of the Bible and in the process enlarged or broadened to include the other members of the Godhead (i.e. the Son and the Holy Spirit). The attribute of him being the sole creator and giver of all things is maintained while such sub-concepts as KĪRĪNYAGA "place of brightness," currently referred to as Mount Kenya, as his dwelling place, MŨGUMO "fig tree" as the place where sacrifices are offered to him, NGOMA "ancestors," etc. being eliminated in light of the new attributed associated with the biblical God. In their place, we find the derivation of new concepts such as IGŨRŨ "heaven," KANITHA "church," and SAITANI "Satan."[42]

As discussed above, other agents within this frame, such as that of MŨTIIRI, which refers to the one who nurses the initiate as he recuperates, is redefined through the process of derivation of new contextual implications to refer to a church worker. The goal of the ritual has also acquired some spiritual bearing within the new [KIROHO] "spiritual" frame as that of getting rid of immaturity as far as one's faith is concerned. There are other benefits that are activated in the blend through the process of completion by the derivation of new contextual implications such as those of forgiveness of sin, becoming a member of the family of God, etc. The beneficiaries include all people groups regardless of their age, sex, and cultural background, as long as they respond in faith, which eliminates the existing assumption from the traditional frame of [IRUA*] of restricting beneficiaries to Kikuyu teenage boys. The object of renewal is of course that of NGORO, which is conceptualized as being the container or storage of evil feelings and behavior as well as the place where feelings or emotions originated from as well as were expressed. As a result of the derivation of new contextual implications, we find that the cause agents are compressed with the role of the Holy Spirit being highlighted in the DS of Romans 2 as the one through whom the beneficiaries are recruited into fellowship and enabled to meet the obligations that are stipulated within the new [KIROHO] frame.

---

42. Kenyatta, *Facing Mount Kenya*, 308–309. According to Kenyatta ("Kikuyu Religion," 324) there are three main groups in the spirit world. The first ones are the spirits of the parents who communicate directly with the living children advising them and also punishing them as they did when they were alive, the second are the clan spirits who are said to watch over the welfare and prosperity of the clan and thus administer justice according to any of the members of the clan as individuals or the clan as a whole, and thirdly the age-group spirits, who can also be referred to as tribal spirits since age-groups unify the clan, who are concerned the activities of their respective particular age-groups.

4.3.2.4.2 The receptor language blended space

The content that appears in the blend is arrived at through three interrelated cognitive processes, namely that of composition, completion, and elaboration, within the relevance theoretic framework. See figure 9 below which highlights the main elements that are projected into the BS.

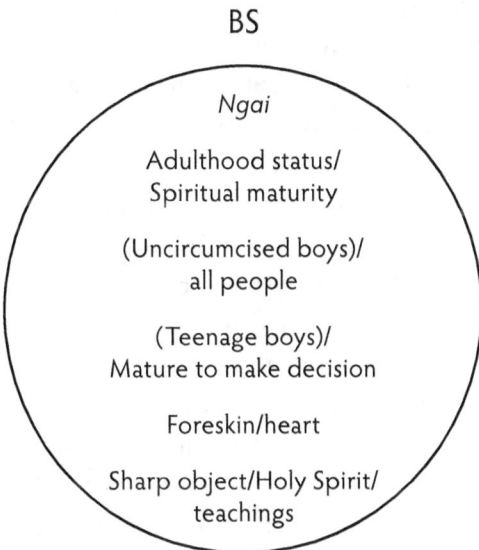

Figure 9: The receptor language blended space

The concept NGAI "God" is projected in the blend from each of the input spaces through the process of composition since the RS dictates that this process is spiritual in nature. In the blend, the concept NGAI* is broadened from the traditional understanding to allow for the extension of this title to include the other members of the godhead. On the other hand, spiritual beings associated with the traditional frame of [IRUA*] such as *ngoma* "ancestors" are eliminated in light of new evidence from the background framing of the nature of the biblical God. Other spiritual beings such as *araika* "angels," *maroho moru* "bad spirits," etc., are derived within the new RS. The idea of *Ngai* being confined on Mount *Kĩrĩnyaga* is now eliminated as a false assumption in light of the new evidence of his dwelling in heaven.

Through the process of derivation of new contextual implications in the blend, we find the fusion of elements with the inference of maturity associated within one's spiritual status. The initiate is expected to exhibit accompanying actions or behaviors such as *kwĩheana mũno kũrĩ Ngai na ũthamaki wake* "to surrender completely to God and [to] his kingdom," *gwĩka wendi wake* "to do his will," *ũthingu* "holiness," among other qualities. A further inference that can be drawn in the blend is that such a person can now be entrusted with leadership responsibilities. Other benefits, which are generated through the process of elaboration generated in the blend, include forgiveness of sin and becoming a member of the family of God.

The beneficiaries and age of the initiates in the blend are arrived at through the process of composition in two different ways, namely, the fusion of elements from both input spaces and/or the projection of a single element as new contextual implications are derived in the BS. As far beneficiaries are concerned, there is the possibility of the fusion of elements from both input spaces as the element *ihĩĩ* "uncircumcised boys" from IS_1 and that of all the people from IS_2 are fused together so that the beneficiaries are inclusive regardless of age, sex, and cultural background with the element "all nations" also projected as a single element into the blend. As far as age is concerned, the element "teenagers" from IS_1 and that of all the "mature enough to make decision" from IS_2 are fused together so it includes both teenagers as well as those who are mature enough to make the decision for (spiritual) maturity and through the projection of a single element into the blend, the element "mature enough to make decision" is also arrived at. Also, through the process of completion in the blend, there is the fusion of elements in that both "foreskin" and "heart" are projected as objects into the blend.

Again, through the process of completion in the blend there is the fusion of elements in the blend as "sharp object" and "teachings" from IS_1 are fused to those of "Holy Spirit" and "teachings" from IS_2. The sharp object is used to get rid of the foreskin and since [IRUA*] is a teaching ritual, the teachings which are now modified within the [KĨROHO] frame, also projected to the blend. The element "Holy Spirit," as a member of the Godhead, is also projected as instrument into the blend. The teachings are modified to prepare the initiates for the new way of life, now that they have become mature members of the society, as well as to equip them with Christian values, beliefs and attitudes. There are some teachings offered in the traditional input of [IRUA*] which are eliminated and thus hindered from entering the blend based on the fact that they are considered as sinful or evil within the new RS. Such include being encouraged to fondle girls in a ritual referred to as *gwĩko*, to participate in the ritual of [KWĨHURA MBIRO] "participating in sex so as to remove the marks left after the wound is healed," bullying of initiates during the seclusion period, singing and dancing to immoral songs, to mention a few.

4.4 Summary

Following the relevance theoretic comprehension procedure, the translation of the metaphorical blend περιτομὴ καρδίας in the context of Romans 2 as "*kũrua ngoro*" "circumcision of the heart" into Kikuyu is problematic. This is because both the elements of adulthood status and spiritual maturity are naturally projected into the blend. These interpretations are inconsistent with the one arrived at in the previous chapter, which narrowed the meaning of this metaphor to that of a cleansing or purging ritual which all people need to undergo so as to be cleansed of their sins. Therefore, the interpretation arrived at which highlights the status of being immature in the faith, needs to be corrected, since it is not the subject that Paul is addressing in the context of Romans 2. The challenge now becomes how best to translate the SL metaphorical blend περιτομὴ καρδίας in the context of Romans 2 to a Kikuyu speaker, guiding them to access the intended assumptions in order to draw the intended conclusions, a concern that is addressed in the next chapter.

CHAPTER 5

Translating the Metaphorical Blend

In this chapter, I will propose how to translate the SL metaphorical blend as arrived at in chapter 3, in light of the misconception that is reflected in the RL blend as discussed in chapter 4. I will first recap the discussions on the contents of the source and receptor language blended spaces, highlight the background framing and relevant metonymic links and inferences entertained in the translation space, including relevant inferences that need to be projected to the receptor language target space (RLTS), before proposing how best to render the metaphor into the RL in the context of Romans 2. I will then propose the procedure for translating a metaphorical blend in light of the proposed complementary approach, before making some concluding remarks.

5.1 The Source Language Blended Space

As discussed in chapter 3, I have argued that the interpretation of the metaphor περιτομὴ καρδίας that is projected to the source language blended space (SLBS) as that of a cleansing or purging ritual. This interpretation arrived at through the derivation of new contextual implications through interaction with existing information as the LXX translators rendered the Hebrew verb מול "he circumcised" with the Greek concept ΚΑΘΑΡΟΣ "to purge" or "to purify." I argued that the apostle Paul as very likely having borrowed the use of this conventional metaphor from the Greek version of the OT since it was the Bible of his time.[1] I also argued that the context of the use of this metaphor

---

1. Stanley, *Paul and the Language of Scripture*, 67.

in the LXX has to do with circumcision being conceptualized as a means of purification with object of removal being reproach, rebellion and iniquity, stubbornness and uncleanness, thus having morality and cultic purity as its salient factors.[2] In light of the additional outer inputs (i.e. the discourse and relevance spaces within the integration process), I have argued that the meaning of the metaphor projected to the SLBS in the context of Romans 2 is that of a cleansing or purging ritual which one needs to undergo so as to be cleansed of their sins.

5.2 The Receptor Language Blended Space

As discussed in chapter 4, the meaning of the metaphor translated as "*irua rĩa ngoro*" "circumcision of the heart" which is erroneously projected into the receptor language blended space (RLBS) is that of spiritual maturity. See the following field responses that were quoted in chapter 3.

(69) *Mũndũ ũgimarĩte na thĩinĩ.*
Person matured on inside
"A person who has spiritually matured."

(70) *Nĩ kũgimara na gũtigana na maũndũ ma tene.*
It.is to.mature and leaving the things of past
"It is maturing and leaving behind [bad] things that one used to do in the past."

(71) *Nĩ mwĩto wa kũgimara kĩroho na gũtigana na*
It.is calling to be.mature spiritually and leaving the
mĩtugo ĩtarĩ ya kĩũngai.
traditions which.not of God
"It is being called/separated so as to become spiritually mature and leaving traditions that are not Godly."

(72) *Nĩ kũgimara mũndũ agatiga gũkorwa arĩ mwana wa*
It.is maturing person abandons to.be a child of

---

2. Lev 19:23; Deut 18:10; 30:6; 10:16.

kĩroho   agatuĩka   mũgima   kĩroho.
spiritual he.becomes mature   spiritually
"It is [the process of] maturing [so that] a person abandons being a spiritual child and becomes mature spiritually."

(73) Ciĩko   ciaku   cikonania   ũgima.
     Actions yours   to.demonstrate maturity
     "It is when one's actions demonstrate that one is mature [spiritually]."

(74) Kũgimara   na   kwĩheana   mũno   kũrĩ   Ngai   na
     to.mature   and   to.surrender   very.much   to   God   and
     ũthamaki   wake.
     kingdom   his
     "To mature and [as a result] surrender more to God and his kingdom."

(75) Nĩ   kũgimara   mũndũ   agatuĩka   mũgima   kĩroho.
     it.is to.mature person becomes   mature   spiritually
     "It is to mature [so that] a person becomes mature spiritually."

This interpretation is arrived at through the process of completion in the blend as respondents seek to derive new contextual information by recruiting their background knowledge which has to do with conceptualizing the ritual of [IRUA*] as a process of achieving adulthood status as the following example points out.

(76) Kũringana   na   mĩtugo   ya   Agĩkũyũ   nĩ   atĩ
     According   to   customs   of   Kikuyu   is   that

     mũndũ   arĩkia   kũgimara   mwena-inĩ   wa
     person   when.he   undergoes.circumcision on.the.side of

     mwana   wa   kahĩĩ   arĩ   wa   mbere   thĩinĩ   wa   mũciĩ
     child   of   boy   if   of   first   in   of   household

ona	*akorwo*	*arĩ wa*	*kĩhinga*	*nda*	
even.if	he	is of	closing	stomach	

anyitagwo atĩ nĩ mũtongoria na akaheo
he.is.perceived as he.is leader and he.is.given

gĩtĩo kĩa mwanya mũciĩ tondũ nĩ
respect which.is special in.homestead because he

mwana wa mũciĩ ndakahika ta mũirĩtu …Mwana
child of home he.will.not.get.married like girl child

wa kahĩĩ endetwo nĩ ithe tondũ akua
of.boy is.loved by his.father because when.he.dies

nĩwe wehokagĩrwo ũtongoria-inĩ mũciĩ ũcio agimara.
he.is entrusted leadership.in homestead that after.circumcision

"According to Kikuyu customs male child who undergoes circumcision whether he be the first born or the last born in the family, he is received as a leader and he is given special respect in that homestead because he stays in the home since he will not go away from the homestead and get married as a girl child does . . . a boy child is loved by his father because when the father dies the boy child is entrusted with the leadership of the homestead since the boy child had undergone circumcision."

There is need for the Kikuyu readers to be guided to arrive at the SL intended interpretation which has to do with a cleansing or purification ritual for Paul is not addressing himself to the process of maturing in faith, an issue which he addresses elsewhere.³ This chapter addresses itself to this challenge of guiding the Kikuyu readers to arrive at the intended SL meaning of the metaphor περιτομὴ καρδίας in the context of Romans 2 so that they can make the right connections within the integration network and as a result draw relevant inferences.

---

3. cf. 1 Cor 13:11; 14:20.

5.3 The Translation Space

McElhanon has proposed a translation model based on conceptual blending which has an additional space, namely that of the translation space. He argues that this space should have "metonymic links with the content of the SL blended space and should allow for inferences to be projected from the translation space to the target space."[4] The translation space will be used here as a platform to enable the comparison of the source and receptor language blended spaces so as to highlight the relevant connections between them with the intended meaning projected to the RLTS, as figure 10 below demonstrates.

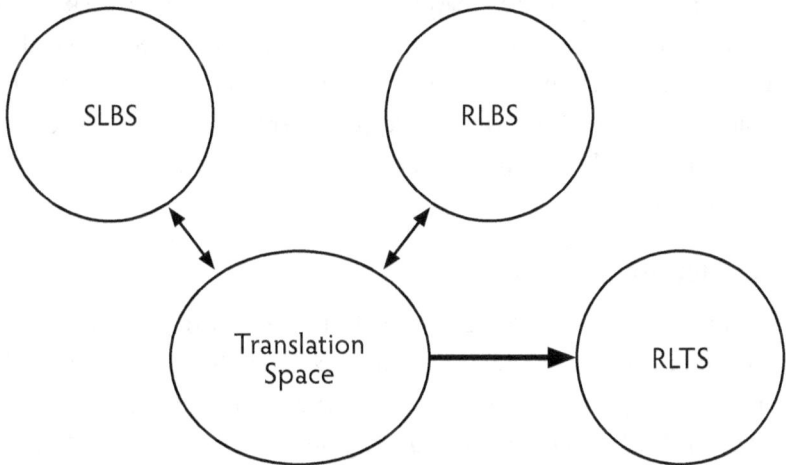

Figure 10: The translation and receptor language target spaces

In this section, I will point out the contextual gaps and metonymic links between the source and target language blended spaces as well as analyze the background framing and highlight the relevant inferences that need to be projected from the translation space to the RLTS. Using the proposed complementary approach, I will also suggest the way forward in terms of putting in place appropriate bridging strategies in order to communicate the intended meaning across the languages.

---

4. McElhanon, "From Simple Metaphors," 69–70.

5.3.1 Target Space Background Framing

The method that is adapted to arrive at the background framing that is projected from the translation space to the target space is that of hyper-framing.[5] In this process, the background framing draws from the background framings of both the SL and RL blended spaces. This means that the resulting RLTS organizing frame includes the two "different (and often clashing) organizing frames" (i.e. that of a purification ritual from the SLBS and that of change of status from the RLBS), thus ending up with its own emergent structure.[6] I will seek to modify or enrich the target readers' existing conceptual framework so as to match the one assumed to have been the most likely one evoked by the first or original readers by analyzing instances where the two background frames overlap as well as where they differ on important aspects. I will then make recommendations on how to bridge the gap so that the target readers can be able to draw the right contextual inferences in the RLTS so as to arrive at the intended meaning of the SL metaphor περιτομὴ καρδίας in the context of Romans 2.

5.3.2 Metonymic Links

As mentioned above, the SLBS and the RLBS are linked in the translation space with each of their respective frames contributing towards the background framing of the RLTS. Between these two blended spaces, there are metonymic links that overlap as well as those that clash. As a result, I will be highlighting in the following sections relevant inferences from both the source and receptor language blended spaces entertained in the translation space and point out relevant ones that need to be accommodated in the RLTS. Such inferences are arrived at within the relevance theoretic framework since the tendency is to maximize the relevance of any element in the integration network by entertaining those that prompt the right network connections and excluding any that warrants unwanted connections.[7]

---

5. Wendland, "Framing the Frames," 34.
6. Fauconnier and Turner, *Way We Think*, 131.
7. Fauconnier and Turner, 334.

5.3.2.1 Metonymic Links from the Source Inputs

There are instances where the background framings of the source and receptor languages allow for the derivation of overlapping inferences across the two languages and other instances where the derived inferences do not match. The striking overlap has to do with the nature of the ritual. The nature of SLBS is that of a spiritual obligation with Jesus Christ as the mediator and every member of God's community expected to undergo this inward spiritual process.[8] When this is integrated with the meaning of the SL metaphor περιτομὴ καρδίας in the context of Romans 2, which has to do with a cleansing or purification ritual, the relevant inference that is entertained in the translation space that needs to be projected to the RLTS is that this process is an inward spiritual process required for those who want to become members of God's community of faith. A comparable inference from the receptor language input space (RLIS) schema is that of fulfilling a social requirement of moving from one status to another in the spiritual realm as well as that of fulfilling responsibilities associated with that status as the following examples point out.

(77) *Nĩ   ũrĩa   mũndũ   ataũkĩragĩrwonĩ Ũkirsto. Ciĩko*
It.is how   person is.revealed   by   Christianity. Actions
ciaku cikonania ũgima.
yours shows   maturity
"[Circumcision of heart] refers to the process whereby Christianity is revealed to a person and his actions show maturity."

(78) *Nĩ   kũgimara mũndũ agatiga gũkorwa   arĩ   mwana wa*
It.is maturing   person abandons to.be a   child of
kĩroho agatuĩka   mũgima   kĩroho.
spiritual he.becomes mature   spiritually
"It is [the process of] maturing [so that] a person abandons being a spiritual child and becomes mature spiritually."

(79) *Mũndũ agarũragwo agakorwo arĩ   mũndũ mwerũ witĩkionĩ*
person is.changed becomes a   person new   in.faith
ona   ningĩ   mĩtugoinĩ nĩguo   onekane na   njĩra

---

8. Williamson, "Circumcision," 123; Byrne, *Romans*, 39; cf. Rom 1:3–4; 3:24.

and	also		in.actions	so.that	he.is.seen	in	way
ya	*ngūrani*	*na*	*ūrīa*	*ararī*	*hau*		*kabere.*
of	different	with	how	he.was	there		before

"It is a person being changed a becoming a new person in faith and also in his actions and is seen in a different way from how he was before."

This RL inference of merely fulfilling a social requirement is mutually incompatible with that projected from the SLBS and if not suppressed is likely to lead the target readers to think of the cleansing or purging ritual as merely fulfilling a social requirement associated one's spiritual maturity. There is need to eliminate this inference from being projected to the RLTS in light of the context of Romans 2 which is that of a cleansing or purification ritual.

Another inference projected from the SLBS to the translation space is the focus of this ritual as being internal, not merely external.[9] Assumptions that have to do with the construal of this ritual as merely physical are eliminated as false in light of Paul's argument within the DS of Romans 2:17–29 that the cleansing ritual is purely a spiritual process as has been argued above. From the RLBS, we find the same internal nature of the ritual being projected to the translation space for the main emphasis of the ritual is expected to be an internal transformation that results to maturity of the individual as examples 69 and 75 quoted above point out. Since the internal nature of the ritual is compatible across the two languages, this inference is entertained in the translation space and also needs to be projected to the RLTS.

One of the inferences likely to be projected into the RLTS from the source language input space (SLIS) is the possibility of arguing that performing the physical ritual of circumcision is no longer necessary. Paul seems to have anticipated such a debate, and goes ahead to eliminate it as false by stating that the Jewish ritual of circumcision has its advantages, one of which has to do with being entrusted with the words of God (Rom 3:1). As pointed out back in chapter 3, in interpreting the ritual within the [ΚΑΙΝΗ ΔΙΑΘΗΚΗ] "new covenant" frame, Paul is careful not to downplay the value of the Jewish circumcision ritual but states that it is insufficient in ushering people into a

---

9. Morris, *Epistle to the Romans*, 143; Rom 2:29.

covenantal relationship with God.[10] A related inference that is also eliminated is that of construing this ritual as being incompatible with faith in Jesus Christ. The example of Paul himself as being circumcised as well as a believer in Jesus Christ eliminates such an inference as false.[11] The parallel attempt to Christianize the concept IRUA* from the SLIS is evidence that the ritual is construed by the receptor language speakers as being compatible with faith in Jesus Christ as the following extract from an interview with a pastor in one of the villages points out. The focus of the church is that of "Christianizing" the ritual, so to speak.

(80) *Rĩrĩa   tuonire itũra   ũrĩa   rĩhuanarĩ, gũkĩambĩrĩria kũgĩa   na*
     When   we.saw village how it.is   it.started   to.have with

   maũndũ ma ikundi citiganĩterĩ, cigoka   na   maũndũ
   things   of groups various   they.come with   things

   rĩngĩ   nĩmaugĩkũyũ, kwĩna   irĩra   nacio,
   sometimes of.Kikuyu   there.are teachings of.those

   kuga   maraheana...   na maũndũ   maingĩ ma
   saying they.are.teaching of things   many   of

   ũũrathoni... rĩu   kanitha ĩkĩoya mũrigo nĩguo   ĩhote   kũgitĩra
   immorarity now Church   took   burden so.that to.be.able to.protect

   rũciaro   kwoguo ĩkĩgĩa   na   mũbango
   generation so   it.initiated   the   process

   wa kũharagĩria   irua.
   of   hosting   circumcision.ritual

---

10. Elliot, *Rhetoric of Romans*, 198; Rom 4:11.
11. cf. Phil 3:5–11.

"When we saw how the ritual was being observed with different groups having varied expectations, some of which had to do with keeping the culture of the Kikuyu people whose teachings were immoral, the church took the responsibility of conducting circumcision rituals as a measure to protect the next generation."

Another inference that is projected from both the source and receptor language blended spaces to the translation space is that of the reversal of status, to the effect that those who are circumcised can be regarded as uncircumcised if they fail to meet the stipulations or obligations of the respective cultural rituals. From the SLBS, there is the possibility of the reversal of one's status if one happens to live contrary to the stipulations symbolized by the ritual.[12] This inference is strengthened in the blend through the process of completion by derivation of new contextual information in light of the attribute of the impartiality of God.[13] This means that anyone who has undergone the cleansing ritual can now assume the status, which initially belonged to a Jew. This leads to the revision of the traditional frame by elimination of previously held assumption of non-Jews as being "outside of God's covenant."[14] Another related inference that has be arrived at in the SLBS through the process of elaboration in the blend is that of the physical ritual of circumcision as no longer fulfilling the role of an identification sign marking one as belonging to the community of God's people. This allows for the construction of an emergent meaning in the SLBS centering on the significance of an individual's inward response through faith.[15] The background frame of the RLBS also allows for the possibility of a circumcised person being referred to as maintaining the former status of childishness if such a person continues to exhibit immaturity of status, as examples below points out.

(81) *Kwaga   ũgima   wa   hakiri   wĩtagwo*
     Lack.of   maturity   of   mind   is.called
     wana,   kwaga   gũkinyanĩra   kĩhakiri, kwaga

---

12. Aletti, *God's Justice in Romans*, 80; cf. Rom 2:26.
13. Rom 2:11; cf. Ps 62:12; Prov 24:12.
14. Moo, *Epistle to the Romans*, 175; cf. Rom 3:30.
15. Dunn, *Romans 9–16*, 48.

childhood	lack.of		achieving.expected.status	of.mind	lack.of
ũgima	na		ũrimũ.		
maturity	and		foolishness		

"Lacking maturity of mind is also referred to as being childish and lacking the expected status in terms of how one thinks, lacking maturity and also being foolish."

The inference of the reversal of status needs to be projected to the RLTS, which opens the possibility of the arriving at an inference that one who has undergone the cleansing or purification ritual but lives contrary to the requirements of the same ritual can beregarded as maintaining the same status as before.

The object of removal which is projected from the SLBS to the translation space is that of sin.[16] The discourse context profiles specific sins such as stealing, committing adultery, robbing temples, among others. When such are integrated with the cleansing/purging role of the ritual in the SLBS, the inference that is projected from the translated space to the RLTS is that a true Jew is one whose sins have been cleansed. On the other hand, the incompatible inference from the RLBS of the object of removal being that of immature actions as the following example points out.

(82)	*Mũndũ*	*agarũragwo*	*agakorwo*	*arĩ*	*mũndũ*	*mwerũ*	*wĩtĩkionii*
person	is.changed	becomes	a	person	new	in.faith
ona	*ningĩ*	*mĩtugoinĩ*	*nĩguo*	*onekane*	*na*	*njĩra*
and	also	in.actions	so.that	he.is.seen	in	way
ya	*ngũrani*	*na*	*ũria*	*ararĩ*	*hau*	*kabere.*
of	different	with	how	he.was	there	before

"It is a person being changed and becoming a new person in faith and also in his actions and is seen in a different way from how he was before."

This element is eliminated and hindered from being projected to the RLTS since the DS of Romans 2:17–29 profiles a different kind of sin that the cleansing or purification process is supposed to take care of. Additional inferences entertained in the translation space from the SLBS that need to be projected to the RLTS are the agency of Jesus Christ as well as that of the Spirit, with

---

16. Winter, "Cutting and Washing," 73; cf. Rom 2:17–24.

the human agency from both input spaces being eliminated as false in light of the evidence that this process is spiritual.[17]

There is an emotive attachment associated with the ritual of circumcision which is projected into the translation space from both the source and receptor language blended spaces. This inference is projected to the SLBS through the process of completion by derivation of background contextual implications since there was a general feeling that those who have undergone this ritual possess something special compared to those who have not.[18] Any Jewish male child who did not undergo the ritual was supposed to be cut off from God's people for not meeting this obligation of the covenant.[19] When this inference is integrated with the content of the SLBS, a further inference entertained in the translation space is that of the cleansing ritual as being mandatory and the same time special for members of the community of faith. The same emotion of bias towards the uncircumcised is projected to the translation space from the RLBS. Among the Kikuyu, there is a hesitation when it comes to entrusting given responsibilities to the uncircumcised, meaning that the circumcised are associated with having some special status as the following example points out.

(83) Ũtongoria   nĩ   ũnyitanĩte   na kũgimara
     Leadership   is   associated   to circumcision
     tondũ   gĩkũyũ matiĩtĩkĩtie   nomatongorio   nĩ kĩhĩĩ.
     because Kikuyu do.not.believe   they.can.be.led by uncircumcised
     "Leadership is associated with those who are circumcised because the Kikuyu do not believe that they can be led by an uncircumcised person."

When this inference of special status interacts with the cleansing ritual, it also leads to derivation of a new contextual implication of this ritual as being special in nature which again needs to be projected to the RLTS.

Within the SLBS there is an additional inference entertained in the translation space of astonishment, which is arrived at through the process of elaboration through the derivation of new contextual implications with the novel

---

17. Robinson, *Studies in Romans*, 7; cf. Rom 3:24.
18. cf. Judg 14:3; 15:18; 1 Sam 14:6.
19. cf. Exod 4:24.

conceptualization of the uncircumcised as having a covenant relationship with YHWH.[20] From the RLBS we find the same attitude of astonishment as people entertain the possibility of an uncircumcised person associating and/or enjoying the same privileges as those who are circumcised as the following example points out.

(84) Rĩu   kwoguo ndũngĩkorwo   ningĩ   mwĩna icera
     Now it.is you.cannot. be   also   you.have.association
     nakĩo   na   ũgĩka   o ũrĩa   kĩreka.   Kwoguo
     with.him and   you.do   as   he.does   therefore
     o   anaake   acio   mũrĩ   naorĩ,   mũtwaranaga
     the.same circumcised those   with   you   you.walk
     nao,   nacio   ihĩĩ   nacio
     with.them and   the.uncircumcised   those
     igagĩtigwo na   ihĩĩ   ciao.
     are.left   other   uncircumcised   ones

"Now when you are circumcised you cannot continue associating with the uncircumcised doing as they do. Therefore you are expected to associate with the circumcised and the uncircumcised to associate with the uncircumcised ones."

The attitude of astonishment when integrated with the meaning of the metaphor in the DS of Romans 2, a further inference of amazement is derived in the translation space as the possibility of a person who has *not* undergone the cleansing ritual enjoying the same blessings as those who have been cleansed is entertained.

There are links that are understood to be cemented when initiates undergo the respective rituals. From the SL background, the eight-day-olds who undergo the ritual of [ΠΕΡΙΤΟΜΗ] are linked back to the patriarchs and as a result enjoined to the everlasting covenant together with all others who have undergone the same ritual.[21] From the RLIS framing background, the relationship between those who undergo the ritual is also cemented with

---

20. Rom 2:11; cf. Ps 62:12; Prov 24:12.
21. cf. Gen 17:9–14; 23–27.

the members forming a *riika* "age group" sharing a close comradeship, as the following proverb points out.

(85) *Riika   rītihithagwo   gīathī*
     (One's) age group   is.not.hidden   meeting
     "One is not supposed to hide anything from his age group."

There are two inferences relating to relationships of members that can be derived when integrated with the cleansing or purification ritual that can be entertained in the translation space. The first one is that the benefactor is linked to the promises given to the patriarchs and the second one is that of the beneficiaries being enjoined with others who have undergone the same cleansing ritual as brothers and sisters in Christ.[22]

There are a number of mutually compatible compressions from the source and target language blended spaces that are entertained in the translation space that are also projected to the RLTS through the vital relations of time, change, identity, and cause-effect. As far as the inner-space relation of time is concerned, the entire life of the individuals undergoing the respective rituals is scaled down to the few minutes in which the ritual is conducted. From the source input space, the entire life of the Jewish male child as one of the community members of God's people is condensed to undergoing the ritual of circumcision, and on the other hand, that of a Kikuyu teenage boy as an adult member of the society is scaled down to the amount of time that the ritual of [IRUA*] takes. When the vital relation of time is integrated with the content of the cleansing or purification ritual and projected from the translation space to the RLTS, the inference that is derived is that of the entire life of the person undergoing the ritual being condensed to the few seconds when this process takes place.

As far as the vital relation of change is concerned, the male child undergoing the circumcision ritual in the SLIS is automatically transformed by a stroke of the knife to be one of those chosen by God to inherit his promises.[23] This same performative function is reflected in the RLIS in that the teenage boy undergoing the ritual of [IRUA*] is automatically transformed to become

---

22. Morris, *Epistle to the Romans*, 68; Rom 3:24; cf. Col 2:11; Heb 1:1–2; 9:11–15.

23. Derouchie, "Circumcision in the Hebrew Bible," 186–196; Williamson, "Circumcision," 123.

an adult member of the society as pointed out earlier in example 76. The initiates are conceptualized as adult members in the respective community despite the manifest differences in terms of age, experiences, etc. When the vital relation of change is integrated in the content of the blend, the inference that is projected to the RLTS through the process of derivation of new contextual implications is that of the immediate transformation that takes place in the life of an individual who has undergone the cleansing ritual, which include the forgiveness of sins and partaking of the blessings that accompany such status.[24]

As far as the vital relation of identity is concerned, we find that from the SLIS the eight-day-old boy is now identified with the patriarchs as well as with the other members of the people who have undergone the same ritual.[25] We also find the same process of identity in the RLBS whereby a Kikuyu teenage boy who has undergone the ritual of circumcision is automatically identified with his respective age group and also as an adult member of the society as the following proverb points out.

(86) *Nyũmba   na   riika   itiumagwo*
     One's family and one's age-set not.abandon
     "One cannot abandon his family or age group."

When this vital relation of identity is integrated with the cleansing ritual in the blend, the inference that is projected to the RLTS through derivation of a new contextual implication is that the one who has undergone the cleansing ritual is automatically identified with the Lord Jesus Christ who is the mediator of the new covenant as well as becomes a member of the body of Christ together with those who have undergone the same ritual.[26] As far as the vital relation of cause-effect is concerned, we find the rituals from the source and receptor input spaces being scaled down to a single composite role with the inference of the cleansing ritual as fulfilling the role of purging one from their sins being projected from the translation space to the RLTS.

There are a couple of additional weaker inferences that can be projected to the translation space and end up enriching RLTS. One such element that

---

24. Moo, *Epistle to the Romans*, 729.
25. Butler, *Joshua*, 58; Williamson, "Circumcision," 122.
26. Murray, *Epistle to the Romans*, 215; cf. Rom 1:8; 3:24; 6:3–5; 1 Cor 12:13.

can be projected from the RLIS and integrated with the content of the SLBS is that of renewal since the initiate of [*IRUA**] is expected to come out as a new person who has delinked himself from the previous stage as pointed out in example 84 above. When this element is integrated with the content of the SLBS in the translation space, the inference that is projected to the RLTS is that a person who has undergone the cleansing ritual is supposed to have nothing to do with the previous status of sinfulness. Another inference from the RLIS that can be entertained in the translation space has to do with the vital relation of intentionality which makes the RLTS even more intelligible. From the RLIS, the boys are eager to undergo the ritual so as to attain the resulting prestigious status and stop being regarded with derision and contempt.[27] When this element is integrated with the content of the SLBS, the inference that is projected to the target space is that of eagerness among those who intend to undergo the cleansing ritual. This inference cannot be derived from the SLIS since the eight-day-old male child lacks intentionality because he is not in a position to consent or dissent to the physical ritual of circumcision.

5.3.2.2 *Metonymic Links from the Target Inputs*

There are also instances where the background framings of the source and receptor target spaces allow for the derivation of shared inferences as well as instances where the inferences are not shared. Within the SL schema, the concept ΚΑΡΔΙΑ "heart" is conceptualized as the seat and function of reason given that it is used mostly in a parallel and synonymous relationship with that of the concept ΝΟΥΣ "mind."[28] The inference of the heart is also associated as being the "center of consciousness, thought or will," an inference that is expected to be projected to the translation space.[29] On the other hand, the function of thinking in the RL is associated with the concept *HAKIRI* "mind" as the following examples point out.

(87) *Kwaga   gwīciria.*
      not   thinking
    "Not thinking/reasoning well."

---

27. Wambūgū, Ngarariga, and Kariūki, *The Agīkūyū*, 85.
28. 2 Cor 3:14–15; Phil 4:7.
29. Banwell, "Heart," 625.

(88) Gwīciria wega.
    to.think well
    "To think/reason well."

When the concept HAKIRI is associated with that of IRUA*, the concept HAKIRI* is narrowed to refer to behaviors that a mature person is associated with, which include making concrete decisions, having a deep understanding of issues, having virtues such as being disciplined, respectful and patient, among other virtues as the following examples point out.

(89) Mūndū ūngītūmīra hakiri/ūūgī na gūtua   matua magima/marūmu.
    Person who.uses   mind   by making decisions mature/stable
    "This is a person who uses his mind to make mature/stable decisions."

(90) | Maciaro | nī | kūgia | na | ūtaūku, | gūkorwo |
|---|---|---|---|---|---|
| Fruits | include | to.have | with | wisdom | to.be |
| wī mūndū | wīna | mūbango | na | wīkinyīire | gūkīra |
| a person | who.has | plans | and | stable | more.than |
| andū | a | riika | rīaku | na | noūthurwo |
| people | of | age group | yours | and | you.can.be.elected |
| ūtongoria-inī | kana | wīhokerwo | ūndū | mūna. | |
| to.lead | or | be.entrusted | issue | certain | |

"Fruits [of one who has matured in the mind] include having wisdom and [good] plans and being stable in life more than one's age-mates and can be elected to lead or be entrusted with certain responsibilities."

Unfortunately, there are other vices that are associated with the uncircumcised, behavior which the circumcised are encouraged to do away with, which are not necessarily sinful from the SL perspective. Such include associating with people who are not circumcised and participating in what is referred to as *waana* "childish games" such as *gūtwara mūbara* "playing with a hoop made of strong bent stick," *kūhūra mbira* "spinning wooden pegs and whipping them with a lash called *kīgūtha*," *kūhūra nyororoka* "skidding in clay mud using trunks from banana stems," and hunting small animals such as birds, rats, squirrels, among other activities. These are eliminated as false in light of the construal of what is sin from the DS of Romans 2.

There are a number of compatible entities that are shared between the SL and RL input spaces when it comes to the conceptualization of the concept translated as "heart." Some of the compatible entities from both Source Language Target Spaces include the heart being conceptualized as a metonymy representing a person,[30] being the source, seat, and place where emotions are expressed,[31] the seat of morality and immorality,[32] as representing the inner life,[33] and also as the center of one's personality and character.[34] When this information is integrated with the cleansing ritual, an additional inference that can be derived and projected into the RLTS is that of a cleansed heart becoming the center of spiritual life and of faith. From the RLTS, the concept NGORO "heart" is conceptualized as a living organ, which indicates whether a person is alive or not (example 91 below), as a metonymy for a person (example 92 below), as a container or storage of qualities, emotions and feelings (example 93 below), and also as the place feelings or emotions are expressed (examples 94 and 95 below).

(91) Nĩmũrwaru biũ   no   ngoro   no   ĩrahũra.
     3sg.sick   much   but   heart   is.still   beating
     "He/she is very sick but is still alive [since the heart is still pumping blood]."

(92) Ngoro   njega.
     Heart   good
     "A good person."

(93) Ngoro   ya   tha.
     Heart   of   mercy
     "A merciful person."

---

30. cf. Ps 73:26; 84:2; Rom 9:1–2.

31. Ryken, Wilhoit, and Longman III, *Dictionary of Biblical Imagery*, 369; Ps 7:9; 26:2; Jer 17:10; 20:12; Rev 2:23.

32. Deut 9:5; Gen 20:5, 6; 1 Kings 8:61; 1 Sam 6:6; cf. Rom 2:5; Exod 7:13, 14, 22; 8:19; 9:12, 35.

33. 1 Sam 12:24; Jer 32:40; Ps 28:7; 112:7; Rom 10:6–10.

34. Banwell, "Heart," 626.

(94) *Ngoro   yakwa   ndĩmwendete.*
    Heart   mine   not.like.him/her
    "My heart does not like him/her."

(95) *E   ngoro   njũru   mũno.*
    He/she.has heart   bad   very.much
    "He/she does not have a welcoming heart."

Availing the necessary SL contextual information is important in assisting the target audience to draw the intended inferences. Such would assist the target audience on the one hand correct wrong inferences and on the other draw the right assumptions which would help them arrive at the intended meaning of the SL metaphor in the context of Romans 2. One such inferences is that of construal of the concept NGORO* as a container or storage of good and evil qualities or characteristics as well as the place where feelings and emotions are initiated and expressed. This would then give rise to an additional inference projected to the translation space which allows the heart to be conceptualized as the place where God reveals himself and where conversion takes place.

5.4 Rendering of the Metaphorical Blend

As established above, there are both mutually compatible entities as well as mismatches across the source and target language blended spaces that are accommodated within the translation space. The challenge now becomes how to address the differences which, if projected in the RLTS, could risk leading to the derivation of erroneous inferences that could end up distorting the message conveyed in the context of Romans 2. It is clear that though the associated concepts in this metaphor between the source and receptor cultures are not entirely mismatched, the relevant inferences drawn in the RL are strong enough to interfere with the message that is conveyed in the context of Romans 2.

I have chosen to render the relevant specific meaning of the SL metaphor within the translation as *gũtherio kwa ngoro* "the cleansing of the heart" and also to provide additional extra-textual information in the glossary so as to maintain a higher degree of meaning resemblance with the original. The purging process is brought out in chapter 4 as to the meaning attached to the ritual of [IRUA*] with the cutting of the foreskin symbolizing getting rid of actions or behavior associated with the uncircumcised. The extra-textual information in the glossary describing the ritual from the SL perspective is intended to enrich the RL cognitive frame by supplying the missing SL relevant information as context adjustment information through the process of hyper-framing.[35] The chosen rendering *gũtherio kwa ngoro* makes the meaning of the metaphor more specific within the current DS of Romans 2. The aim of this rendering is to bring out the implicated premise of the metaphorical blend as that of a cleansing or purifying ritual so as to guide the target audience to draw the intended inferences from the SL background framing. The suggested rendering of the metaphor is given below, with the asterisk representing information to be found in appendix I.

²⁸*Nĩ gũkorwo gũtuĩka Mũyahundi to kũhingia mĩtugo ya kĩũyahudi, na kũrua kwama to tu kĩmwĩrĩ,* ²⁹no Mũyahundi kũna nĩ ũria arĩwe ngoro thĩinĩ, na kũrua kwama nĩ gũtherio kwa ngoro* na njĩra ya Roho Mũtheru ti watho. Mũndũ ta ũyũ akumagio nĩ Ngai no ti.*

For it.is to.be Jew not.only to.fulfill customs of the.Jewish and circumcision real not only bodily but a.Jew true.one is who the.one heart inside and circumcision true is be.cleansed of heart by means of Spirit Holy not Law Person like this is.praised by God but not

"For one to be a Jew is not only to fulfill the Jewish customs and real circumcision is not only that of the body but a true Jew is one who is one in the heart and true circumcision is the cleansing of the heart, by means of the Holy Spirit not [by fulfilling] the Law. A person like this is praised by God but not [by] man."

---

35. Wendland, "Framing the Frames," 34.

One mismatch that is rectified by providing the extra-textual information in the glossary has to do with the object of removal. From the SLBS, the object that is projected to the translation space is that of sin, with the current SLDS profiling specific kinds of sins such as stealing, committing adultery, robbing temples, etc.[36] When this projected element is integrated with the cleansing/purging role of the ritual in the SLBS, the major inferences projected to the target space is that a true Jew is one whose sins have been cleansed. The information in the glossary is informed by the need to suppress the projection of the wrong objects from the RLBS, such as *waana* "childish behavior," also referred to as *ūhīī* "behavior of one who has not undergone [IRUA*]," and any other object that does not fit into the category of sin from the biblical perspective.

The information in the glossary also includes the appropriate cross-references regarding the ritual of circumcision, which goes a long way in enriching the RL cognitive environment. This information brings to the attention of the RL readers that the Jewish ritual of circumcision is centered on meeting a religious obligation required of every Jewish eight-day-old male descendant in order to become one of God's chosen people. Information is also provided on the historical nature of the Jewish ritual tracing it back to the covenant made between God and Abraham. This additional information shapes the cognitive environment of the receptor audience and assists them in accessing the right assumptions so as to draw the intended inferences.

The source background knowledge provided in the glossary that the uncircumcised are not able to participate in religious ceremonies builds on shared knowledge with that of the receptor audience since an uncircumcised person is hindered from participating in certain social activities of the community as pointed earlier in example 76. Such a person could also not participate in sacrifices as well as in leading communal prayers. It is considered an abomination for such a person to marry or even father children for such was conceptualized as an abomination which would attract divine punishment upon the whole community. Generally, the extra-textual information provided in the glossary is intended to assist the target readers to make the important links to arrive at the interpretation of this ritual as having the salient factor of a cleansing ritual as far as the context of Romans 2 is concerned.

---

36. cf. Rom 2:21–22.

5.5 Procedure for Translating a Metaphorical Blend

In this section, I present a procedure of translating a metaphorical blend based on the steps that I have used in the rendering of the SL metaphor περιτομὴ καρδίας into Kikuyu. This procedure is based on McElhanon's five steps of interpreting a conceptual blend that are developed and modified to a total of eight steps in light of the complementary approach proposed in this work.[37]

1. This step, which corresponds to McElhanon's first step, requires one to work from the blended space(s) with the goal of describing the respective input spaces and the background framing(s) from which the input spaces are derived.[38] One is also required to establish the argument(s) made within the DS in order to see how profiled related concepts within the context influence the meaning of the metaphor(s).
2. In the second step, which corresponds to McElhanon's fifth step, the translator is expected to extract the structure that is common to the mental spaces, suggesting cover terms and entering such in the GS.[39] This step is helpful in accounting for the presumed commonality shared among the other spaces. At the same time, because the blend is metaphoric, one is to map the metonymic links between the entities in the corresponding input spaces.
3. The third step is that of establishing which of the input spaces is serving as the primary space that provides the organizing frame or scenario for the events depicted in the blended space.
4. The fourth step is to establish within the relevance theoretic framework which elements/entities within these input spaces are projected to the blend as well as those which are hindered from doing so. There are those that will be strengthened through provision of further evidence, those that will be eliminated in light of new evidence and new contextual implications derived through interaction with existing information.
5. The fifth step, which corresponds to McElhanon's third and fourth steps, requires one to find out what the content of the virtue or

---

37. McElhanon, "From Simple Metaphors," 50, 69–70.
38. McElhanon, 50.
39. McElhanon, 50.

imaginary world which is accommodated in the blended space is.[40] The content of the blend is expected to have been adapted to meet the goals of the blend's creator through the processes of composition, completion, elaboration, and compression. In running the blend, one is expected to work within the relevance theoretic framework to recruit entities from input spaces and integrate them with the content of the blend in order to allow the drawing of additional inferences projected to the target space.

6. For step 6, one is to compare the contents of the source and receptor language blended spaces in the translation space and draw relevant connections taking note of the similarities and differences in terms of entities as well as inferences resulting from the process of running the blend. Also compare the gaps between the source inputs between the two languages and establish the metonymic links and find inferences that are relevant to the original text and how they are similar or different to those of the target language, and in the process take note of any resulting erroneous conceptions. Repeat the same process as far as the target inputs are concerned.
7. The seventh step is to take note of relevant inferences that are projected from the translation space to the RLTS again within the relevance theoretic framework.
8. The last step is to look for the best way to render the meaning of the metaphor into the RL. This might include the need to enrich or correct the RL frames by use of extra-textual materials such as footnotes, illustrations, glossary, etc., to avoid derivation of wrong inferences.

5.6 Summary

In this chapter, I have proposed how to translate the SL metaphorical blend as arrived at in chapter 3 in light of the misconception that is reflected in the RL translation blend as discussed in chapter 4. I have argued for the option of rendering the metaphor using the specific meaning of a cleansing ritual and

---

40. McElhanon, 50.

bridging the conceptual gap by providing the relevant SL context adjustment information as extra-textual material. I have also discussed the metonymic links in the translation space and highlighted relevant inferences that are projected to the RLTS. I have also proposed steps that a translator can follow in translating a metaphorical blend in light of the suggested complementary approach which adhere to the overarching relevance theoretic framework.

CHAPTER 6

Conclusions and Recommendations

This chapter summarizes the answers to the questions raised at the beginning of the study as well as gives some recommendations for further research.

6.1 Conclusions

Metaphors in general pose a great challenge to a translator, since their translatability depends on reproducing particular cultural experiences and semantic associations from source to target cultures. I have demonstrated this by pointing out the cognitive frames that are activated by the associated concepts in the metaphors περιτομὴ καρδίας and its rendering as kūrua ngoro and suggested the need to guide the target audience to draw the originally intended contextual assumptions and inferences. To adequately equip a translator for this task, I have proposed a complementary approach between Conceptual Integration Theory and Relevance Theory as a rewarding conceptual undertaking in the translation of metaphorical blends. This approach helps to address the underlying integration process such as generating mental spaces from the respective background frames, and constraining projections and inferences to and from the blend, among other integration processes. I have argued that the mapping process in Conceptual Integration Theory does not adequately address the emergent meaning issue as well as how the target audience(s) are able to arrive at the inferences that are author intended. To bridge this gap, I have argued that the integration process is driven within the relevance theoretic framework, which forms the basis of determining which background knowledge framing is activated and how the entire intergration process is constrained.

I have demonstrated that the apostle Paul is inducing his readers into the process of frame shifting by accentuating the change of background assumptions and implications associated with the concepts associated in the metaphor περιτομὴ καρδίας. To this end, I have pointed out how this traditional frame is modified and replaced with a new one within the Discourse Space of Romans 2. Using the suggested complementary approach between Conceptual Integration Theory and Relevance Theory, I have argued for the lexical adjusted meaning of the metaphor περιτομὴ καρδίας as that of a cleansing or purification ritual, which people need to undergo to be cleansed of their sins. I have included the two additional outer spaces in the integration process, namely the discourse and relevance spaces, which affect the interpretation of any given metaphor. These spaces tend to constrain the drawing of the right inferences that are author intended with the goal of eliciting the right responses from the audience. I have pointed out the salient concepts as well as the relevant aspects of the background framing that end up being (semi-)activated, which in one way or another, influence the underlying conceptual framework that shapes the meaning of the entire argument in the discource space. The relevance space comes in handy in that it addresses the pragmatic factor in the integration process by encouraging connections that maximize relevance and exclude those that prompt unwanted connections by seeking the achievement of cognitive effects. Using the suggested complementary approach, I have detailed the entire integration process in both the source and receptor languages and how relevant elements and inferences are selected and projected from the translation space to the receptor language target space.

From the field research conducted within the receptor culture, I have pointed out that the ritual frame of [IRUA*] generally activates the organizing frame of [KŪGIMARA] "entering adulthood status," which is recruited in the interpretation of the metaphor translated as *kūrua ngoro* in the context of Romans 2. This means that the contextual assumptions that are activated within this background framing of the associated concepts do not match with those activated within the source culture leading to the derivation of the wrong meaning. This is because the first interpretation arrived at in the blend is that of adulthood status leading to the assumption that metaphor περιτομὴ καρδίας in Romans 2:29 has to do with spiritual maturity, which is not consistent with the meaning arrived at in the source language blended space. I have pointed out the need for the target audience to be guided so that the first interpretation that they arrive at is the intended meaning that is consistent with the principle of relevance. To bridge this conceptual gap, I have suggested the need to render the metaphor using the specific meaning focused on within the current discourse space, which has to do the cleansing or purification ritual, as well as provide the necessary source language context adjustment information as extra-textual material. In light of the proposed complementary approach, I have proposed eight steps that a translator can follow so as to render a given metaphorical blend across languages.

6.2 Further Recommendations

This work is intended to encourage translators to broaden the understanding and application of cognitive linguistics to translation by suggesting a complementary approach between Conceptual Integration Theory and Relevance Theory to interpretation and translation of metaphorical blends. Any further attempt to refine what is presented here is a welcome idea. Using the suggested methodological approach, it would be interesting to analyze metaphorical blends in different kinds of genres keeping an eye on how the process of frame shifting takes place. The discoveries made in this work can be incorporated as a theoretical basis for translating other figures of speech as well such as humor, irony, compound words, collocations, idioms, and the like.

Appendix A

Questionnaire

1. *Tanjĩra   igũrũ   rĩa   irua   rĩa   ũgĩkũyũ.*
   tell.me   about   of   circumcision   according to.Kikuyu[custom]
   Tell me about the ritual of circumcision according to Kikuyu custom.

2. *Ũtaũku   waku   wa   ithugunda 'hakiri' nĩguo ũrĩkũ? No*
   understanding yours   of   concept   mind   is   which can
   ũhe   ngerekano?
   you.give   examples
   What is your understanding of the concept "mind"? Can you give me some examples?

3. *Ũtaũku   waku   wa   ithugunda "ngoro" nĩguo ũrĩkũ? No*
   understanding yours   of   concept   "heart" is   which can
   ũhe   ngerekano?
   you.give   examples
   What is your understanding of the concept "heart"? Can you give me some examples?

4. *Ũtaũkagĩrwo   atĩa   nĩ   ciugo   kũrua   hakiri?*
   Your.understanding is.which   of   words   circumcision   mind
   What is your understanding of the words "circumcision of mind"?

5. *Kũringana na gĩcunji kĩa kĩrĩkanĩro kiu twathoma,*
   According to text of Bible which we.have.read
   wataũkĩrwo atĩa nĩ ciugo kũrua ngoro?
   your.understanding is.which of saying circumcision heart
   According to the biblical text that we have read, what is your understanding of the saying "circumcision of heart"?

Appendix B

Irua rĩa Gĩgikũyũ

1. *Mwanake amenyekanaga atĩa nĩakinya wa kũgimara?*
   male.child was.known how he.is.ready to be.circumcised?
   How did people know that a boy child was ready for the circumcision ritual?

   Angĩabĩrĩria kũrera tũnyamũ tũtũ, ĩ twa njegeke, rĩu
   when.he.starts to.grow things this, that.is of arm pit, now
   When he starts to grow puberty hair under his armpits,

   ũcio no atuĩke no arue.   Rĩrĩa kĩmwana gĩa kinyia
   that.one Is can.be to.be circumcised. when boy is arrives
   he is ready to be circumcised. When the boy becomes

   mĩaka ikũmi na ĩtano kana ikũmi na ĩtandatũ, tiga Rĩu
   years Ten and five or ten and six, except now
   fifteen or sixteen years old, except that

   Marakĩrua tondũ mwana nĩathiĩ sekondarĩ, Agathiĩ
   they.get.circumcised because child is.going to.secondary, he.goes
   these days they get circumcised because they are transiting to secondary school, and so

Akarua ena mīaka ikūmi na īīrī, no hau kabere
and.gets.circumcised with years ten and two, but there before
he is circumcised when he is twelve, but before

kīmwana kīaruaga kīna kuma mīaka ikūmi na ītandatū,
boy was.circumcised he.has from years ten and six,
a boy child would be circumcised when he was sixteen

na mūgwanja, na īnana. Ona kūrī na Arīa
and [ten and] seven, and [ten and] eight. Even there.is with Those
and seventeen and eighteen years old. Even some might

Makinyagia mīaka kībaū kūringana na ūrīa ithe Atarī
who.go.up.to years twenty according to how father he.has.no
go up to twenty years depending on whether the father was able to pay

na ūhoti. Na rīu mūndū ūyū akinyia hau
with ability. And now person this when.he.arrives there
for the ritual. When a boy child attains this age

Atuīka nī egūthii kūgimaraī, nīwe Weonaga
when.he.becomes is he.will.go to.be.circumcised, it.is.he who.saw.himself
he goes to be circumcised, and it is him who sees signs

kīmwīrī gīake, ta kīambīrīria kūmeria huyo na Acoke
body his, like starting to.grow public hair and he.also
in his body, such as that of growing public hair and when

athikīrīrie one ūrīa araragia nīambīrīria kūruruma, Rīu
analyses and sees how he.speaks if.he.starts to.talk.with.base, Now
he speaks with a deep voice

nīamenya no agimare.
he.knows that he.can.be.circumcised.
he knows that he is ready to be circumcised.

2. *Wīra wa mūtiiri   warī ūrīkū?*
   work of god father   was which?
   What was the work of a circumciser?

   Na mūtiiri   nī amathagwo wagūtira   mūndū ūcio.
   And god father was looked.for to.stand.with person that.one.
   A godfather was sought to nurse the initiate.

   Na tiūndū   mūhūthū nītondū wa gūtiira   mūndū Harī
   And was.not.issue easy   because to stand.with person it.was
   It was not easy to be a godfather because to be one was a big

   ona mūrigo   nītondū nīguo   ūmūrūgamīrīrerī Ūgatigana
   a   responsibility because so.that you.stand.with.him you.will.be.done.with
   responsibility because when you become one you will have to continue with the

   nake nginya rīrīa akahona.   Mūtiiri   ethagwo   nī kīmwana
   him Only   when he.recuperates. godfather was.sought by Boy
   responsibility until the initiate recuperates. A god father was sought by the boy

   gīkī kīrathiī   kūgimara   na agetha   mwanake   Ūrīa
   that who.is.to.be be.circumcised and he.looks circumcised.one Who
   who is undergoing the ritual and he looks for one who

   onaga Nī mūgima na ena mītugo   īrīa yagīrīire, Mūndū
   he.sees Is mature and with character which is.good, Person
   is mature and of good character, a person

   Wīkindīire   na mūhoreri mūndū ūtarī   ngūī   Ūngīmūhe
   who.is.settled and humble   person with.no trouble who.can.give.him
   who is settled and humble with no bad track record and one who is able to teach

kīrīra   wega.   Acaria   mūndū ūciorī, agagīthiī Akamūtwara
teachings well.   When.he.gets person that,   he.goes   he.takes.him
him well. When he gets such a person, the god father takes him to

rūūī   Na   agacoka agoka   akamūthondeka   agatigīrīra Nī
to.river And then   he.comes he.looks.after.him until   He
the place of circumcision and looks after him until he is

ahona.   Ahona   nīhagīcokaga gūkarīo ngūkū īkaheo
recovers. when.he.is.healed then   there.is hen   to.be.given
recovers. When he does so, he slaughters a hen for his

mūtiiri.   Ngūkū īno īkīrīo   nīguo Mwanake
god father. hen   this when.it.is.being.eaten so.that circumcised.one
god father. When this hen is being eaten the initiate is

aikaragio thī   agakīrwo rīu nīūragimarire   mūtugo wa
is.seated down he.is.told now he.has.matured actions of
being given advice now that he has undergone the ritual that he should
stop behavior

Ihīī   ūtigane naguo nīwatuīka   mūndū mūgima.
uncircumcised.ones to.stop them   he.has.become person mature.
of the circumcised now that he has become an adult.

Ūrūgamagīrīre mītugo īno   ndūgacoke gūcera   na   Aria
to.take.on   actions these not   to.associate with Those
He is not supposed to have the character or actions associated with the

Mūraceraga   nao   matarī aruu   kwoguo rīu
who.you.were.associating with not   circumcised for   now
uncircumcised but from now on

Ūrīthiaga na   aria   aruu.   Kwoguo ūyū mūtirani Nī
to.associate with the ones circumcised. so   this god father Is
only associate with the circumcised ones. Therefore this god father is

Wakŭmŭhe kĭrĭra   nĭgetha agĭe   na mĭtugo   ĭrĭa
to.give.him teachings so that he.acquires with character which
to teach him so that he acquires good character

yagĭrĭire tondŭ   nĭ   agimara oima   na   mwena ŭrĭa
is.good   because he.is an adult has.left from side   that
because the initiate is now an adult and has moved from one status

oka   ngathĭ ĭno. Ithe   nĭ   acokaga o ho
he.comes status this. father he.is then   at same time
to another. When the father of the now circumcised son

Ona   mwanake   wake nĭ agimara na ena   mĭtugo
when.he.observes circumcised.one his is an adult and he.has actions
observes that his son has acquired adulthood status and he has good actions,

mĭegarĭ, nĭ   acokaga akamŭrutĭra   mbŭri ya ihaki,
good,   he.is then   he.gives.on.his.behalf goat of recognition,
he provides a goat on behalf of his son so that his son can be recognized

nĭgetha athiĭ   ahake   aanake   arĭa   angĭ   nĭguo
so that he.can give.to circumcised.ones those others so.that
by the other circumcised young people from previous age-groups and

Mwanake   ŭyŭ etĭkĭrio   nĭ aanake   rĭrĭa nyĭmbo
circumcised.one this can.be.allowed by circumcised.ones when Songs
can be allowed by these previous age-groups so that when there are ceremonies to sing and dance

Cianagwo   kŭingĭra aine   rwĭmbo.
were sung/dance he.enters to.sing/dance songs.
he is allowed to do so.

3. *Ĩ   nayo mbũri ya kĩama?*
   what about goat of elders.court?
   What can you tell me about the goat that is given to the elders?

   Mwanake acoka agũrana,   mbũri ya kĩama   nĩwe   ũkerutĩra
   male.child when he.marries, goat of elders.court it.is.he to.give
   When the now circumcised man marries, he is supposed to give a goat to the elders

   tondũ   ndangĩrutĩrwo   nĩ ithe   atarĩ   Aragĩa
   because it.cannot.be.given.on.his.behalf by father.his he.has.no he.has
   because a father cannot give this goat on his behalf for now he has

   na   mũtumia. Atarĩ   na   mũtumia arutĩrwo   nĩ Ithe
   with wife.   if.he.has.no with wife   if.it.is.given by father.his
   a wife. It is only if he has no wife that such a goat might be given by his father

   Nĩekwaga   matathi   na   mũthĩgi kũria akainũkia.
   he.will.lack part.of.goat.meat and rod   where he.will.take.home.
   and even then he will not be given the part of the goat meat and rod that is given for one to take home.

   Anengerwo   guoko   kwa mbũri ĩrĩa   arutire
   when.is.given front.leg of goat which he.has.given
   One is given the front leg of the goat which he has given to the elders court

   Ainũkio   nĩ mũthuri na   matathi   na   mũthĩgi.
   to.be.taken.home by elder   with part.of.goat.meat and rod.
   and is accompanied home by an elder with the part of the meat and the rod.

   Mũthĩgi ũyũ ti   wa mbara   no   nĩwaharia   angĩthiĩ
   rod   this not for fighting but it.is.for.where he.can.go
   This rod is not for fighting but it is to be used whenever he is

atūmwo   kīama   tondū   nīatuīka   mūthuri wa Kīama
being.sent elders.court because he.has.become man of elders.court
sent by the elders because he has become one of the elders

no   Athiī   rīu akīhuraga ime   nīkīo   wūiguaga athuri
now he.can now removing morning dew that.is.why you.hear elders
and he can use it to remove the morning dew on the paths and that is why you hear the elders

makiuga nīmekwenda   rūbia rwa ime,   tondū   Kīama
saying they.would.like coins of morning dew, because elders.court
say that they want to be paid some money because of the morning dew, for such work

Gīathiagwo   kīroko   tene.
it.was.attended morning early.
was done very early in the morning.

4. *Wīra wa mūtiiri   ūthiraga   na   irua?*
work of god father is.it.finished with circumcision?
Does the work of the god father get completed after the circumcision ritual?

Wīra wake ndūthiraga   na   irua.   Ūngīka   Ūūru
work his it.is.not.finished with circumcision. If.you.do bad.action
His work is not finished after the circumcision ritual. If you [the initiate] does a bad deed

mūndū atūmagīrwo   ūrīa   wamūtiirire. Ūngīcoka
person was.sent.to.him one who was.his.god father. if.you.then
the one who is sent to resolve the matter is one's god father. If you do not

Ūreme   ūcio,   nīegūkwīra rīu kumanagia na
not.listen that.one, will.tell.you now from   with
listen to your god father, he might tell you that from now on

hau   ndarī   nawe   tondū   nīona   niekūmūthūkīria
that.time he.is.not with.you because he.has.seen you.will.destroy.his
he is not on your side because he is worried that you will destroy his good

rītwa.   Na   nīkīo   Gīkūyū kīūragia atīrīrī, Ūceraga
reputation. And that.is.why Kikuyu asks   this, you.associate
reputation. This is why the Kikuyu have a saying state that one does not have to associate

naū   ūtagūtonyaga ndūgīra? Ūguo nī kuuga atī Mūthiaga
with.who you.do.not   listen?   that is to.say that you.associate
with a person who does not listen to advice. That is to say that why do you associate

naū   ūyū   ūtagūtaraga?   Kwoguo Ingīgūtara
with.who that.one who.does.not.advise.you? so   if.I.give.you.advice
with a person who does not incline to advise? Therefore if I give you advice

na   ndūnjiguaga   rīu   tongīgūikīrie   moko!
and you.do.not.listen now I.can.throw.to.you hands!
and you do not listen or adhere to it, I am entitled to give up on you!

5. *Riika   rīarī rīa wīra ūrīkū?*
   age-group was of   work which?
   What was the need of having age-groups?

   Riika   nī   arīa   mathiīte   hamwe   rūūī
   age-group was those.ones who.have.gone together to.river
   An age-group comprises of those who undergo the ritual of circumcision together

   Makaruanīra   na nīkuga   atī thamake īria Twaita
   circumcised.together and it.is.to.say that blood which we.shed
   and they persevere together and this means that we shed blood together

tūrī Nawe hau handū hena gwatanīro nene mūno.
with with.you there place there.is unity big very.
with you in that place unites us and binds us together very strongly.

Gūitanīra thakame mūthenya ūmwe nī igongona iritū.
to.shed.together blood day same is ceremony great.
To shed blood at the same day is a great ceremony.

Hakoragwo hena gītīo kīnene mūno gatagatī ka andū arīa
there.was with respect great very between of people who
There was great respect between those who

Maruīte hamwe. Mūndū wa riika tene
are.circumcised together. person of age-group sometime.ago
are circumcised together. Sometime ago, a person who shared the same age-group with another

nīathiaga kwa mūndū wa riika rīake na kūu nī
would.go to person of age-group his and there is
would go to the homestead of his age-mate and

egūkoma. Athiī ahanda itimū na mwene mūciī Akore
spend night when.he.goes he.plants spear and owner house he.sees
spend the night there. He would go and plant his spear on the door of the wife of the owner of the

itimū Na amenye nī rīa wakiinī wake, kūu
spear And he.knows it.is of age-mate his, there
homestead and when the owner comes and sees the spear he knows that it belongs to one of his

ndangīingīra! Nīmwītīkīrīku aciare mwana kūu.
he.cannot.enter! he.is.accepted to.bear child there.
age-mates, and he cannot enter his wife's house! It was okay for the age-mate to have children there.

6. *Wakiinī nīwe thiari?*
   Wakiinī it.is.he close.age-mate?
   Is *Wakiinī* the same as *thiari*?

   Aca. Wakiinī nī ūrīa mwatemirwo nake No
   no. *Wakiinī* is one who you.were.cut.together with.him But
   No. A *Wakiinī* is one who you were cut together but

   Thiari nī mūndū ūrīa mūkūrū gūgūkīra no ti
   Thiari is person who is.older than.you but not
   thiari is a person who is older than you but not

   Kūraihanīria mūno, nīkuuga atī aruīte mbere waku ta
   with.gap big, it.is.to.say that he.is.circumcised before you like
   with a big gap, that is to say someone who underwent circumcision before you with a duration

   mīaka Īrī kana ītatū ūguo.
   years Two or three around.
   of around two or three years.

7. *Warua no wīrwo wī Mūgima*
   when.you.get.circumcised can it.be.said that.you.are Mature
   When you get circumcised, can it be said that you have matured

   hakiri?
   in.mind?
   in your thinking?

   No ūrue no ūkorwo ūtarī mūgima hakiri.
   you.can be.circumcised but you.can.be with.no mature in.mind.
   No you can be physically circumcised but not be mature in mind.

   Mūndū angīrua na atuīke ndūrīka Ambaga
   person if.he.is.circumcised and he.becomes with.bad behavior First
   A person who is circumcised and then becomes of bad behavior is first

Gwītīrwo   arīa   maruīte   nao   Na
he.is.called.for.him the.ones who.are.circumcised together.with.him And
spoken to by his age-mates and

Angīmarema   ithe   erwo   mūndū ūcio   Agetīrwo
if.he.does.not.listen father.his when.told person that.one it.is.called.on.him
if he does not listen and the father is informed about it, a family meeting is convened

nyūmba ona   mūhīrīga wao na   hau   nīho
house   and. also clan   his and there it.is.when
and also his clan is informed and he is expected to

Arīagīrwo mbūri tondū   nī   rūrūrīko.
he is fined goat   because he.is disobedient.
be fined a goat because he has become disobedient.

Angīaga   kūgarūrīra akahingwo   nī riika   kuuga atī
if.he.does.not rectify   he.is.banned by age-group to.say that
If he does not change his behavior he is banned by his age-group meaning that

matikanyitanīra   handū   kwoguo we arīkoragwo   e   mbogo
they.will.not.associate anywhere so   he will.always.be like buffalo
they will not associate anywhere so he becomes like a buffalo

ta   yanduīki e   wiki. Akerwo angīkagarūrīra
which.is alone he.is alone. he.is.told that.when.he.changes
which walks alone. He is toke that when he decides to change

Ūgoka   na thenge na njohi nīguo tūkūhingūre.
he.is.to.come with he.goat and acohol so.that they.can.take.him.back.
he can come with a he goat and some traditional beer so that they can take him back.

Angĩthiĩ na mbere na ũtũrĩka kuoyagwo Mũguĩ
if.he.goes and ahead with being.disobedient they.were.taken Arrows
If he continues with his disobedience, a bow and arrows

na Ũta gũkerwo "ĩ ngaiĩ ngania nĩ atũrema Kĩmuoe
and Bow it.is.said "oh god this.one is not.listening take.him
were taken and it is said, "Oh God this one does not listen to advice so take him and we have

rĩu ndamũikia na kĩano!" Mũguĩ ũgaikio Kuonania
now I.have.thrown.him with loop!" arrows are.thrown to.symbolize
thrown him away with a loop." Arrows were then thrown to symbolize

atĩ we nĩwateo, kĩu nĩkĩrumi kĩnene na
that he he.is.excommunicated, that.it a curse great and
that he is excommunicated and this symbolizes a big curse and

Ndũngĩthiĩ hanene ũtakuĩte.
you.cannot.go far before dying.
one cannot go far without losing his life.

8. *Mũrera mariika nũ?*
one.who.brings.up age-groups is.who?
Who is a *mũrera mariika*?

Nĩ mũndũ ũrĩa ũruĩte harĩa kabere no
it.is person who has.been.circumcised there before but
It is a person who has been circumcised a while ago but

atũraga aceraga na ciana iria irarua na
he.always associates with younger.one who are.getting.circumcised and
continues to associate with younger age-groups and

kuoguo Nĩ mũndũ wonekaga ndarĩ na thiri. Ndĩna
therefore it.is person who.seems not.to.have with secret. I.have
therefore is not a person who keeps secrets. Such a person is married

mūtumia no ndīracera na aanake   arīa matarī
wife   but I.associated with circumcised.ones who not.have
but continues to associate with other age-groups after his who are not

atumia. Ūcio   nī mūndū ūtarī   gītīo.
wives. that.one is person with.no respect.
married. Such a person has no respect

9. Andū arīa maregaga kūrua   Nīmaruithagio
people who refuse   to.be.circumcised were.they.circumcised
People who refuse to be circumcised were they circumcised

kīa hinya?
by force?
by force?

Ĩĩ mūno.   Ona thoguo   ndegwītio mbeca Cia
yes very.much.so. Even your.father is.not.asked money Of
Yes indeed. Even your father was not requested to provide money for

cuka. Mbeca icio cikūhothanio hau hau ūkaruithio   kīa
sheet. money that it.will.be.raised there there to.be.circumcised By
buying a sheet to cover oneself as he recuperated. That money was raised there and then and you will

hinya. Gīgīkūyū   mūndū ūtarī muruu   nī mūgiro.
force. According.to.Kikuyu.custom person not   circumcised is taboo.
circumcised by force. According to the Kikuyu customs not to be circumcised is a taboo.

Irua   nī kīndī kīrathime tondī   ona mwathani Jīsū
Circumcision is thing blessed   because even Lord   Jesus
Circumcision is blessed because the Lord Jesus

aciaro   anina thikū inyanya o   nake ndagīthire akīrua.
after.birth after days eight   even him he.was   circumcised.
eight days after birth and even him he was circumcised.

Ũtongoria nĩ ũnyitanĩte na kũgimara tondũ Gĩkũyũ
leadership is associated with circumcision because according.to.Kikuyu
Leadership is associated with circumcision because according to the Kikuyu customs

Matiĩtĩkĩtie no matongorio nĩ kĩhĩĩ.
they.do.not.believe they.can.be led by uncircumcised.person.
they do not believe they can be led by the uncircumcised.

10. *Andũ matwaragwo rũũĩ nĩkĩ?*
    people were.taken to.river why?
    Why were people take to the river?

    Nĩguo maingĩra rũũĩ kĩroko tene makiumĩra
    so.that they.immerse in.river morning early as.they.come.out
    So that they can immerse themselves in the river very early in the morning so that

    Megũkorwo magandĩte.
    they.are anesthetized.
    they can be anesthetized.

11. *Ĩĩ mũndũ angĩrĩra akĩrua?*
    what.about person who.cries when.getting.circumcised?
    What about a person who cries when undergoing the ritual?

    Mbara ĩrĩa ũkuona hau nĩ ndĩtũ mũno. Irua
    fight which he.will.see there is big very. Circumcision
    He will be beaten very much. Circumcision

    Rĩakoragwo rĩrĩ iritũ nĩguo mũndũ omĩrĩrie
    it.was with difficult so.that person would.be.courageous
    was a difficult ritual so that the person undergoing it will come out courageous

mŭtŭtĭreinĭ. Ndŭngĭruta thiri ona atĭa! Irŭgi
in.life.   you.cannot.give.out secret even how! uncircumcised girls
when facing life issues. You cannot give out secrets at any cost! Only uncircumcised girls

Nĭacio mathiaga makonania mena guoya
were.the.ones who   would.show they feared
could show that they fear when undergoing the ritual.

makĭrua.   Irua   rĭarĭaka,   Mwainŭka
when.getting.circumcised. circumcision when.finished, you.would.go.home
When circumcision is over, one would go home

Kŭrugĭtwo iruga inene mŭno, njŭgŭ ona Meru
it.was.prepared feasting big very, peas and also ripe bananas
and a great feast was prepared which include peas and ripe bananas which

matigathira!
would.be.in.plenty!
Were in great supply.

12. *Mŭruithia arĭ mŭndŭ wa gĭthemba kĭrĭkŭ?*
    circumciser was person of kind which?
    What kind of a person was a circumciser?

Kwarĭ mbarĭ ya aruithia kwoguo ti mŭndŭ o ŭguo.
there.was family of circumcisers so not person any one.
There was a specific family of people with this trade and so it was not any person.

Uumĭte mbarĭ ĭyo noguo ŭgŭcoka ŭbundithie ciana Ciaku
coming family that so.that you.then you.teach children Yours
One would have to come from that family so as to teach your children

ona wenda.   No nginya ūkorwo   ūkinyīte   makinya ma
if   you.want. it.is must   you.should.be have followed steps   of
if you want. It is a must that one should have followed the steps of

ūthuri tondū   ndūngūkūruithania   we ūtarī mūruu!
elders because you.cannot.circumcise you not having.been.circumcised!
elders because you cannot be allowed to circumcise if you have not been circumcised yourself!

Nonginya makorwo marī   na   atumia na   makaruta   mbūri
It.is.must they.be   having with wives   and they.have.given Goats
It is a must that such people should be married and they have offered offerings of goats

Magīūka   kwūrutwo   wīra ūcio.
has.they.come to.be.taught work that.one.
as they come to be taught that work.

Appendix C

Joshua 5:2–9 Matt-LXX Comparison

verse	MT/BHS		LXX (Rahlfs)
2a	הַהִיא בָּעֵת אָמַר יְהוָה אֶל־יְהוֹשֻׁעַ עֲשֵׂה לְךָ חַרְבוֹת צֻרִים	At that time the Lord said to Joshua, "Make for yourself **flint knives**	Ὑπὸ δὲ τοῦτον τὸν καιρὸν εἶπεν κύριος τῷ Ἰησοῖ Ποίησον σεαυτῷ μαχαίρας πετρίνας ἐκ πέτρας ἀκροτόμου
2b	מֹל וְשׁוּב בְּנֵי־אֶת־יִשְׂרָאֵל שֵׁנִית׃	and **return** and circumcise the sons of Israel [a second time]."	καὶ καθίσας περίτεμε τοὺς υἱοὺς Ισραηλ.
3	וַיַּעַשׂ־לוֹ יְהוֹשֻׁעַ חַרְבוֹת צֻרִים וַיָּמָל־אֶת־יִשְׂרָאֵל בְּנֵי גִּבְעַת אֶל־הָעֲרָלוֹת׃	So Joshua made [for himself] flint knives, and circumcised the people of Israel at hill of foreskins.	καὶ ἐποίησεν Ἰησοῦς μαχαίρας πετρίνας ἀκροτόμους καὶ περιέτεμεν τοὺς υἱοὺς Ισραηλ ἐπὶ τοῦ καλουμένου τόπου Βουνὸς τῶν ἀκροβυστιῶν.
4a	הַדָּבָר וְזֶה מָל אֲשֶׁר־יְהוֹשֻׁעַ	and this is the reason why Joshua **circumcised**	ὃν δὲ τρόπον περιεκάθαρεν Ἰησοῦς
4b	הָעָם כָּל־הַיֹּצֵא מִמִּצְרָיִם	all the people **who had come out from Egypt**,	τοὺς υἱοὺς Ισραηλ, ὅσοι ποτὲ ἐγένοντο ἐν τῇ ὁδῷ
4c	כָּל הַזְּכָרִים ׀ אַנְשֵׁי הַמִּלְחָמָה בַּמִּדְבָּר מֵתוּ בַּדֶּרֶךְ בְּצֵאתָם מִמִּצְרָיִם	all the **males, the men of war,** had died in the wilderness during the journey after they went out from Egypt.	

	Comments
And about this time the Lord said to Joshua, "Make to yourself **stone knives from sharp stone,**	The LXX specifies that the kind stones used were worked on i.e. polished/sharpened. The translation here is quite free.
and **sit down** and circumcise the sons of Israel.	The LXX read ושב "sit down" and not ושוב "again" thus a mistake by the translator. The LXX has no reference to second circumcision.
and Joshua made sharp swords of stone and circumcised the sons of Israel **in the place called the "Hill of foreskins."**	The decision to point to the reader that the referent to the "Hill of foreskins" is a place is a good translation practice.
And this is the way in which Joshua **purified**	The LXX has a different interpretation to the circumcision event.
the sons [of Israel]; **as many as at some time were born on the way,**	The LXX focus different i.e. on those born on the way.
	The LXX description of the groups is shorter

verse	MT/BHS		LXX (Rahlfs)
5	מֵלִים כִּי־ הָיוּ הַיֹּצְאִים הָעָם וְכָל־ הַיִּלֹּדִים הָעָם בַּדֶּרֶךְ בַּמִּדְבָּר בְּצֵאתָם מִמִּצְרַיִם לֹא־ מָלוּ׃	Although all the people who came out had been circumcised, all the boys [born] in the wilderness on the way after they had come out of Egypt had not been circumcised.	καὶ ὅσοι ποτὲ ἀπερίτμητοι ἦσαν τῶν ἐξεληλυθότων ἐξ Αἰγύπτου, πάντας τούτους περιέτεμεν Ἰησοῦς·
6a	כִּי אַרְבָּעִים שָׁנָה	For forty years	τεσσαράκοντα γὰρ καὶ δύο ἔτη
6b	הָלְכוּ בְנֵי־יִשְׂרָאֵל בַּמִּדְבָּר	the sons of Israel walked in the wilderness,	ἀνέστραπται Ισραηλ ἐν τῇ ἐρήμῳ τῇ Μαδβαρίτιδι,
6c	עַד־תֹּם כָּל־הַגּוֹי אַנְשֵׁי הַמִּלְחָמָה הַיֹּצְאִים מִמִּצְרַיִם אֲשֶׁר לֹא־שָׁמְעוּ יְהוָה בְּקוֹל נִשְׁבַּע אֲשֶׁר יְהוָה לָהֶם לְבִלְתִּי הַרְאוֹתָם אֶת־הָאָרֶץ אֲשֶׁר נִשְׁבַּע יְהוָה לַאֲבוֹתָם לָתֶת לָנוּ אֶרֶץ ת חָלָב זָבַת וּדְבָשׁ	until **all** the nation, the men of war who came out of Egypt, **perished** [for] not obeying the voice of the Lord. To them the Lord swore that he would not let them see the land that he had sworn to their fathers to give us, a land flowing with milk and honey.	διὸ ἀπερίτμητοι ἦσαν οἱ πλεῖστοι αὐτῶν τῶν μαχίμων τῶν ἐξεληλυθότων ἐκ γῆς Αἰγύπτου οἱ ἀπειθήσαντες τῶν ἐντολῶν τοῦ θεοῦ, οἷς καὶ διώρισεν μὴ ἰδεῖν αὐτοὺς τὴν γῆν, ἣν ὤμοσεν κύριος τοῖς πατράσιν αὐτῶν δοῦναι ἡμῖν, γῆν ῥέουσαν γάλα καὶ μέλι

	Comments
and **as many as were uncircumcised of them that came out of Egypt**, all these Joshua circumcised;	The LXX implies that not all that went out of Egypt were circumcised. This means that those that were uncircumcised from Egypt as well as those that were born in the wilderness were circumcised together. There seems to be a motive behind the MT rendering that *all* were circumcised.
for forty **and two** years	Since the Israelites rebelled two years after leaving Egypt, the LXX might have added these two years on top of the forty they wondered in the wilderness (cf. Num 10:11–12)
Israel wondered in the wilderness [**of Madbaritidi,**]	Possibly a misreading of a reduplicated *mdbr* "desert"? this then could be attributed to a mistake by the translator.
therefore **most** of the fighting men that came out of **the land of** Egypt, **were uncircumcised**, who disobeyed the commands of God; concerning whom also he determined that they should not see the land, which the Lord swore to their fathers to give us, a land flowing with milk and honey.	The LXX maintains the interpretation that *most* and not *all* of the men coming out of Egypt were circumcised.

verse	MT/BHS		LXX (Rahlfs)
7	וְאֶת־בְּנֵיהֶ֞ם תַּחְתָּ֣ם הֵקִ֣ים מָ֣ל אֹתָ֣ם יְהוֹשֻׁ֑עַ כִּי־עֲרֵלִ֣ים הָי֔וּ כִּ֛י לֹא־מָ֥לוּ אוֹתָ֖ם בַּדָּֽרֶךְ׃	and it was their sons, whom he raised up in their place that Joshua circumcised, for they were uncircumcised, because they had not circumcised them on the way.	ἀντὶ δὲ τούτων ἀντικατέστησεν τοὺς υἱοὺς αὐτῶν, οὓς Ἰησοῦς περιέτεμεν διὰ τὸ αὐτοὺς γεγενῆσθαι κατὰ τὴν ὁδὸν ἀπεριτμήτους.
8	וַיְהִ֛י כַּאֲשֶׁר־תַּ֥מּוּ כָל־הַגּ֖וֹי לְהִמּ֑וֹל וַיֵּשְׁב֥וּ תַחְתָּ֛ם בַּֽמַּחֲנֶ֖ה עַ֥ד חֲיוֹתָֽם׃	And it was when **all the nation** had finished to be circumcised, they **stayed in their place** in the camp until they recovered.	περιτμηθέντες δὲ ἡσυχίαν εἶχον αὐτόθι καθήμενοι ἐν τῇ παρεμβολῇ, ἕως ὑγιάσθησαν.
9	וַיֹּ֤אמֶר יְהוָה֙ אֶל־יְהוֹשֻׁ֔עַ הַיּ֗וֹם גַּלּ֛וֹתִי אֶת־חֶרְפַּ֥ת מִצְרַ֖יִם מֵעֲלֵיכֶ֑ם וַיִּקְרָ֞א שֵׁ֣ם הַמָּק֤וֹם הַהוּא֙ גִּלְגָּ֔ל עַ֖ד הַיּ֥וֹם הַזֶּֽה׃	And the Lord said to Joshua, "Today I have rolled away from you the reproach of Egypt." And he called the name of that place Gilgal **until this day.**	καὶ εἶπεν κύριος τῷ Ἰησοῖ υἱῷ Ναυη Ἐν τῇ σήμερον ἡμέρᾳ ἀφεῖλον τὸν ὀνειδισμὸν Αἰγύπτου ἀφ' ὑμῶν. καὶ ἐκάλεσεν τὸ ὄνομα τοῦ τόπου ἐκείνου Γαλγαλα.

	Comments
and in their [place] he replaced with their sons, whom Joshua circumcised, because those who were born on the way were not circumcised.	
And having been circumcised they rested on the spot lying down in the camp till they became healthy.	
And the Lord said to Joshua **the son of Naue**, "On this very day I have removed the reproach of Egypt from you. And he called the name of that place Galgala."	LXX mentions the name of Joshua's father (possibly showing some respect to the oral tradition) and omits the closing formula "until this day"

Appendix D

The Vulgate for Joshua 5:4–9[1]

English

5:4 Now this is the cause of the second **circumcision**: All the people that came out of Egypt that were males, all the men fit for war, died in the desert, during the time of the long going about in the way:

5:5 Now these were all circumcised. But the people that were born in the desert,

5:6 During the forty years of the journey in the wide wilderness, were uncircumcised: till **all they were consumed** that had not heard the voice of the Lord, and to whom he had sworn before, that he would not show them the land flowing with milk and honey.

Latin

haec autem causa est secundae circumcisionis omnis rrant qui egressus est ex Aegypto generis rrant universi bellatores viri mortui sunt in deserto per longissimos viae circuitus

qui omnes circumcisi rrant rrant autem qui natus est in deserto

Per quadraginta annos itineris latissimae solitudinis incircumcisus fuit donec consumerentur qui non audierant vocem Domini et quibus ante iuraverat ut ostenderet eis terram lacte et melle manantem

---

1. http://www.latinvulgate.com/verse.aspx?t=0&b=6&c=5

5:7	The children of these succeeded in the place of their fathers, and were circumcised by Josue: for they were uncircumcised even as they were born, and no one had circumcised them in the way.	horum filii in locum successerunt rrant et circumcisi rrant Iosue quia sicut nati fuerant in praeputio rrant nec eos in via aliquis circumciderat
5:8	Now after they were all circumcised, they remained in the same place of the camp, until they were healed.	Postquam autem omnes circumcisi sunt manserunt in eodem castrorum loco donec sanarentur
5:9	And the Lord said to Josue: This day have I taken away from you the reproach of Egypt. And the name of that place was called Galgal, until this present day.	Dixitque Dominus ad Iosue hodie abstuli obprobrium Aegypti a vobis vocatumque est nomen loci illius Galgala usque in praesentem diem

Appendix E

Kikuyu Government

1489–1523	*Manjiri*
1523–1557	*Mamba*
1557–1591	*Mindi*
1591–1625	*Tene*
1625–1659	*Agu*
1659–1693	*Manduti*
1693–1727	*Cuuma*
1727–1761	*Ciira*
1761–1795	*Mathathi*
1795–1829	*Ndemi*
1829–1863	*Iregi*
1863–1897	*Maina*
1897–1931	*Mwangi*
1931–1965	*Irũngũ*

NB: Each parliament lasted for thirty-four years.

Appendix F

Kikuyu Age-Groups

Kīa mūgwī	"of the arrow"	1840
Kīrūgwe or mūhīa	"millet"	1841
Ndūnyū ya iregi		1842
Mīruna aka	"lovers of girls"	1843
Mathaga	"ornaments"	1844
Kamau		1845
Gīkunyi	"barterer"	1846
Gītaū		1847
Kīanderi	"year of the eagles"	1848
Kīmani	"eating of beans"	1849/50
Kīnūthia		1851
Karanja	"famine of small bones"	1852
Njūgūna	"club"	1853
Gīchūgūma	"big club"	1854
Theuri		1855
Ng'ang'a		1856/57
Njoroge		1858
Ndiang'ui		1859
Ndegerege		1860
Wainaina	"courageous"	1861
Ndirangū	"prohibiting war"	1862

Wanyūtū	"of the wolves"	1863
Njīhia	"famine of kīmūrūri"	1864
Ngūnjiri	"ornaments of the head"	1865
Nguo ya nyina	"clothes of the mother"	1866
Manyeki	"blades of herbs"	1867
Nguchu	"earrings"	1868
Maguchia mūkūrū	"old thieves of clothes"	1869/70
Gīthūkū	"measles"	1871
Gathūita		1872
Mūthige	"wild dog"	1873
Njaūre	"thief"	1874
Yūyū		1875
Ngūgī	"clod"	1876
Rūharo	"dysentery"	1877
Ndaho	"seizure"	1878
Koinange		1879
Ngatha-inya		1880
Ngūrūrū	"kind of bird"	1881
Ngūciara		1882
Nguthūka	"quick"	1883
Mūhaguya	"famine of the necklaces"	1884
Kīrogi	"poisoner"	1885
Gachenga	"kind of chalk"	1886
Mbūrū	"chalk"	1887
Kīnyaga	"year of the ostrich"	1888
Kahiū	"knife"	1889
Kīa mūhīa	"year of millet"	1890
Ngigī	"locusts"	1891
Ngoma na mūro	"sleeping with weeding stick"	1892
Nūmīkū		1893
Mūtūng'ū	"small pox"	1894
Mwahūra	"thief"	1895
Kīroko	"morning"	1896

Kĩenjeku	"shaved heads"	1897
Nũthi	"jiggers"	1898
Mũnyeero	"leper"	1899
Ndimũ	"kind of chalk"	1900
Njangiri	"wanderers"	1901
Kamande (athũngũ)		1902
Gatego (ndũng'ũ)	"syphilis"	1903
Machai	"iron sheets"	1904
Nyũtũ	"wolves"	1905
Ngara	"mice"	1906
Njege (Nyarigi)	"porcupines"	1907
Gĩthĩi	"maize mill"	1908
Makanga	"cotton clothes"	1909
Kanoria	"kind of disease"	1910
Njaramba	"courageous"	1911
Ũhere	"scabies"	1912
Mbaũni	"gold"	1913
Gatuthĩ	"kind of weed"	1914
Biringi	"whistle"	1915
Gĩchũguo		1916
Kĩa riũa	"year of famine"	1917
Kĩhiũ mwĩrĩ		1918
Kĩnyotoku		1919
Manoti	"currency notes"	1920
Gathetha	"beads necklace"	1921
Bendera	"flag"	1922
Nuthu		1923
Gichithi	"cow tail used as ornament"	1924
Karebe	"Ghana gold"	1925
Ngigĩ	"year of locusts"	1926
Mukwanju		1927
Ndege	"year of aeroplane"	1928
Mũgwongo	"elephant tusk"	1929

Mamboleo	"modern practices"	1930
Magoko	"wattle bark"	1931
Ngigĩ	"year of locusts"	1932
Njanekanini		1933
Kenyabathi		1936

Appendix G

Research on *Kūgimara hakiri*

1. *Mūndū ūngītūmīra hakiri/ūūgī   na gūtua Matua*
   Person who.uses mind/wisdom and makes Decisions

   magima/marūmu
   mature/stable

2. *Ti   kūrua   tu;   ona   gūtuīka Mūndū*
   Not to.be.circumcised only; even.though even.if Person

   Arua   eragwo nīagimara. Noūkorwo wī mūgima
   when.he.is.circumcised is.said he.is.mature. you.could be mature

   kīūga,   Ūrue   no wage   ūgima   wa hakiri.
   physically, be.circumcised but not.have maturity of mind.

3. *Nī kūgīa meciria makinyanīru na mītugo mīgima.*
   it.is to.have thoughts sound   and actions mature.

4. *No   wage kūgimara   mwīrī/kūrua no ūkorwo wī*
   you.can lack circumcision physical   but you.are with

   mūūgī. No ūgīkūyū   gīthomo kīa   mūtūrīre
   wisdom. but Kikuyu.customs teachings concerning life

gĩtiaheagwo   Ihĩĩ   na   ũthĩinĩĩ.
is.not.given   uncircumcised.ones with   depth.

5. Gũikarania na   andũ   ũthome   nĩũtarĩkaga,
   associating with people who.are.taught you.benefit,

   ũkaroreka   ũkoneka   wĩ   mũgima hakiri.
   you.are.observed you.are.found that.you.are mature in.mind.

6. He   ũgĩ   wa mũciarĩre no   hatarĩ   Na
   there.is wisdom of birth   but without With

   Kĩrĩra   kĩa mũtũrĩre ndũrĩ   mũgima   hakiri.
   teachings of   life   I.have.no mature of.mind.

7. Kũgimara hakiri kumanaga na   ũmenyo   ũrĩa
   maturing in.mind results   from knowledge which

   umanaga na   gũthikĩrĩria, kuona   na   kũria.
   Comes   from listening,   observing and asking.

8. Kĩrĩra   kĩu kĩhoyagwo   kuuma kũrĩ andũ   Arĩa
   teachings that is.requested from   from people the ones

   akũrũ.
   elderly.

9. Maciaro nĩ kũgia na   ũtaũku,   gũkorwo
   Fruit   is to.be with understanding,   to.be

   wĩ   mũndũ wĩna mũbango na wĩkinyĩire gũkĩra   andũ
   that.you.are person with life.plans and stable more.than people

   a   riika   rĩaku na   noũthurwo   ũtongoria-inĩ kana
   of age-group yours and you.can.be.chosen in.leadership or

   wĩhokerwo   Ũndũ mũna.
   be.entrusted Issue certain.

10. | Wagimara | hakiri | wīragwo | wīna | īgī | Wa
    when.you.mature | in.mind | you.are.said | to.have | wisdom | To

    kūrugūra/gūtaūra maūndū. | Ūgagītuo | mūndū wa igūrū.
    discern issues. | you.are.made | person of importance.

    Mūndū wothe Mūtīīku kana mūtongoria no nginya
    person every Respected or leader can must

    angīakorirwo Na kīheo gīkī.
    to.have.been With gift that.

11. Ūngīkorwo na mīario īīkinyīrīte na mīgima, kiugo
    if.you.are with words good and mature, Word

    gīaku gīgatīīka.
    your is.respected.

12. Ihīī itiagīrīirwo gūkorwo kīrathi-inī Gīkī kīa
    uncircumcised.boys are.not.allowed to.be in.class That of

    andī agima hakiri tondū itingīaheirwo Morutani
    people mature in.mind because they.could.not.be.given Teachings

    maya na mītaratara-inī ya gūikarania na athuri matarwo.
    these and procedures of associating with elders to.be.taught.

13. Mūtiiri waku warua nīagīrīirwo Nī
    godfather yours when.you.get.circumcised is To

    gūgūtara Igūrū rīa mūtūrīre ūgimare tombo na
    advise.you concerning of life you.mature thoughts and

    mwīrī.
    physically.

14. Ūkorwo wīna ciugo ciīna njīra cingīteithīrīria to
    you.be with words with substance which.can.advise not

Kwaria   o   ŭguo.
to.speak manner   anyhow

15. Ũũgĩ   wa gĩthomo   tiguo ũgima   wa Hakiri
    Wisdom of formal.education   is.not maturity of Mind

    nĩkĩo   cĩĩtagwo   hakiri   cia gĩthomo.
    that.is.why   they.are.called knowledge of formal.education.

16. Ndũngĩhota   gũthathaũra maũndũ ma ũndũire/mũtũtĩre
    you.cannot.be.able to.eĩplain issues of Traditions

    kana ma mũtũrĩre tiga   ũkorwo na   ũũgĩ   ũyũ.
    or   of Life   eĩcept you.are with wisdom this.

17. Ũngĩkinya   mbere ya andũ   na kwĩnyihia
    if.you.come   before of people and you.humble.self

    ũreke   ũtwarwo   nĩ athuri ũtige   gwĩtua   kĩmenyi.
    you.allow   to.be.sent by elders you.stop   making.self   you.know.

18. Ũgimaraga   na   njĩra ya kũhoya   kĩrĩra
    if.you.mature with way   of requesting teachings

    kĩa   ũndũire   na   mũtaratara wa gwĩka maũndũ.
    concerning   traditions/customs   and procedures of to.do things.

19. Mĩtugo   yaku   na   mĩario   nĩyo   yonanagia
    Actions   yours   and   words   they.are the.ones.showing

    ũgima   kana kwaga   ũgima   thĩinĩ waku.
    maturity or   lack.of maturity   inside of.you.

20. Waga   ũgima   wa tombo   kana hakiri   Wĩragwo
    if.you.lack   maturity of thoughts or   mind   you.are.said

    ndũrĩ   Na   ũgima   kana hakiri   na   wĩ
    you.have.no   With maturity or   knowledge and that.you.are

Wa wana.
Of childhood.

21. Gwĩtua nĩwe ũũĩ mũno, kwaga
to.make.oneself you.are knowlegeable very, lack.of

ũkirĩrĩria, ũtaũku na gĩtĩo nĩ ndariri ya Kwaga
being.humble, understanding and respect are signs of lack.of

ũgima Tondũ ndũrĩ na ũtaũku kana ĩmenyo.
maturity Because you.have.no with understanding or wisdom.

22. Meciria nĩ methugundaà wĩna meciria marĩkũ?
Wisdom is concepts you.have thoughts which?

23. Kũgimara ti ũũgĩ wa mũciarĩre nĩ kĩrathi Kana
maturing not wisdom of birth is school Or

kĩrĩra kĩheanagwo.
teachings you.are.given.

24. Hakiri, ũũgĩ, kana ũgima we nĩwe
thinking, wisdom, or maturity you you.are.the.one

ũthondekaga Na kwĩmenyerera ũrĩa ũreka.
to.make.them And you.be.careful what you.do.

25. Kũhoya kĩrĩra kĩa ũndũire na mũtaratara
to.request teachings of traditions/customs and procedures

wa gwĩka maũndũ nĩũkũhotithagia kũgimara.
to to.do things enables.you to.mature.

26. Atarani no nginya makorwo marĩ agima na
advisors it.is must they.be having mature and

me gatũ. Mũndũ ũtarĩ mũgima ndangĩkũhe kĩrĩra
having status. person not mature cannot.give teachings

gīkinyanīru.
good.

27. Kūgimara meciria   nī kūhūthiīra ūūgī   kana ūgima,
    maturing thoughts   is to.use   wisdom or   maturity,

    gūtua   Matua   marūmu na   magima.
    to.make Decisions stable and mature.

28. Kīūga   kīa mwīrī   na mīaka mīingī ndiugaga
    appearance of physically and years many   do.not.show

    No   nginya ūkorwo wī   mūgima hakiri. Mūndū mūnini
    That must you.are with mature in.mind. Person younger

    na mīaka kana kīūga   no ohīge   Kana agimare
    of years or   physical.appearance can be.wise Or   be.mature

    Hakiri gūkīra   ūrīa   wīna kīūga   kana
    in.mind more.than one who has   physical.appearance Or

    mīaka mīingī. Ona   gūtuīka wīna   mīaka mīingī niwagīrīirwo
    years many. Even if you.have years   many   you.should

    gūkorwo wī   mūgima,   ūtarīkīte   na ūkohīga.
    to.be   with maturity, you.be.advised and you.are.wise.

29. Kīrathi kīa andū othe nī kīa o   mūhaka He
    School of people all is of with must   To

    mūndū oro wothe agimara   hakiri.
    person any every to.mature in.mind.

30. Mūtongoria o   wothe no nginya akorwo arī   mūūgī na
    Leader   any every is must   to.be   with wisdom and

    mūgima   hakiri.   Mataro na   ciīko   ciake Nīcirūmbūyagia
    maturity of.mind. advise and   actions   his   he.looks.after.them

mūno.	
very.much.	

31. | Mūtiiri | arūgamagīrīra | o | mūndū | kīrui | gīake |
    |---------|---------------|---|-------|-------|-------|
    | godfather | nurses | | each | person | initiate | his |

nīūndū	wa	mataro.
because	of	giving.advise.

32. | Kūrua | nī | kūgimara | ngoro, | kūnyita | na |
    |-------|-----|----------|--------|---------|-----|
    | to.be.circumcised | is | to.mature | in.heart, | to.hold.to | and |

gūthingata	kīrīra.
apply	teachings.

33. | Kīrīra | hīndī | īyo | gītirī | | thoni, | tondū | Nī |
    |--------|-------|-----|--------|---|--------|-------|-----|
    | teachings | time | that | it.did.not.have | | shame, | because | it.is |

kumbūra	Maūndū	cararūkū.
to.reveal	Things	inside.out.

34. | Mūtiiri | waku | no | atūmwo | gūtara | ūrīa |
    |---------|------|-----|--------|--------|------|
    | godfather | yours | can | be.sent | to.advise | same.way |

atariire	angīogoma	kana	Ahong'oke	mūtūrīre-inī	Tondū
he.advised	if.he.disobeys	or	goes.astray	in.life	Because

nīoī	kana	nī	ūtūrīka	kana	nīkūrigwo.
he.knows	if	is	being.disobedient	or	not.understanding.

35. | Kūira | ngūrano | nīkūimbīrwo |
    |-------|---------|-------------|
    | rejecting | advice | is.fatal |

36. | Kūruithio | nī | kūhingūrīrwo | mūrango | wa | Kūgimara |
    |-----------|-----|--------------|---------|-----|----------|
    | to.be.circumcised | is | to.be.opened | door | of | to.mature |

hakiri	kana	kūheo	kīrīra.
in.mind	or	to.be.given	teachings.

37. *Ũngĩgimara   hakiri   kana   tombo   wĩragwo*
    if.you.mature in.mind   or   thoughts you.are.said

    kũrua   gwaku   gũtinorĩra   thĩ;   wĩ   mũgima.
    circumcision yours   has.not.been.lost down; you.are mature.

38. *Kũgimara mwĩrĩ   ti   kuuga ũhikanie, ũtongorie,*
    maturing physically not to.say you.marry, you.lead,

    ũtuĩke   mũthigari; no   nginya ũtarwo   ũhĩge.
    to.be   warrior;   it.is must   to.be.advised to.be.wise.

39. *No nginya ũrũmĩrĩre   mũtaratara wa maũndũ ma*
    it.is must you.follow   procedures of things of

    mũtũrĩre Ũũhĩge   ũtanaingĩrĩra   maũndũ ma ũgima.
    life   to.be.wise before.entering issues of maturity.

40. *Ũngĩonania ũgima   wa hakiri athuri Nĩmagwethaga*
    if.you.show maturity of mind   elders seek.for.you

    magũtare   kana makũingĩrie   maũndũ-inĩ nawe   ũkona
    to.advise.you   Or   to.initiate.you to.status and.you you. get

    Mweke wa gũthoma.
    Chance of learning.

41. *Kwaga   ũgima   wa hakiri wĩtagwo wana,   Kwaga*
    lack.of maturity of mind   is.called childhood, lack.of

    gũkinyanĩra kĩhakiri, kwaga   ũgima   na ũrimũ.
    maturing   in.mind, lack.of maturity and foolishness.

42. *Wagimara   kana warua   Wĩrĩgagĩrĩrwo*
    when.you.mature   or   when.you.get.circumcised you.are.expected

    ũkorwo Ũgĩĩkua   na ũgima,   watithia   wĩragwo
    to.be carrying.yourself   with maturity, if.you.cease   you.are.said

Wīna   wana.
to.have childhood.

43. Motongoria-inī mothe nonginya ūgima   wa hakiri
    leadership   all   it.must maturity of mind

    ūrorwo   na   ūthingatwo.
    be.sought and be.natured.

44. Kūgimara mwĩrĩ   gūkūhingūragīra mūrango wa kūgimara
    maturing physically opens.for.you   door   of maturing

    hakiri.   Nīgūkūhingūrīra   mūrango wa kīrathi kīrīra-inī.
    in.mind. is.to.open.for.you door   of school of.teaching.

45. Kūgimara hakiri nīgūkonainie na   mīaka, kīrīra na
    maturing mind   has.to.do   with years, teachings and

    ūndūire.
    traditions/customs.

46. Kūrua   kwa mwĩrĩ   tikuo kūgimara;
    to.be.circumcised of   physically is.no maturity;

    kūhingūragīra mūndū mūrango wa kīrīra   ūhīga   na
    it.opens   person door   of teachings to.be.wise and

    ūgimare.
    you.mature.

Appendix H

Research on *Kũrua Kwa Ngoro*

1. *Nĩ gũtigana na maũndũ moru kana merirĩria ma mwĩrĩ.*
   it.is to.leave those things bad or desires of flesh.

   Mũndũ ta ũyũ ndatongoragio nĩ merirĩria mwa mwĩrĩ no
   person like this is.not.led by desires of flesh but

   atongoragio nĩ roho.
   is.led by spirit.

2. *Nĩ kũgimara na gũtigana na maũndũ ma tene nĩguo mũndũ*
   it.is to.mature and to.leave those things of former so.that person

   eharĩrĩrie nĩtondũ wa mũtũrĩre ũrĩa ũroka wa mũndũ mũgima
   prepares because of life that is.coming of person mature

   Nĩguo ahote gũthurania wega na ũũru thĩinĩ wa mũtũrĩre.
   so.that he.is.able to.choose good and bad in of life.

3. *Nĩ kwerũhio kwa ngoro. Kũhingũra mĩrango ya ngoro Nĩguo*
   it.is to.be.renewed of heart. to.open doors of heart so.that

   Ngai athamake. Nĩ kũgimara mũndũ agatiga gũkorwo arĩ mwana
   God rules. it.is to.mature person to.leave to.be be child

269

wa kīroho   agatuīka mūgima kīroho.
of spiritual to.be   mature spiritually.

4. Nī   ūrīa mūndū ataūkīragīrwo   nī Ūkirsto.   Ciīko   Ciaku
   it.is That person made.to.understand by Christianity. actions Yours

   cikonania   ūgima.
   show   maturity.

5. Nī kweheria gīko   kuma ngoro. Nīta   gūtheria ngoro.
   it.is to.remove impurity from heart. it.is.like to.cleanse heart.

   Ngai aroraga ngoro   kwoguo no   nginya īkorwo ī theru.
   God looks.at heart So   it.is   must   to.be   cleansed.

6. Harī Ayahudi, no   nginya mūndū angīaruire   nīguo akorwo
   to   Jews,   it.is must   person to.be.circumcised so.that to.be

   arī ūmwe wa andū a Ngai kūringana na ūrīa Ngai aathire
   be one of people of God according to how God commanded

   Iburahīmu. No Paūrū Ameraga   atī kūrua   kwa mwīrī
   Abraham.   But Paul was.telling.them that circumcision of flesh

   ti   kwa bata   angīkorwo matiramwathīkīra.   Kūrua
   not of importance If   they.will.not.obey.him. to.be.circumcised

   kwa ngoro nī gwathīkīra Maathani   ma Ngai
   of heart is to.obey   commandments of God.

7. Ūhonokio   ūmanagia   na thīinī wa mūndū no ti kumanagia na
   Salvation comes.from inside of person but not from

   ciīko   cia mūndū gūtekūmakania kana mūndū nī mūruu kana
   actions of person not.considering or person is bad   or

   ti   mūruu. Kūrua   kwa mwīrī nī ikinya rīa kerī
   not bad.   to.be.circumcised Of flesh is step   of second

8. *Mūndū ndekūbatarania akorwo arī mūyahundi nīguo atuīke*
   person is.not.required to.be be Jew so.that he.becomes

   mwana wa Ngai. Kīrīa kīrabatarania nī ngwatanīro ya mūndū na
   child of God. what is.needed is fellowship of person with

   Ngai. Paūlū aragia igūrū rīa andū a ndūrīrī arīa
   God. Paul was.speaking concerning people of nations those

   matiganaga na Ūkristo nītondū matiarī Aruu na
   who.abandon Christ because they.were.not circumcised and

   ameraga atī ona matua matua ma gwathīkīra
   was.telling.them that even.if they.make decisions of to.obey

   Mathani ma Ngai nī ciana cia Ngai makorwo Marī
   commandments of God they.are children of God if.they Are

   aruu kana matarī aruu.
   circumcised or they.are.not circumcised.

9. *Mūndū agarūragwo agakorwo arī mūndū mwerū wītīkionī Ona*
   person is.expected to.be be person new in.faith and.also

   ningī mītugoinī nīguo onekane na njīra ya ngūrani na ūrīa
   also in.actions so.that to.be.seen in way of different with how

   ararī hau kabere.
   he.was there before.

10. *Nīkūgimara kīroho. Nī kūhonoka na kūmenya wega na ūūru.*
    to.mature spiritually. it.is to.be.saved and to.know good and bad.

11. *Nīkweheria maūndū marīa moru, mehia, na kwaga Gūthinga*
    it.is.to.remove things those bad, sins, and lacking Righteousness

    kuma ngoroinī ya mūndū. Nī gūthambia ngoro ya mūndū.
    from heart.inside of person. it.is to.cleanse heart of person.

12. *Nĩkũgarũrwo   kuma kĩũmwĩrĩ mũndũ agatuĩka wa kĩroho.*
    it.is.to.be.changed from the.flesh person to.be   of spiritual.

13. *Nĩ mwĩto wa kũgimara kĩroho   na gũtigana na mĩtugo*
    it.is a.call of to.mature spiritually and to.leave the culture

    (culture) ĩtarĩ   ya kĩũngai.
    (culture) that.is.not of godly.

14. *Nĩ kũgĩa na   kĩrĩkanĩro (covenant) na   Ngai.*
    it.is to.have with covenant (covenant) with God.

15. *Nĩ kũgimara mũndũ agatuĩka mũgima kĩroho.*
    it.is to.mature person to.be   mature spiritually.

16. *Nĩ gũthambio   kumanagia na mehia. Kũgarũrwo*
    it.is to.be.cleansed from   sins. to.be.changed

    kumanagia na wĩhia mũndũ agatuĩka mũthingu.
    from   sins person to.be   righteous.

17. *Nĩ kũgarũrwo   (conversion) mũndũ agatiga gũkorwo arĩ*
    it.is to.be.changed (conversion) person to.leave to.be   be

    Mwĩhia agatuĩka mũndũ mũthingu. Nĩkwamũkĩra (accepting) Ngai
    Sinner to.be   person righteous. it.is.to.receive (accepting) God

    na gwĩtĩkĩra atongorie ũtũro waku ũkũringithania na   mũtũtĩre
    and to.accept to.be.led life yours to.compare   with life

    wa kĩũndũire ũrĩa mũndũ atongoragio nĩ andũ.
    of common   which person is.led   by people.

18. *Nĩ kũhonoka na gĩtherio   ngoro nĩ Roho.*
    it.is to.be.saved and to.be.cleansed heart by Spirit.

19. *Nĩ kuma ngathĩ ĩmwe (one level) na gũthiĩ ĩngĩ   ũndũ*
    it.is from level one (one level) and to.go another thing

ūkonainie   na   maūndū   marīa ūreka   nīguo   ūkorwo   ūrī
concerning   with things   those you.do   so.that you.are   are

mūndū wīna   ūngai   thīinii wake.   Nī   kūgarūrwo   thīinii
person who.has godliness inside him.   it.is to.be.changed inside

wa ūndū   mwerū   na   kūrūmagīrīra watho   wa Ngai
of thing new   and   to.follow   commandment   of God

o guo   wiki.
that   only.

20. Kūhitūkīra   kūbatithio   nīguo   mūndū   agimaraga ngoro.
    Through   to.be.circumcised so.that person   to.mature heart.

    Gūtuīka mwana   wa Ngai nī gwītīkīra Jīsū   ta mwathani   na
    to.be   child   of God is to.accept Jesus as lord   and

    mūhonokia.   Roho (spirit)   citī   cikahonokio   na   njīra
    savior.   Spirit (spirit) ours   to.be.saved   through way

    ya ūtugi.
    of grace.

21. Kūgimara   thīinii   wa   Kristo
    Maturity   inside   of   Christi

22. Mūyahudi   ūrīa   wama   ūruīte   ngoro   thīinii
    Jew   who   is.true   circumcised   heart   inside

23. Mūndū   ūgimarīte   na thīinii
    person   who.has.matured   inside

24. Kūmenyagīrīra   mītugo   īrīa   ītarī   ya   ūngai
    to.take.care.of actions   which   that.is.not of   godliness

25. Kūhingūka   maitho ma   kīroho   ūkera   Ngai niwega
    to.be.closed eyes   of   spiritual   to.tell God thankyou

26. *Kũgimara ngoro na ũndũ war oho no ti ũhoro Mwandĩke*
    Maturity heart and thing of.spirit but not information Written

27. *Kũgimara ũtegũtwarĩrĩrio nĩ makũmbĩ thĩinĩ wa wĩtĩkio*
    Maturity not.to.be.led by waves inside of faith

28. *Kũgimara na kwĩheana mũno kũrĩ Ngai na ũthamaki wake*
    to.be.mature and to.offer.oneself much to God and kingdom His

29. *Gũtinio (kweheria) ũmũndũ wa kĩmwĩrĩ*
    to.remove (to.remove) personality of flesh

30. *Ũũ nĩ kũgimara kwa ngoro*
    it is to.mature of heart

31. *Nũ kwĩruta kũrĩ Jesũ na gwĩka wendi wake*
    it.is to.surrender to Jesus and to.do will his

32. *Nĩ ũhonokio thĩinĩ wa Kristo na ũndũ wa roho wa Ngai*
    it.is salvation inside of Christi through thing of spirit of God

33. *Nĩ kĩranĩro atĩ nĩwĩheanĩte harĩ Jesũ ta mũhonokia*
    it.is covenant that you.have.surrendered to Jesus as savior

34. *Kũgimara meciria na gwĩtigĩra Ngai*
    Maturity mind and believing God

35. *Nĩ gũtigana na maũndũ maria ma tene kuma Wahonoka*
    it.is to.leave from things those of former from when.you.got.saved

36. *Nĩ ũhonokio*
    it.is salvation

37. *Nĩ gwathĩkĩra watho*
    it.is to.obey commandment(s)

38. *Nĩ gũkinyanĩra thĩinĩ wa roho mũtheru*
    it.is to.be.complete in.sphere of spirit holy

39. Nĩ   kũgimara   ngoro   na   kũmenya   ũrĩa   Ngai   arenda
    it.is to.mature heart   and to.know   what   God   wants

40. Nĩ   ũrĩa   mũndũ   angĩingĩra   kĩrĩkanĩro-inĩ   na   Ngai
    it.is how   person   can.enter   covenant   with God

41. Nĩ   kweheria   wĩhia   wa   ngoro   na   kũhonokio   nĩ   Ngai
    it.is to.remove   sins   of   heart   and to.be.saved   by   God

42. Nĩ   kũhonokio   biũ   nĩ   thakame   ya   Jesũũ
    it.is to.be.saved   completely   by   blood   of   Jesus

43. Nĩ   kũgarũrĩra   maũndũ   ma   tene   na   gũtuĩka   mũndũ   Mwerũ
    it.is to.change   things   of   former   and to.be   person New

44. Nĩ   kũgarũrwo   na   ũkerũhio   na   thĩinĩ
    it.is to.be.changed   and   to.be.renewed   inside

45. Ni   kũmenya   Ngai   ũrĩa   wama   thiinũ   ngoro.
    it.is to.know   God   who   is.true inside   heart.

46. Kũrua   ngoro   nĩkũgimara   kĩ   ngoro   kwoguo   mataro
    to.be.circumcised   heart   is.to.mature   of   heart   so   advice

    Maku   kana   ciugo   Iria   waragiarĩ,   waragia   ũhoro
    Yours or   words   Which   you.speak,   you.speak   information

    mũgima   ti   kwaria   Wana   ũkaragia   Ũhoro
    mature   not   speaking   immaturity   you.speak   information

    mũbarĩrĩre.   Ngoro   ndĩngĩgimara   hakiri   Ĩkorwo   ĩtagimarĩte.
    well.weighed.   heart   cannot.mature   mind   to.be   not.mature.

Appendix I

Glossary Entries on *Kūrua* and *Ngoro*

Kūrua gwa Kīyahundi: Kūringana na mītugo ya kīyahundi, irua rīa arūme rītiakonainie na kūgimara mūndū agatigana na waana agatuīka mūndū mūgima. Īndī nī mūtugo wa kīndini wahingagio harī mwana wa kahīī ena thikū inyanya kuma gūciarwo ta rūūri atī nīatuīka ūmwe wa rūruka rūrīa rūcagūre nī Ngai, rūrīa arī ruo rwa Kīyahundi, na nīngī nīatuīka mūgai wa irathimo iria Ngai erīire Iburahīmu na rūciarwo rwake (Kīambīrīria 17:1-27; Luka 1:59). Irathimo ici ciakonainie na gūtherema maingīhe na ningī magae būrūri wa Kanani ūrīa erīire maithe mao. Kūrua rwarī rūūri rwa gwītīkīra kūhingia mathani marīa Ngai amahete. Mūyahundi kwaga kūrua kwarī kūregana na watho wa Ngai na mūndū ta ta ūyū ndataragwo ta ūmwe wa rūrīrī rūrīa Ngai athurīte tondū ndangīarutīire Ngai magongona kana anyitanīre na andū arīa angī tondū ti ūmwe wa arīa Ngai athurīte. Ayahundi monaga andū arīa matarī aruu ta marī na mūgiro na matarī na kīene tondū matiarī na kīrīkanīro na Ngai kīrīa rūūri rwa kīo rwarī irua. Kūrūmīrīra mūtugo ūyū wa atī mūndū ndagīatuīkire ūmwe wa rūrīra rūrīa Ngai athurīte kana amūkīre irathimo iria cierīirwo Iburahīmu atambīte kūrua, andī arīa matarī Ayahundi meragwo no nginya mambe marue nīguo matuīke arūmīrīri a Mwathani Jesū Kristo (Atūmwo 15:1-5). No Paūlū andīkīte marūainī make atī irathimo cia Ngai no ciamūkīrwo nī arīa meheanīte kūhingia mathani ma Ngai na marī na wītīkio ta wa Iburahīmu, makorwo maruīte kana mataruīte (Warumi 4:1ff).

Free translation: Jewish circumcision: According to the customs of the Jewish people, male circumcision has nothing to do with a person leaving

277

childish behavior behind and transiting to adulthood status. It was a religious ritual which was performed on an eight-day-old male child after birth as a sign that he had become one of the members of the tribe chosen by God, which is the Jewish tribe, and that he has become an inheritor of the blessings which God promised to Abraham and his descendants (Gen 17:1–27). These blessings have to do with the promise that they will multiply and be many and also that they will inherit the land of Canaan which he had promised to their fathers. Circumcision was a sign of accepting to obey the commandments that God had given them. To refuse to circumcise was to disobey the command of God and a person like that could not be allowed to participate in religious ceremonies or to fellowship with other people, since he was not counted as one of the people chosen by God. The Jews viewed the uncircumcised as being unclean and with no value or as inferior because they did not have a covenant relationship with God whose sign is circumcision. Following this tradition, that one could not become one of the chosen people and inherit the blessings which were promised to Abraham without first being circumcised, the people who were not Jews were told that they had undergo circumcision so that they could become followers of the Lord Jesus Christ. But Paul wrote in his letters that the blessings of God can be received by those who have given themselves to obey the commands of God and have the faith like that of Abraham, whether circumcised or not (Rom 4:1ff).

Ngoro: Ngoro kūringana na Kīyahundi nī kīīga gīa gwīciria nakīo na kwoguo kīīga kīria nūndū atūmagīra gwīthugunda, kūririkana, gūtua matua, na ciīko ingī nyingī iria meciria makuruhanagio nacio (Wakorintho wa Kerī 3:3:14–15; Wafilipi 4:7). Muoyo wa mūndī ūkoragwo ūkuruhanītio na ngoro na ningī nī kuo mawaganu mothe makoragwo na nīkīo ngoro yagīrīirwo nī kīgarūra nī hinya wa Ngai.

Free translation: Heart: According to Jewish thinking, the heart is the part of the body where reasoning, remembering, making decisions, and other actions associated with the mind take place (2 Cor 3:14–15; Phil 4:7). The life of a person is associated with the heart as well as all evil things and that is why the heart needs to be converted by the power of God.

Bibliography

Aaron, D. H. *Biblical Ambiguities: Metaphor, Semantics, and Divine Imagery.* Leiden: Brill Academic, 2001.

Aichele, George F., Fred W. Burnett, Elizabeth A. Castelli, Robert M. Fowler, David Jobling, Stephen D. Moore, Gary A. Phillips, Tina Pippin, Regina M. Schwartz, and Wilhelm Wuellner. *The Postmodern Bible.* New Haven, CT: Yale University Press, 1995.

Allen, Leslie C. *Jeremiah: A Commentary.* Louisville; London: Westminster John Knox, 2008.

Aletti, Jean Noël. *God's Justice in Romans: Keys for Interpreting the Epistle to the Romans.* Translated by Peggy Manning Meyer. Roma: Gregorian & Biblical Press, 2010.

Allwood, Jens. "Meaning Potentials and Context: Some Consequences for the Analysis of Variation in Meaning." In *Cognitive Approaches to Lexical Semantics*, edited by Hubert Cuyckens, René Dirven, and John R. Taylor, 29–65. Berlin: Mouton de Gruyter, 2003.

Alo, A. A. "Translating the Metaphor Φῶς in Lugbarati (Matthew 4:12–17): A Relevance Theory Perspective." Dissertation, Africa International University, Nairobi, Kenya, 2011.

Auld, A. Graeme. *Joshua: Jesus Son of Nauē in Codex Vaticanus.* Leiden: Brill, 2005.

Banwell, B. O. "Heart." In *The Illustrated Bible Dictionary*, edited by J. D. Douglas, 625–626. Leicester: Inter-Varsity Press, 1980.

———. "Kidneys." In *The Illustrated Bible Dictionary*, edited by J. D. Douglas, 850. Leicester: Inter-Varsity Press, 1980.

Barcelona, Antonio. "Introduction: The Cognitive Theory of Metaphor and Metonymy." In *Metaphors and Metonymy at Crossroads: A Cognitive Perspective*, edited by Antonio Barcelona, 1–28. Berlin: Mouton de Gruyter, 2003.

Barclay, William. *The Letter to the Romans.* Revised edition. Philadelphia, PA: Westminster Press, 1975.

Barnett, Paul. *The Second Epistle to the Corinthians*. Grand Rapids: Eerdmans, 1997.

Barnwell, Kathrine. *Bible Translation: An Introductory Course in Translation Principles*. Dallas: SIL International, 1975.

Barrett, C. K. *A Commentary on the Epistle to the Romans*. London: Black, 1977.

Barsalou, Lawrence W. "Frames, Concepts, and Conceptual Fields." In *Frames, Fields, and Contrasts: New Essays in Semantic and Lexical Organization*, edited by Adrienne Lehrer and Eva Feder Kittay, 21–74. New Jersey: Lawrence Erlbaum Associates, 1992.

Baumann, Gerlinde. *Love and Violence: Marriage as Metaphor for the Relationship between YHWH and Israel in the Prophetic Books*. Collegeville, MN: Liturgical Press, 2003.

Beeby, H. D. *Hosea: Grace Abounding*. Grand Rapids: Eerdmans, 1989.

Beekman, John, and John Callow. *Translating the Word of God*. Grand Rapids: Zondervan, 1974.

Beet, Joseph Agar. *A Commentary on St. Paul's Epistle to the Romans*. 10th edition. Salem, OH: Allegheny Publications, 1982.

Behm, J. "The Greek Term διαθήκη." In *Theological Dictionary of the New Testament*, vol. 2, edited by Gerhard Kittel, 124–134. Grand Rapids: Eerdmans, 1964.

Berkley, Timothy W. *From a Broken Covenant to Circumcision of the Heart: Pauline Intertextual Exegesis in Romans 2:17–29*. Atlanta: SBL Press, 2000.

Bernat, David A. *Sign of the Covenant: Circumcision in the Priestly Tradition*. Atlanta: SBL Press, 2009.

Bertone, John A. *"The Law of the Spirit": Experience of the Spirit and Displacement of the Law in Romans 8:1–16*. New York: Lang, 2005.

Black, Carl Clifton. *The Rhetoric of the Gospel*. St. Louis, MO: Chalice Press, 2001.

Black, Matthew. *Romans*. New Century Bible Commentary. 2nd edition. London: Marshall, Morgan & Scott, 1989.

Black, Max. "How Metaphors Work: A Reply to Donald Davidson." In *On Metaphor*, edited by S. Sacks, 181–192. Chicago: University of Chicago Press, 1979.

———. *Models and Metaphors: Studies in Language and Philosophy*. Ithaca: Cornell University Press, 1962.

Blakemore, Diane. *Understanding Utterances: An Introduction to Pragmatics*. Oxford: Blackwell, 1992.

Bloch, Abraham P. *The Biblical and Historical Background of Jewish Customs and Ceremonies*. New York: KTAV, 1980.

Blumenthal, Fred. "The Circumcision Performed by Zipporah." *The Jewish Bible Quarterly* 35, no. 4 (2007): 255–259.

Bock, Darell L. *Luke*. IVP New Testament Commentary Series. Downers Grove: InterVarsity Press, 1994.
Boeije, Hennie. *Analysis in Qualitative Research*. London: Sage, 2010.
Boeve, Lieven. "*Linguistica Ancilla Theologiae*: The Interest of Fundamental Theology in Cognitive Semantics." In *The Bible Through Metaphor and Translation: A Cognitive Semantic Approach*, vol. 15, edited by K. Feyaerts, 15–35. Bern: Lang, 2003.
Booth, W. C. "Ten Literal Theses." In *On metaphor*, edited by S. Sacks, 173–174. Chicago: University of Chicago Press, 1979.
Brandt, Line. "Explosive Blends: From Cognitive Semantics to Literary Analysis." Thesis, Roskilde University, Denmark, 2000.
Brandt, Line, and Per Age Brandt. "Making Sense of a Blend: A Cognitive-Semiotic Approach to Metaphor." *Review of Cognitive Linguistics* 3 (2005): 216–249.
Bratcher, Robert G., and Barclay M. Newman. *A Translator's Handbook on the Book of Joshua*. New York: United Bible Societies, 1983.
Bray, Gerald, ed. *Romans*. Ancient Christian Commentary on Scripture. Downers Grove: InterVarsity Press, 1998.
Brettler, Marc Zvi. *God Is King: Understanding an Israelite Metaphor*. Sheffield: Sheffield Academic, 1989.
Brown, Francis, S. R. Driver, and Charles A. Briggs. *The Brown-Driver-Briggs Hebrew and English Lexicon*. Peabody, MA: Hendrickson, 2007.
Brown, Gerlad Grover. *Christian Response to Change in East African Traditional Societies*. Woodbrooke Occasional Papers 4. London: Friends Home Service Committee, 1973.
Bruce, F. F. *I & II Corinthians*. The New Century Bible Commentary. Grand Rapids: Eerdmans, 1983.
Buchanan, G. W. "Circumcision." In *The Oxford Companion to the Bible*, edited by Bruce Metzger and Michael Coogan. New York: Oxford University Press, 1993.
Butler, Trent C. *Joshua*. Word Biblical Commentary 7. Waco, TX: Word, 1983.
Byrne, Brendan. *Romans*. Sacra Pagina Series, vol. 6. Collegeville, MN: Liturgical Press, 1996.
Caird, G. B. *The Language and Imagery of the Bible*. London: Duckworth, 1980.
Cameron, Lynne. *Metaphor in Educational Discourse*. London: Continuum, 2003.
Cervel, M. Sandra Peña. *Topology and Cognition: What Image-Schemas Reveal about the Metaphorical Language of Emotions*. München: Lincom Europa, 2003.
Charmaz, Kathy. *Constructing Grounding Theory: A Practical Guide through Qualitative Analysis*. Thousand Oaks, CA: SAGE, 2006.
Charteris-Black, Jonathan. "A Contrastive Cognitive Perspective on Malay and English Figurative Language." In *Meaning through Language Contrast*, vol. 2,

edited by K. M. Jaszczolt and Ken Turner, 141–157. Amsterdam; Philadelphia: John Benjamins, 2003.

Chingota, Felix. "Leviticus." *Africa Bible Commentary*, edited by Tokunboh Adeyemo, 129–168. Nairobi: WorldAlive, 2006.

Chomsky, Noam. *Language and the Problems of Knowledge: The Managua Lectures*. Cambridge, MA: MIT Press, 1988.

Christensen, Duane L. *Deuteronomy 21:10–34:12*. Word Biblical Commentary 6. Nashville, TN: Thomas Nelson, 2002.

Classen, Carl Joachim. *Rhetorical Criticism of the New Testament*. Boston: Brill, 2002.

Clements, Ronald Ernest. *Exodus*. The Cambridge Bible Commentary Series. Cambridge: Cambridge University Press, 1972.

Coggins, R. J., and S. P. Re'emi. *Israel among the Nations*. Grand Rapids: Eerdmans, 1985.

Cohen, Eugene J. *Guide to Ritual Circumcision and Redemption of the First-Born Son*. New York: KTAV, 1984.

Cohen, Shaye J. D. *The Beginnings of Jewishness: Boundaries, Varieties, Uncertainties*. Berkley: University of California Press, 1999.

Cotter, David W. *Genesis*. Berit Olam: Studies in Hebrew Narrative and Poetry. Collegeville, MN: Liturgical Press, 2003.

Coulson, Seana. *Semantic Leaps: Frame-Shifting and Conceptual Blending in Meaning Construction*. Cambridge: Cambridge University Press, 2001.

Coulson, Seana, and Marta Kutas. "Frame-Shifting and Sentential Integration." *Technical Report* CogSci. UCSD-98.03. Department of Cognitive Science, UCSD, 1–32. Sand Diego, CA, 1998. http://www.cogsci.ucsd.edu/~coulson/Papers/coulson-kutas98.pdf.

Coulson, Seana, and Todd Oakley. "Blending and Coded Meaning: Literal and Figurative Meaning in Cognitive Semantics." *Journal of Pragmatics* 37, no. 10 (2005): 1510–1536. www.sciencedirect.com.

Creswell, John W. *Qualitative Inquiry and Research Design: Choosing among Five Traditions*. Thousand Oaks: SAGE, 1998.

Dancygier, Barbara. "What Can Blending Do for You?" *Language and Literature: International Journal of Stylistics* 15, no. 1 (2006): 5–15.

Danker, Frederick W., ed. *A Greek-English Lexicon of the New Testament and Other Early Christian Literature*. 3rd ed. Chicago: University of Chicago Press, 2000.

Davidson, D. "What Metaphors Mean." In *On Metaphor*, edited by S. Sacks, 29–45. Chicago: University of Chicago Press, 1979.

Dawes, Gregory W. *The Body in Question: Metaphor and Meaning in the Interpretation of Ephesians 5:21–33*. Boston: Brill, 1998.

Delaney, Carol L. *Abraham on Trial: The Social Legacy of Biblical Myth*. Princeton, NJ: Princeton University Press, 1998.

Derouchie, Jason S. "Circumcision in the Hebrew Bible and Targums: Theology, Rhetoric, and the Handling of Metaphor." *Bulletin for Biblical Research* 14, no. 2 (2004): 175–203.

deSilva, David A. "Circumcision." In *Dictionary of Scripture and Ethics*, edited by J. B. Green, 139–140. Grand Rapids: Baker, 2011.

De Troyer, Kristin. *Rewriting the Sacred Text: What the Old Greek Texts Tell Us about the Literary Growth of the Bible.* Atlanta: SBL Press, 2003.

de Vaux, Roland. *Ancient Israel: Its Life and Institutions.* London: Darton, Longman & Todd, 1961.

Dewey, David. *A User's Guide to Bible Translations: Making the Most of Different Versions.* Downers Grove: InterVarsity Press, 2004.

Dille, Sarah J. *Mixing Metaphors: God as Mother and Father in Deutero-Isaiah.* New York: T & T Clark, 2004.

Dines, Jennifer M. *The Septuagint.* Edited by Micahel A. Knibb. London: T&T Clark, 2004.

Dirven, René, and Marjolyn Verspoor. *Cognitive Exploration of Language and Linguistics.* Amsterdam; Philadelphia: John Benjamins, 1998.

Dunn, James D. G. "Spirit." In *The New International Dictionary of New Testament Theology*, vol. 3, edited by Colin Brown, 693–717. Milton Keynes: Paternoster Press, 1986.

———. *Romans 9–16.* Word Biblical Commentary 38B. Waco, TX: Word Books, 1998.

Durham, J. I. *Exodus.* Word Bible Commentary 3. Waco, TX: Word Books, 1987.

Eller, Vernard. *In Place of Sacraments: A Study of Baptism and the Lord's Supper.* Grand Rapids: Eerdmans, 1972.

Elliot, Neil. *The Rhetoric of Romans: Argumentative Constraint and Strategy and Paul's Dialogue with Judaism.* Sheffield: JSOT Press, 1990.

Evans, Barrie, and Alina Krajewska. "'Equivalence' in the Presence of 'Otherness.'" *The Bible Translator* 57, no. 3 (2006): 138–153.

Evans, C. A. *Luke.* New International Biblical Commentary. Peabody, MA: Hendrickson, 1990.

Evans, Vyvyan, and Melanie C. Green. *Cognitive Linguistics: An Introduction.* Edinburgh: Edinburg University Press, 2006.

Fauconnier, Giles. *Mappings in Thought and Language.* Cambridge: Cambridge University Press, 1997.

———. *Mental Spaces: Aspects of Meaning Construction in Natural Language.* 2nd ed. Cambridge: Cambridge University Press, 1994.

Fauconnier, Giles, and Eve. Sweetser, eds. *Spaces, Worlds and Grammars.* Chicago, IL: University of Chicago Press, 1996.

Fauconnier, Giles, and Mark Turner. "Conceptual Integration Networks." *Cognitive Science* 22, no. 2 (1998): 133–187.

———. *The Way We Think: Conceptual Blending and the Mind's Hidden Complexities*. New York: Basic Books, 2002.

Faust, Avraham. *Israel's Ethnogenesis: Settlement, Interaction, Expansion and Resistance*. London: Equinox, 2006.

Fedders, Andrew, and Cynthia Salvadori. *Peoples and Cultures of Kenya*. Nairobi: Transafrica, 1979.

Fillmore, C. "Frame Semantics." In *Linguistics in the Morning Calm*, edited by Linguistic Society of Korea, 111–138. Soul: Hanshin, 1982.

———. "Frames and the Semantics of Understanding." *Quaderni di semantic* 6, no. 2 (1985): 222–253.

Fillmore, Charles J., and Beryl T. Atkins. "Towards a Frame-Based Lexicon: The Semantics of RISK and Its Neighbors." In *Frame, Fields and Contrasts: New Essays in Semantic and Lexical Organization*, edited by Adrienne Lehrer and Eva Feder Kittay, 75–102. Hillsdale, NJ: Lawrence Erlbaum, 1992.

Fitzmyer, Joseph A. *Romans: A New Translation with Introduction and Commentary*. The Anchor Bible. New York: Doubleday, 1993.

Fox, Michael V. "The Sign of the Covenant: Circumcision in the Light of Priestly 'ôt Etiologies.'" *Revue Biblique* 81, no. 4 (1974): 557–596. https://www.academia.edu/2253026/_The_Sign_of_the_Covenant_Circumcision_in_the_Light_of_the_Priestly_ot_Etiologies_Revue_Biblique_81_1974_557_96.

Fredriksen, P. "Judaism, the Circumcision of Gentiles, and Apocalyptic Hope: Another Look at Galatians 1 and 2." In *The Galatians Debate*, edited by Mark D. Nanos, 235–260. Peabody, MA: Hendrickson, 2002.

Freedman, David Noel, and David Miano. "People of the New Covenant." In *The Concept of the Covenant in the Second Temple Period*, edited by S. E. Porter and J. C. R. de Roo, 7–26. Leiden; Boston: Brill, 2003.

Friedman, Robert A. "Circumcision of the Heart." *Jew for Jesus* 1, no. 6 (1981). https://www.jewsforjesus.org/publications/issues/issues-v01-n06/circumcision-of-the-heart.

Gachiri, Ephigenia W. *Female Circumcision: With Reference to the Agikuyu of Kenya*. Nairobi: Paulines Publications Africa, 2000.

———. *Rite of Passage for Christian Boys*. Nairobi: Paulines Publications Africa, 2006.

Gärdnefors, Peter. "Some Tenets of Cognitive Semantics. In *Cognitive Semantics: Meaning and Cognition*, edited by Jens S. Allwood and Peter Gärdnefors, 19–36. Amsterdam; Philadelphia: John Benjamins, 1999.

Garland, David E. *2 Corinthians*. The New American Commentary. Nashville, TN: Broadman & Holman, 1999.

Gatheru, R. Mugo. *Child of Two Worlds*. London: Routledge & Kegan Paul, 1966.

Gay, L. R., Geoffrey E. Mills, and Peter W. Airasian. *Educational Research: Competencies for Analysis and Applications*. 8th ed. Upper Saddle River, NJ: Pearson, 2006.

Georgakopoulou, Alexandra, and Dionysis Goutsos. *Discourse Analysis: An Introduction*. 2nd edition. Edinburgh: Edinburgh University Press, 2004.

Gifford, E. H. *Romans*. Minneapolis: James Family Publishing, 1977.

Githura, J. N. "Factors That Influence the Perceptions and Attitudes of Adolescent Boys Towards the Church after Going Through Initiation Rite in Magumu Area." Thesis. Africa International University, Nairobi, Kenya, 2010.

Godet, Frederic L. *Commentary on Romans*. Grand Rapids: Kregel, 1977.

Goldberg, Harvey E. *Jewish Passages: Cycles of Jewish Life*. Berkley: University of California Press, 2003.

Goossens, Louis. "Metaphtonymy: The Interaction of Metaphor and Metonymy in Expressions of Linguistic Action." In *Metaphor and Metonymy in Comparison and Contrast*, edited by René Dirvén and Ralf Pörings, 349–377. Berlin: Mouton de Gruyter, 2003.

Goslinga, C. J. *Joshua, Judges, Ruth*. Translated by Ray Togtman. Grand Rapids, MI: Zondervan, 1986.

Gräbe, Petrus J. *New Covenant, New Community: The Significance of Biblical and Patristic Covenant Theology for Contemporary Understanding*. Milton Keynes: Paternoster, 2006.

Grady, Joseph, Todd Oakley, and Seana Coulson. "Blending and Metaphor." In *Metaphor in Cognitive Linguistics*, edited by Raymond W. Gibbs, Jr. and Gerard J. Steen. Amsterdam: John Benjamins, 1999. http://cogweb.ucla.edu/CogSci/Grady_99.html

Gray, John, ed. *Joshua, Judges and Ruth*. London: Nelson, 1967.

Green, Joel B. *Hearing the New Testament: Strategies for Interpretation*. Grand Rapids, MI: Eerdmans, 2010.

Grimes, Barbara F., and Raymond G. Gordon, Jr., eds. *Ethnologue: Languages of the World*. Vol. 1, 14th ed. Dallas, TX: SIL International, 2000.

Gross, C. D. "Circumcision in the New Testament: Translating without Embarrassment." *The Bible Translator* 50, no. 4 (1999): 422–427.

Gruenwald, Ithamar. *Rituals and Ritual Theory in Ancient Israel*. Leiden: Brill, 2003.

Gunkel, Hermann. *Genesis*. Translated by Mark E. Biddle. Macon, GA: Mercer University Press, 1997.

Gutt, Ernst-August. *Relevance Theory: A Guide to Successful Communication in Translation*. Dallas, TX: SIL International, 1992.

———. *Translation and Relevance: Cognition and Context*. Oxford; Cambridge, MA: Blackwell, 1991.

Haldane, Robert. *Exposition of the Epistle to the Romans*. London: Banner of Truth Trust, 1958.

Hamilton, Victor P. *The Book of Genesis: Chapters 18–50*. Grand Rapids, MI: Eerdmans, 1995.

Hamlin, E. John. *Inheriting the Land: A Commentary on the Book of Joshua*. Grand Rapids, MI: Eerdmans, 1983.

Harries, K. "The Many Uses of Metaphor." In *On Metaphor*, edited by S. Sacks, 165–172. Chicago: University of Chicago Press, 1979.

Harvey, John D. *Listening to the Text: Oral Patterning in Paul's Letters*. Grand Rapids: Baker Books, 1998.

Hayes, Christine Elizabeth. *Gentiles Impurities and Jewish Identities: Intermarriage and Conversion from the Bible to the Talmud*. Oxford: Oxford University Press, 2002.

Hays, Richard B. *Echoes of Scripture in the Letters of Paul*. New Haven, CT: Yale University Press, 1998.

Hegg, Tim. "Circumcision as a Sign: The Theological Significance." Evangelical Theological Society Northwest Regional Meeting. 21 April 1990. https://www.academia.edu/4529165/Circumcision_as_a_sign_the_theological_significance.

Hendriksen, William. *Romans*. New Testament Commentary. Edinburgh: Banner of Truth Trust, 1980.

Hennink, Monique, Inge Hutter, and Ajay Bailey. *Qualitative Research Methods*. Los Angeles: SAGE, 2011.

Hill, Harriet S. "Communicating Context in Bible Translation among the Adioukrou of Cote D'Ivoire." Dissertation, Fuller Theological Seminary, USA, 2003.

Hoffman, L. A. "Circumcision." In *The Encyclopedia of Judaism*, vol. 1, edited by Jacob Neusner, 89–95. Leiden: Brill, 2000.

Howe, Bonnie. *Because You Bear This Name: Conceptual Metaphor and Moral Meanings of 1 Peter*. Leiden: Brill, 2006.

Huey Jr., F. B. *Jeremiah, Lamentations*. The American Commentary, vol. 16. Nashville, TN: Broadman, 1993.

Hugenberger, Gordon Paul. *Marriage as a Covenant: A Study of Biblical Law and Ethics Governing Marriage Developed from the Perspective of Malachi*. Leiden: Brill, 1994.

Hyatt, James Philip. *Exodus*. The New Century Bible Commentary. London: Marshall, Morgan and Scott, 1971.

Ibáñez, Francisco J. M. "The Role of Mappings and Domains in Understanding Metonymy." In *Metaphor and Metonymy at the Crossroads: A Cognitive Perspective*, edited by Antonio Barcelona, 109–132. Berlin: Mouton de Gruyter, 2003.

Ironside, H. A. *Lectures on the Epistle to the Romans.* Neptune, NJ: Loizeaux Brothers, 1970.

Janzen, W. *Exodus.* Waterloo, ON: Herald Press, 2000.

Jobes, Karen H., and Moisés Silva. *Invitation to the Septuagint.* Grand Rapids, MI: Baker, 2000.

Johnson, Mark. *The Body in the Mind: The Bodily Basis of Meaning, Imagination, and Reason.* Chicago: University of Chicago Press, 1987.

Kanogo, Tabitha. *Squatters and Roots of Mau Mau 1905–63.* London: James Currey, 1987.

Keach, Benjamin. *Preaching from the Types and Metaphors of the Bible.* Grand Rapids, MI: Kregel, 1972.

Keener, Craig S. *Romans.* A New Covenant Commentary. Eugene, OR: Cascade, 2009.

Keil, C. E. "The Books of Samuel." In *Commentary on the Old Testament*, vol. 2, edited by C. F. Keil and F. Delitzsch. Edinburgh: T & T Clark, 1866–1891. Reprinted, Peabody, MA: Hendrickson, 1996.

Kennedy, George A. *A New History of Classical Rhetoric.* Princeton, NJ: Princeton University Press, 1994.

———. *New Testament Interpretation through Rhetorical Criticism.* Chapel Hill, NC: University of North Carolina Press, 1984.

Kenyatta, Jomo. *Facing Mount Kenya: The Tribal Life of the Gikuyu.* London: Secker & Warburg, 1938.

———. "Kikuyu Religion, Ancestor-Worship, and Sacrificial Practices." *Journal of the International African Institute* 10, no. 3 (1937): 308–328.

Kertész, Andras. *Cognitive Semantics and Scientific Knowledge: Case Studies in the Cognitive Science of Science.* Amsterdam; Philadelphia: John Benjamins, 2004.

Kinoshita, J. "Romans – Two Writings Combined: A New Interpretation of the Body of Romans." In *Novum Testamentum* 7 (1965): 258–277.

Kirika, G. M. "Aspects of the Religion of the Gikuyu of Central Kenya before and after the European Contact, with Special Reference to Prayer and Sacrifice." Dissertation, University of Aberdeen, Scotland, 1988.

Kittay, Eva Feder. *Metaphor: Its Cognitive Force and Linguistic Structure.* Oxford: Clarendon, 1987.

Klein, William W., Craig L. Blomberg, and Robert L. Hubbard, Jr. *Introduction to Biblical Interpretation.* Rev. ed. Nashville: Nelson, 2004.

Kline, Meredith G. *By Oath Consigned: A Reinterpretation of the Covenant Signs of Circumcision and Baptism.* Grand Rapids, MI: Eerdmans, 1968.

Kövecses, Zoltan. *Metaphor in Culture: Universality and Variation.* Cambridge: Cambridge University Press, 2005.

Kugel, James L. *Traditions of the Bible: A Guide to the Bible as It Was as the Start of the Common Era.* Cambridge, MA: Harvard University Press, 1998.

Kümmel, Werner Georg. *Introduction to the New Testament.* Rev. ed. Translated by Howard Clark Kee. Nashville: Abingdon, 1975.

La Fontaine, J. S. *Initiation: Ritual Drama and Secret Knowledge across the World.* Manchester: Manchester University Press, 1985.

Lakoff, George. "Cognitive Semantics." In *Meaning and Mental Representations,* edited by Umberto Eco, Marco Santambrogio, and Patrizia Violi, 119–154. Bloomington: Indiana University Press, 1988.

———. *Women, Fire, and Dangerous Things: What Categories Reveal about the Mind.* Chicago: University of Chicago Press, 1987.

Lakoff, George, and Mark Johnson. *Metaphors We Live By.* Chicago: University of Chicago Press, 1980.

Lakoff, George, and Mark Turner. *More than Cool Reason: A Field Guide to Poetic Metaphor.* Chicago: University of Chicago Press, 1989.

Lampe, G. W. H., ed. *A Patristic Greek Lexicon.* Oxford: Clarendon, 1961.

Lane, W. L. *Hebrews 1–8.* Word Biblical Commentary 47A. Dallas, TX: Word Books, 1991.

Langacker, Ronald W. *Cognitive Grammar: A Basic Introduction.* Oxford: Oxford University Press, 2008.

———. *Concept, Image and Symbol: The Cognitive Basis of Grammar.* Berlin; New York: Mouton de Gruyter, 1991.

———. *Foundations of Cognitive Grammar.* Vol. 1. Stanford: Stanford University Press, 1987.

———. *Foundations of Cognitive Grammar.* Vol. 2. Stanford: Stanford University Press, 1991.

Larson, Mildred L. *Meaning-Based Translation: A Guide to Cross-Language Equivalence.* New York: University Press of America, 1984.

Leakey, L. S. B. *The Southern Kikuyu before 1903.* Vol. 2. New York: Academic Press, 1977.

Lee, Jae-Hun. *Paul's Gospel in Romans: A Discourse Analysis of Rom 1:16–8:39.* Leiden: Brill, 2010.

Leezenberg, Michael. *Contexts of Metaphor.* Oxford, UK: Elsevier, 2001.

Liddell, H. G., and R. Scott. *A Greek-English Lexicon: With a Revised Supplement.* Oxford: Clarendon, 1996.

Link, H. G. and J. Schattenmann. "καθαρός." In *The New International Dictionary of New Testament Theology,* vol. 3, edited by C. Brown, 102–108. Grand Rapids, MI: Zondervan, 1978.

Livesey, Nina E. *Circumcision as a Malleable Symbol.* Tübingen: Mohr Siebeck, 2010.

Longenecker, Richard N. *Galatians.* World Biblical Commentary 41. Dallas, TX: Word, 1990.

López, A. R. "Applying Frame Semantics to Translation: A Practical Example." *Translators' Journal* 47, no. 3 (2002): 312–350.

Louw, J. P., and Eugene A. Nida, eds. *Greek-English Lexicon of the New Testament Based on Semantic Domains*. 2 vols. New York, NY: United Bible Societies, 1988.

Luc, A. "לֵב." In *The New International Dictionary of Old Testament Theology & Exegesis*, vol. 2, edited by Willem A. VanGemeren, 749–754. Grand Rapids, MI: Zondervan, 1997.

Luomanen, Petri, Ilkka Pyysiäinen and Risto Uro. "Introduction: Social and Cognitive Perspectives in the Study of Christian Origin and Early Judaism." In *Explaining Christian Origins and Early Judaism: Contributions from Cognitive and Social Science*, edited by Luomanen, Pyysiäinen and Uro, 1–33. Leiden: Brill, 2007.

Lyall, Francis. *Slaves, Citizens, Sons: Legal Metaphors in the Epistles*. Grand Rapids, MI: Academie Books, 1984.

MacCormac, Earl R. *A Cognitive Theory of Metaphor*. Cambridge, MA: MIT Press, 1985.

Macquarrie, John. *God Talk: An Examination of the Language and Logic of Theology*. London: SCM Press, 1967.

Marcos, Natalio Fernández. *The Septuagint in Context: An Introduction to the Greek Versions of the Bible*. Translated by Wilfred G. E. Watson. Leiden: Brill, 2000. Reprinted, Atlanta: SBL Press, 2010.

Marshall, Catherine, and Gretchen B. Rossman. *Designing Qualitative Research*. 5th edition. Thousand Oaks, CA: SAGE, 2011.

McComiskey, Thomas Edward. *The Minor Prophets: An Exegetical and Expository Commentary*. Grand Rapids, MI: Baker Books, 1992.

McConville, G. J. "בְּרִית." In *New International Dictionary of Old Testament Theology and Exegesis*, vol. 1, edited by Willem A. VanGemeren, 746–755. Grand Rapids, MI: Zondervan, 1997.

McElhanon, Kenneth A. "From Simple Metaphors to Conceptual Blending: The Mapping of Analogical Concepts and the Praxis of Translation." *Journal of Translation* 2, no. 1 (2006): 31–81.

———. "From Word to Scenario: The Influence of Linguistic Theories upon Models of Translation." *Journal of Translation* 1, no. 3 (2005): 29–67.

McFague, Sallie. *Metaphorical Theology: Models of God in Religious Language*. London: SCM Press, 1982.

———. *Speaking in Parables: A Study in Metaphor and Theology*. London: SCM Press, 2002.

McKnight, Scott. *A Light among the Gentiles: Jewish Missionary Activity in the Second Temple Period*. Minneapolis: Fortress, 1991.

Merrill, Eugene H. *Deuteronomy*. New American Commentary. Nashville: Broadman & Holman, 1994.

Mertens, Donna M. *Research and Evaluation in Education and Psychology*. 3rd ed. Thousand Oaks, CA: SAGE, 2010.

Milgrom, Jacob. *Leviticus 17–22: A New Translation with Introduction and Commentary*. New York: Doubleday, 2000.

———. *Leviticus 23–27: A New Translation with Introduction and Commentary*. New York: Doubleday, 2001.

Miller, James C. *The Obedience of Faith, the Eschatological People of God, and the Purpose of Romans*. Atlanta: SBL Press, 2000.

Mitchell, M. "Rhetorical and New Literary Criticism." In *Oxford Handbook of Biblical Studies*, edited by J. W. Rogerson and J. M. Lieu, 615–633. Oxford: Oxford University Press, 2006.

Moberly, R. W. L. *Genesis 12–50*. Sheffield: Sheffield Academic Press, 1992.

Mojola, Aloo O. "Bible Translation in Africa: What Implications Does the New UBS Perspective Have for Africa? An Overview in the Light of the Emerging New UBS Translation Initiative." *Acta Theologica* 22, no. 1, Supplement 2 (2002): 202–213.

Moo, Douglas J. *The Epistle to the Romans*. Grand Rapids, MI: Eerdmans, 1996.

Moreno, Rosa E. Vega. *Creativity and Convention: The Pragmatics of Everyday Figurative Speech*. Philadelphia, PA: John Benjamins, 2007.

Morris, Leon. *Luke*. Tyndale New Testament Commentaries. Rev. ed. Leicester, UK: Inter-Varsity Press, 1988.

———. *The Epistle to the Romans*. Grand Rapids, MI: Eerdmans, 1988.

Moseley, Christopher, and R. E. Asher, eds. *Atlas of the World's Languages*. London: Routledge, 1994.

Mugenda, Olive M., and Abel G. Mugenda. *Research Methods: Quantitative and Qualitative Approaches*. Nairobi: Acts Press, 1999.

Mugo, E. N. *Kikuyu People: A Brief Outline of the Customs and Traditions*. Nairobi: Kenya Literature Bureau, 1982.

Muraoka, T. *A Greek-English Lexicon of the Septuagint*. Louvain: Peeters, 2009.

———. *A Greek-English Lexicon of the Septuagint: Chiefly of the Pentateuch and the Twelve Prophets*. Louvain: Peeters, 2002.

Muriuki, Godfrey. *A History of the Kikuyu: 1500–1900*. London: Oxford University Press, 1974.

———. *People Round Mount Kenya: Kikuyu*. Nairobi: Evans Brothers, 1985.

Murray, J. M. "The Kikuyu Female Circumcision Controversy, with Special Reference to the Church Missionary Society's 'Sphere of Influence.'" PhD dissertation, University of California, 1974.

Murray, Jocelyn. *The Epistle to the Romans*. Grand Rapids, MI: Eerdmans, 1997.

Naylor, Peter. *Ezekiel: A Study Commentary*. Darlington, UK: EP Books, 2011.

Nelson, Richard D. *Deuteronomy: A Commentary*. Louisville, KY: Westminster John Knox, 2002.

———. *Joshua: A Commentary*. Louisville, KY: Westminster John Knox, 1997.

Neusner, Jacob, and William Scott Green, eds. *Dictionary of Judaism in the Biblical Period: 450 B.C.E. to 600 B.C.E.* Peabody, MA: Hendrickson, 1996.

Newman, Barclay, and Eugene A. Nida. *A Translator's Handbook on Paul's Letter to the Romans*. London: United Bible Societies, 1973.

Newmark, Peter. *A Textbook of Translation*. New York: Prentice Hall, 1988.

Nida, Eugene A. *Towards a Science of Translating: With Special Reference to Principles and Procedures Involved in Bible Translating*. Leiden: Brill, 2003.

Nida, Eugene A., and Charles Russell Taber. *The Theory and Practice of Translation*. Leiden: Brill, 1969.

Nielsen, Kristen. *There Is Hope for a Tree: The Tree as Metaphor in Isaiah*. Sheffield, UK: Sheffield Academic Press, 1989.

Njiraini, N. W. "Mentoring: The Role of the Mutiiri in Traditional Kikuyu Society with Implications for Mentoring in Presbyterian Church of East Africa St. Andrew's Church." Thesis. Africa International University, 2004.

Noh, Eun-Ju. *Metarepresentation: A Relevance-Theory Approach*. Amsterdam: John Benjamins, 2000.

Norrick, Neal R. "Discourse and Semantics." In *The Handbook of Discourse Analysis*, edited by D. Schiffrin, D. Tannen, and H. E. Hamilton, 76–99. Oxford: Blackwell, 2001.

Nygren, Anders. *Commentary on Romans*. Translated by C. C. Rasmussen. Philadelphia: Fortress, 1949.

Olofsson, Staffan. *The LXX Version: A Guide to the Translation Technique of the Septuagint*. Stockholm: Almqvist & Wiksell International, 1990.

Osborne, Grant R. *Romans*. Downers Grove, IL: InterVarsity Press, 2004.

Patton, Michael Q. *How to Use Qualitative Methods in Evaluation*. Newbury Park, CA: SAGE, 1987.

Petruck, Miriam R. L. "Frame Semantics and the Lexicon: Nouns and Verbs in the Body Frame." In *Essays in Semantics and Pragmatics in Honor of Charles J. Fillmore*, edited by M. Shibatani and S. Thompson, 279–297. Amsterdam: John Benjamins, 1995.

Pink, Arthur Walkington. *Gleanings in Joshua*. Chicago: Moody Press, 1964.

Plumer, William S. *Commentary on Romans*. Grand Rapids, MI: Kregel, 1979.

Porter, Stanley E. "The Concept of Covenant in Paul." In *The Concept of the Covenant in the Second Temple Period*, edited by Stanley E. Porter and J. R. de Roo, 269–285. Leiden: Brill, 2003.

Pyysiäinen, I. *How Religion Works: Towards a New Cognitive Science of Religion*. Leiden: Brill, 2001.

Quell, G. "διαθήκη." In *Theological Dictionary of the New Testament*, vol. 2, edited by Gerhard Kittel, 106-124. Grand Rapids, MI: Eerdmans, 1964.

Radden, Günter. "How Metonymic Are Metaphors? In *Metaphor and Metonymy at the Crossroads: A Cognitive Perspective*, edited by Antonio Barcelona, 93-108. Berlin: Mouton de Gruyter, 2003.

Reed, Jeffrey T. "Discourse Analysis." In *Handbook to Exegesis of the New Testament*, edited by Stanley E. Porter, 189-217. Boston: Brill, 1997.

Richards, I. A. *The Philosophy of Rhetoric*. London: Oxford University Press, 1936.

Robbins, Vernon K. "Conceptual Blending and Early Christian Imagination." In *Explaining Christian Origins and Early Judaism: Contributions from Cognitive and Social Science*, edited by Petri Luomanen, Ilkka Pyysiäinen, and Risto Uro, 161-195. Leiden: Brill, 2008.

Robinson, Thomas. *Studies in Romans: Expository and Homiletical*. Grand Rapids, MI: Kregel, 1982.

Routledge, William S., and Katherine Routledge. *With a Prehistoric People: The Akikuyu of British East Africa*. London: Frank Cass & Co., 1968.

Ryken, Leland, James C. Wilhoit, and Tremper Longman III, eds. *Dictionary of Biblical Imagery*. Downers Grove, IL: InterVarsity Press, 1998.

Saeed, John I. *Semantics*. 2nd ed. Oxford: Blackwell, 2003.

Sagi, Avraham, and Tsevi Zohar. *Transforming Identity: The Ritual Transition from Gentile to Jew - Structure and Meaning*. New York: Continuum, 2007.

Sakenfeld, Kathrine Doob. *The New Interpreter's Dictionary of the Bible: A-C*. Vol. 1. Nashville: Abingdon, 2006.

Sasson, Jack M. "Circumcision in the Ancient Near East." *Journal of Biblical Literature* 85, no. 4 (1966): 473-476.

Schmid, Hans-Jörg. "Conceptual Blending, Relevance and Novel N+N-Compounds." In *Windows of the Mind: Metaphor, Metonymy and Conceptual Blending*, edited by Sandra Handl and Hans-Jörg Schmid, 119-245. Berlin: de Gruyter, 2011.

Schneider, Tammi J. *Judges*. Berit Olam: Studies in Hebrew Narrative and Poetry. Collegeville, MN: Liturgical Press, 2000.

Schreiner, Thomas R. *Romans*. Baker Exegetical Commentary on the New Testament. Grand Rapids, MI: Baker Books, 1998.

Shedd, William G. T. *A Critical and Doctrinal Commentary on the Epistle of St. Paul to the Romans*. Grand Rapids, MI: Zondervan, 1967.

Skinner, John. *Critical and Exegetical Commentary on Genesis*. 2nd ed. Edinburgh: T & T Clark, 1963.

Smith, Carlota S. *Models of Discourse: The Local Structure of Texts*. Cambridge: Cambridge University Press, 2003.

Smit, J. "The Letter of Paul to the Galatians: A Deliberative Speech." In *The Galatians Debate*, edited by Mark D. Nanos, 39–59. Peabody, MA: Hendrickson, 2002.

Soggin, J. Alberto. *Israel in the Biblical Period: Institutions, Festivals, Ceremonies, Rituals*. Translated by John Bowden. Edinburgh: T & T Clark, 2001.

———. *Joshua: A Commentary*. Translated by R. A. Wilson. London: SCM Press, 1972.

Sorg, T. "Heart." In *The New International Dictionary of New Testament Theology*, vol. 2, edited by C. Brown, 180–184. Grand Rapids, MI: Zondervan, 1986.

Sohn, Seock-Tae. *YHWH, the Husband of Israel: The Metaphor of Marriage between YHWH and Israel*. Eugene, OR: Wipf & Stock, 2002.

Soskice, Janet Martin. *Metaphor and Religious Language*. Oxford: Clarendon, 1985.

Sperber, Dan, and Deirdre Wilson. *Relevance, Communication and Cognition*. 2nd ed. Oxford: Blackwell, 1995.

Stanley, Christopher D. *Arguing with Scripture: The Rhetoric of Quotations in the Letters of Paul*. New York: T & T Clark, 2004.

———. *Paul and the Language of Scripture: Citation Technique in the Pauline Epistles and Contemporary Literature*. Cambridge: Cambridge University Press, 1992.

Stott, John R. W. *The Message of Romans*. Leicester, UK: Inter-Varsity Press, 2001.

Strauss, Anselm L., and Juliet M. Corbin. *Basics of Qualitative Research: Techniques and Procedures for Developing Grounded Theory*. London: SAGE, 1998.

Strawn, Brent A. *What Is Stronger than a Lion?: Leonine Image and Metaphor in the Hebrew Bible and the Ancient Near East*. Fribourg, Switzerland: Vandenhoeck & Ruprecht Göttingen; Academic Press Fribourg, 2005.

Stuhlmacher, Peter. *Paul's Letter to the Romans*. Translated by Scott J. Hafemann. Louisville, KY: Westminster John Knox, 1994.

Tate, W. Randolph. *Biblical Interpretation: An Integrated Approach*. 3rd edition. Peabody, MA: Hendrickson, 2008.

Tendahl, Markus. *A Hybrid Theory of Metaphor: Relevance Theory and Cognitive Linguistics*. Basingstoke: Palgrave Macmillan, 2009.

Tendahl, Markus, and Raymond W. Gibbs, Jr. "Complementary Perspectives on Metaphor: Cognitive Linguistics and Relevance Theory." *Journal of Pragmatics* 40, no. 11 (2008): 1823–1864.

Thompson, Marianne Meye. "'Mercy upon All': God as Father in the Epistle to the Romans." In *Romans and the People of God*, edited by Sven K. Soderlund and N. T. Wright, 203–216. Grand Rapids, MI: Eerdmans, 1999.

Tobin, Thomas H. *Paul's Rhetoric in Its Contexts: The Argument of Romans*. Peabody, MA: Hendrickson, 2004.

Toews, John E. *Romans*. Believers Church Bible Commentary. Scottdale, PA: Herald Press, 2004.

Tov, Emmanuel. *The Greek and Hebrew Bible: Collected Essays on the Septuagint.* Leiden: Brill, 1999.

Tracy, D. "Metaphor and Religion: The Test Case of Christian Texts." In *On Metaphor*, edited by S. Sacks, 89–104. Chicago: University of Chicago Press, 1979.

Tsang, Sam. *From Slaves to Sons: A New Rhetoric Analysis on Paul's Slave Metaphors in His Letter to the Galatians.* New York: Lang, 2005.

Turner, Victor. *The Ritual Process: Structure and Anti-Structure.* Chicago: Aldine, 1969.

van der Meer, Michaël N. *Formation and Reformulation: The Redaction of the Book of Joshua in the Light of the Oldest Textual Witness.* Leiden: Brill, 2004.

van der Watt, Jan Gabriel. *Family of the King: Dynamics of Metaphor in the Gospel according to John.* Leiden: Brill, 2000.

van Gennep, Arnold. *The Rites of Passage.* Translated by Monika B. Vizedom and Gabrielle L. Caffee. Chicago: University of Chicago Press, 1960.

van Wolde, Ellen. *Reframing Biblical Studies: When Language and Text Meet Culture, Cognition, and Context.* Winona Lake, IN: Eisenbrauns, 2009.

Wallace, Daniel B. *Greek Grammar beyond the Basics.* Grand Rapids, MI: Zondervan, 1996.

Wambũgũ, Hillary, James Mwangi Ngarariga, and Peter Muriithi Kariũki. *The Agĩkũyũ: Their Customs, Traditions and Folklore.* Nairobi: Wisdom Graphics Place, 2006.

Watson, Duane F. "The Contributions and Limitations of Greco-Roman Rhetorical Theory for Constructing the Rhetorical and Historical Situations of a Pauline Epistle." In *The Rhetorical Interpretation of Scripture: Essays from 1996 Malibu Conference*, edited by Stanley E. Porter and Dennis L. Stamps, 125–151. JSNT Supplement Series 180. Sheffield: Sheffield Academic Press, 1999.

Wedderburn, A. J. M. *The Reasons for Romans.* Minneapolis: Fortress, 1991.

Weiss, Robert Stuart. *Learning from Strangers: The Art and Method of Qualitative Interview Studies.* New York: Free Press, 1994.

Wendland, Ernst R. "Framing the Frames: A Theoretical Framework for the Cognitive Notion of 'Frames of Reference.'" *Journal of Translation* 6, no. 1 (2010): 27–50.

———. *Life-Style Translating: A Workbook for Bible Translators.* Dallas, TX: SIL International, 2006.

Wenham, Gordon J. *The Book of Leviticus.* New International Commentary on the Old Testament. Grand Rapids, MI: Eerdmans, 1979.

———. *Genesis 16–50.* Word Biblical Commentary 2. Dallas, TX: Word Books, 1994.

Westermann, Claus. *Genesis 12–36: A Commentary.* Trans. John Scullion. Minneapolis: Fortress, 1985.

Wikberg, Kay. "Studying Metaphors Using a Multilingual Corpus." In *Meaning through Language Contrast*, vol. 2, edited by Katarzyna M. Jaszczolt and Ken Turner, 109–123. Philadelphia: John Benjamins, 2003.

Williams, Jenny, and Andrew Chesterman. *The Map: A Beginner's Guide to Doing Research in Translation Studies*. Manchester: St. Jerome Publishing, 2002.

Williamson, P. R. "Circumcision." In *Dictionary of the Old Testament Pentateuch*, edited by D. Alexander and D. W. Baker, 122–125. Downers Grove, IL: InterVarsity Press, 2002.

Wilson, D. "Parallels and Differences in the Treatment of Metaphor in Relevance Theory and Cognitive Linguistics." *Intercultural Pragmatics* 8, no. 2 (2011): 177–196.

———. "Relevance and Understanding." In *Language and Understanding*, edited by Gillian Brown, Kirsten Malmkjaer, Alastair Pollitt and John Williams, 35–58. Oxford: Oxford University Press, 1994.

Wilson, D., and D. Sperber. "Relevance Theory." In *The Handbook of Pragmatics*, edited by L. Horn and G. Ward, 607–662. Oxford: Blackwell, 2004.

———. "A Deflationary Account of Metaphors." In *Meaning and Relevance*, edited by D. Wilson and D. Sperber, 97–122. Cambridge: Cambridge University Press, 2012.

Wilson, D., and Robyn Carston. "Metaphor, Relevance, and the 'Emergent Property' Issue." *Mind and Language* 21, no. 3 (2006): 404–433.

———. "A Unitary Approach to Lexical Pragmatics: Relevance, Inference and Ad Hoc Concepts." In *Pragmatics*, edited by Noel Burton-Roberts, 230–259. Basingstoke: Palgrave, 2007.

Wilss, Wolfram. *Knowledge and Skills in Translator Behavior*. Amsterdam: John Benjamins, 1996.

Winter, Richard. "Cutting and Washing: Circumcision and Baptism: Highly Appropriate Symbols in our Erotic Culture." *Presbyterion* 26, no. 2 (2000): 67–83.

Witherington III, Ben. *The Paul Quest: The Renewed Search of the Jew of Tarsus*. Downers Grove, IL: InterVarsity Press, 1998.

———. *Paul's Letter to the Romans: A Social-Rhetorical Commentary*. Grand Rapids, MI: Eerdmans, 2004.

Wolff, Hans Walter. *Anthropology of the Old Testament*. Philadelphia: Fortress, 1974.

Woudstra, Marten H. *The Book of Joshua*. Grand Rapids, MI: Eerdmans, 1981.

Wuellner, W. "Paul's Rhetoric of Argumentation in Romans: An Alternative to the Donfried-Karris Debate over Romans." In *The Romans Debate*, edited by Karl P. Donfried, 128–146. Peabody, MA: Hendrickson, 1991.

Yao, Mingjun. "Application of Frame Theory in Translation of Connotation in Chinese Ancient Poems." *Theory and Practice in Language Studies* 2, no. 6 (2012): 1141–1146.

Yri, Kjell Magne. "Recreating Religion: The Translation of Central Religious Terms in the Light of a Cognitive Approach to Semantics." In *The Bible through Metaphor and Translation: A Cognitive Semantic Approach*, vol. 15, edited by K. Feyaerts, 187–203. New York: Lang, 2003.

Zee, Leonard J. V. *Christ, Baptism and the Lord's Supper: Recovering the Sacraments for Evangelical Worship*. Downers Grove, IL: InterVarsity Press, 2004.

Zeitlin, Solomon. "Who Is a Jew? A Halachic-Historic Study." *The Jewish Quarterly Review* 49, no. 4 (1959): 241–270.

Ziesler, John. *Paul's Letter to the Romans*. London: SCM Press, 1989.

Langham Literature, with its publishing work, is a ministry of Langham Partnership.

Langham Partnership is a global fellowship working in pursuit of the vision God entrusted to its founder John Stott –

> *to facilitate the growth of the church in maturity and Christ-likeness through raising the standards of biblical preaching and teaching.*

Our vision is to see churches in the Majority World equipped for mission and growing to maturity in Christ through the ministry of pastors and leaders who believe, teach and live by the word of God.

Our mission is to strengthen the ministry of the word of God through:
- nurturing national movements for biblical preaching
- fostering the creation and distribution of evangelical literature
- enhancing evangelical theological education

especially in countries where churches are under-resourced.

Our ministry

Langham Preaching partners with national leaders to nurture indigenous biblical preaching movements for pastors and lay preachers all around the world. With the support of a team of trainers from many countries, a multi-level programme of seminars provides practical training, and is followed by a programme for training local facilitators. Local preachers' groups and national and regional networks ensure continuity and ongoing development, seeking to build vigorous movements committed to Bible exposition.

Langham Literature provides Majority World preachers, scholars and seminary libraries with evangelical books and electronic resources through publishing and distribution, grants and discounts. The programme also fosters the creation of indigenous evangelical books in many languages, through writer's grants, strengthening local evangelical publishing houses, and investment in major regional literature projects, such as one volume Bible commentaries like the *Africa Bible Commentary* and the *South Asia Bible Commentary*.

Langham Scholars provides financial support for evangelical doctoral students from the Majority World so that, when they return home, they may train pastors and other Christian leaders with sound, biblical and theological teaching. This programme equips those who equip others. Langham Scholars also works in partnership with Majority World seminaries in strengthening evangelical theological education. A growing number of Langham Scholars study in high quality doctoral programmes in the Majority World itself. As well as teaching the next generation of pastors, graduated Langham Scholars exercise significant influence through their writing and leadership.

To learn more about Langham Partnership and the work we do visit **langham.org**

www.ingramcontent.com/pod-product-compliance
Lightning Source LLC
Chambersburg PA
CBHW070234240426
43673CB00044B/1788